HOUSTON

"Houston's Enterprises" by Maureen Bayless Balleza

Windsor Publications, Inc.
Chatsworth, California

HOUSTON

CONTEMPORARY PORTRAIT BY GARY TAYLOR

GATEWAY TO THE FUTURE

Windsor Publications, Inc.—Book Division
Managing Editor: **Karen Story**
Design Director: **Alexander D'Anca**
Photo Director: **Susan L. Wells**
Executive Editor: **Pamela Schroeder**

Staff for *Houston: Gateway to the Future*
Manuscript Editor: **Mary Jo Scharf**
Photo Editor: **Larry Molmud**
Editor, Corporate Profiles: **Melissa W. Patton**
Production Editor, Corporate Profiles: **Una FitzSimons**
Customer Service Manager: **Phyllis Feldman-Schroeder**
Editorial Assistants: **Elizabeth Anderson, Dominique
Jones, Kim Kievman, Michael Nugwynne, Kathy B.
Peyser, Theresa J. Solis**
Publisher's Representatives, Corporate Profiles:
L. Burroughs, C. Parks, W. Healey
Layout Artist, Corporate Profiles: **Chris Murray**

Designer: **Christina L. Rosepapa**

Windsor Publications, Inc.
Elliot Martin, Chairman of the Board
James L. Fish III, Chief Operating Officer
Michele Sylvestro, Vice President/Sales-Marketing
Mac Buhler, Vice President/Acquisitions

Library of Congress Cataloging-in-Publication Data
Taylor, Gary, 1947-
Houston, gateway to the future : a contemporary portrait /
by Gary Taylor.
p. 264 cm. 23x31
Includes bibliographical references and index.
ISBN 0-89781-379-0
1. Houston (Tex.)—Civilization. 2. Houston (Tex.)—De-
scription—Views. 3. Houston (Tex.)—Economic conditions.
4. Houston (Tex.)—Industries. I. Title.
F394.H85T38 1991   90-45851
976.4'141'06--dc20   CIP

■ *Title spread: Photo by Bob Rowan/Progressive Image
Photography*

■ *Right: Photo by Bob Rowan/Progressive Image
Photography*

■ *Following page: The individual in this photo appears
to have walked all the way from downtown. Photo by Bob
Rowan/ Progressive Image Photography*

For my late father—
a St. Louis entrepreneur
who should have moved to Houston
before I was born.

CONTENTS

PART

1

GATEWAY TO THE FUTURE

■ *Photo by James Blank*

1

THE
PAPER CITY

For civic leaders gathered at John Carlos' City Exchange on April 4, 1840, the situation could not have looked more grim. This first generation of city leadership was learning the hard way how quickly boom can turn to bust. It seemed only yesterday that their four-year-old enterprise—the city of Houston—stood on the brink of prosperity as the "First City" of the upstart Republic of Texas. Business had flourished in the Republic's first capital, and population had exploded from nothing to more than 2,000, with an estimated 100 immigrants arriving weekly.

Tradesmen of all sorts could be seen mingling with diplomats on the muddy streets, where settlers from the surrounding farmlands came to exchange their produce for necessities of life. The hero of the war for independence from Mexico, General Sam Houston, called this namesake city his home and lived there as president of Texas in a two-room log cabin. Just five years before there had been nothing but swampy land at the fork of Buffalo and White Oak bayous. Overnight, it seemed, a dynamic city had sprouted to stake its claim on the future.

Now, just as quickly, that promising future seemed at risk. A new presidential administration in 1839 had decided to move the capital to another unfinished city named Austin, on the western frontier. That fall, 30 wagons headed out with the Republic's archives and Houston's claim as the seat of government. Meanwhile, 10 percent of the city's population were dying from Yellow Fever in an epidemic that threatened to ruin the city's reputation as a safe place to live. Neighboring Harrisburg, a town eager to create its own boom, was aggressively promoting plans to organize an import company and attract set-

■ *Amateur performers put on a circus in the Houston YMCA gym. Courtesy, Harris County Heritage Society*

tlers. The currency of the financially strapped Republic had been devalued to 10 cents on the U.S. dollar, creating the most competitive business environment in Houston's brief history.

As if those twists of fate were not enough, over the winter three unexpected tragedies had added their depressing impact to that meeting on April 4. On February 6 the steamship *Emblem* had become the first ship to sink in the waters of Buffalo Bayou, adding fuel to criticism that Houston lay too far up the river for serious development as a port. Four days later another boat, the *Rodney*, had been damaged by rising water in the same area, only to be followed in March by the sinking of the *Brighton*, the victim of a snag. While damning the bayou's reputation as an efficient, natural highway for commerce, the steamboat mishaps had created even more significant and immediate problems. The river channel was blocked east of Houston, denying travelers easy passage upstream beyond its rival Harrisburg.

For those leaders who gathered to discuss a solution, the city's future sat in their hands. One of Houston's two founders, John Kirby Allen, had died in 1838. His brother, Augustus Allen, was destined to leave the city in 1843, never to return. At this crucial time of crisis in 1840, relocation probably loomed as a viable alternative. The Texas frontier resembled a garden of community development with opportunistic villages springing up everywhere. Many would vanish as ghost towns, falling victim to one form of catastrophe or another. Houston might today be recalled among them except for the response to this first crisis.

Instead of giving up, the young city's leaders organized their first chamber of commerce and launched a three-year effort to clear the riverway of obstructions. With their optimism and their reluctance to surrender, they responded in a way that's become the primary theme throughout Houston's cyclical history. They reviewed the city's past, brief as it was in 1840, and renewed their faith in a vision born of ambition.

From its start as nothing more than a land promoter's dream, Houston has grown in the track of dynamic individuals who seized opportunity where none seemed to exist, defied the odds against success, and turned positive events to greater advantage. It has also been a place where they could salvage their dreams despite apparent disadvantages of geography and nature. Houston's story is symbolic of the American frontier and of the American ideals that continue pushing the nation forward to whatever frontiers lie ahead.

Houstonians acknowledge with a smile the image of their city's birth. Its founding fathers—the Allen brothers—were primarily high-pressure land promoters who combined a good sales pitch with marketing genius to put Houston on the map.

In August of 1836, with Santa Anna's Mexican Army vanquished and the Republic of Texas springing to life, a map was about the only place that Houston could be found. It was a paper city existing only in the vision of these two brothers from New York who had just purchased for $5,000 some 2,200 acres of land at the fork of Buffalo and White Oak bayous, about 50 miles above the open waters in the Gulf of Mexico and the Republic's budding port city of Galveston. They planned to subdivide the parcel, attract settlers and investors, and build—according to their advertisements—"the great interior commercial emporium of Texas."

The Allens hardly fit the image of rough-cut frontiersmen. They were pioneers of a different sort, seeking fortune rather than independence. Augustus was a prodigy, trained as an engineer, and John Kirby boasted a reputation as a fastidious dresser. They migrated to Texas from New York in 1832 while both were in their twenties, and by 1835 land speculation had placed them among the largest landowners in the Mexican colony.

Although they didn't join the Texas forces then fighting for independence, they served as fundraisers for Sam Houston's ragtag army and viewed their friend's victory as an opportunity for

■ *John Kirby Allen (shown) and his brother, Augustus, who had come to Texas from New York in 1832, founded the city of Houston on Buffalo Bayou. Two years after the city's founding, John Kirby Allen passed away. Courtesy, Harris County Heritage Society*

greater prosperity. Some detractors have tried to paint the Allens as New York con-artists, but more sympathetic historians view them as models for this Jacksonian era with its atmosphere of aggressive commercial expansion. Whatever the case may be, two things are certain. Despite their use of misleading advertisements to get Houston off the ground, they did make good on most of their developmental promises. And they set the tone of entrepreneurial hustle that has characterized the generations following them.

Heralding their location as the head of navigation on Buffalo Bayou, the Allens neglected to note it had actually been their fourth choice for development—after Galveston Island, a spit of land now called Morgan's Point, and the village of Harrisburg, burned by the Mexican Army in its April pursuit of Sam Houston's revolutionaries. Until they learned that a cotton planter had used the Buffalo-White Oak fork in 1826 as a shipment point, the Allens believed Harrisburg, at the fork of Buffalo and Brays bayous, to be the head of navigation on this important waterway. But their attempts to purchase the ruins of Harrisburg failed. Land titles there were in dispute, and they couldn't wait for litigation to clarify things.

Patience had little virtue for fortune seekers in those days of the Republic. Texas beckoned magnetically in the wake of the Mexican defeat at San Jacinto on April 21, 1836. Now a new army had invaded, but it sought to build rather than destroy. It was an army of entrepreneurs and promoters like the Allens, and paper cities were popping up all over the Southeast Texas countryside as these guerrillas of capitalism marched into the frontier determined to carve enterprise from the wilderness.

Besides the competition from these rival towns, the Allens faced another challenge. Mainstream commercial leaders of early Texas had long believed the Brazos River—not Buffalo Bayou—would become the region's primary riverway. The largest river between the Rio Grande and the Red River, the Brazos attracted much of the early farming development in Texas. Stretch-

ing 840 miles into the interior from its mouth near present-day Freeport, the Brazos was billed as the new Mississippi by Texans of the 1820s. It would later prove too wild for early navigational development. But to the Allens in 1836 it appeared that their plans for developing a city on Buffalo Bayou required quick action to circumvent the reputation of the Brazos. Fortunately, they possessed marketing talents that provided an edge.

They demonstrated those talents with two brilliant promotional coups, illustrating the kind of foresight that has characterized Houston throughout its commercial history. Indeed, everything about the city's creation indicates the touch of developers who were at least a century ahead of their time. First, the Allens chose the perfect name for a city located near the scene of the battle that made Sam Houston a hero. The leading candidate in the Republic's first presidential election, Houston returned the favor by boosting the Allens' efforts in their second goal: to make Houston the capital of Texas.

They realized their city would need a foundation industry and an identity. So they focused on the Republic's need for a temporary capital and prepared what had to be one of this nation's earliest economic development incentive packages. Elected to serve as a congressman in the first Texas House of Representatives, J.K. Allen argued his case for Houston in person.

With a crucial vote on November 30, 1836, the Texas Congress selected Houston over other contenders. At that time, not a single building had been completed there. In fact, the first boatload of settlers drawn to Houston by the Allens' ads floated right past their destination, unable to see the stakes that marked the full extent of construction there. But the Allens had promised to build a $10,000 capitol building at their own expense and to provide housing for legislators at a nominal charge. This early investment paid additional dividends, attracting settlers to work on the construction projects.

By May of 1837, the capitol still lacked a roof, but Congress was in session anyway with tree branches lashed together overhead while construction continued. Houston boasted rows of tent homes and the future looked bright enough for the state's pioneer paper, the *Telegraph and Texas Register,* to move there from Columbus.

"The selection of the site, the naming of the place, the presentation of the advantages of securing the temporary location of the seat of government, constitute a high testimonial to the shrewdness and sagacity of the promoters of the city of Houston," noted Anson Jones, the Republic's last president, in his memoirs.

There proved to be more to Houston than just hype in those days of the infant Republic of Texas. As the frontier developed, the advantages of Buffalo Bayou over the Brazos as a commercial waterway quickly became apparent. In contrast to other major streams, the Buffalo ran east-west, pointing toward the Brazos. Not much more than a peaceful creek, it was wide and deep from its fork with the San Jacinto River, narrowing finally at Harrisburg for the last few miles to Houston. Farmers quickly discovered their quickest route to market lay overland, from the Brazos Valley into Houston and to the Main Street landing the Allens built, which emptied into Buffalo Bayou. No wonder the city quickly attracted its first of several nicknames as early settlers labeled it "The Bayou City."

When those farmers arrived in Houston they found a town ahead of its time. The Allens had plotted their city with the streets much wider than the norm for those days. Texas Avenue, the main thoroughfare, stood 100 feet wide while other streets, including Main, were mapped at 80-foot widths. The brothers divided 128 acres in 62 blocks, with the rest of their land in reserve for later expansion. Agents greeted all newcomers, hawking town lots at prices ranging to $3,000 each.

"I could not understand where so many people could be lodged," noted naturalist John James Audubon during a visit in those exciting days. "I soon learned that the prairie was dotted with tents."

Houston became a haven for opportunists. The collection of gamblers, drifters, and other undesirables prompted another early visitor to report: "Houston is the greatest sink of dissipation and vice that modern times have known." While the wild side attracted the most attention, however, early Houstonians were building a cultural foundation, with a primitive theater and numerous service organizations, including the Philosophical Society of Texas, created in 1837 by 26 intellectuals for the "collection and diffusion of correct information regarding the moral and social condition of our country."

That first generation of leadership already had an edge in early 1840, when it looked to

■ *Relatively few of Houston's high-school-aged youth attended Central High in the waning years of the nineteenth century. The 1895 building included tall windows that provided adequate light for the classrooms and a gymnasium for the physical education of students. Courtesy, Harris County Heritage Society*

many as if this phenomenon on Buffalo Bayou was just another frontier flash in the pan, destined to die with the migration of the capital to Austin. But too many commercial cornerstones had been laid in its first four years, and Houston's leaders stood committed to further growth. Besides organizing their chamber of commerce, they raised funds to clear the bayou of its obstructions. More important, they lobbied the Republic for a law empowering them to preserve and improve navigation on the bayou above Harrisburg, a development that placed within their grasp the ability to create a truly commercial riverway.

In fact they even managed to turn the movement of the capital to their advantage. Austin's location on the Colorado River soon enhanced Buffalo Bayou's transportation image even further when settlers in the new capital discovered the Colorado navigable for just a short distance. That meant they could not bypass Houston. Expansion westward to construct Austin actually brought more commercial traffic through Houston as merchants there aggressively pursued opportunities to serve new customers in Austin.

At the same time, the city leaders altered the city charter to allow construction of wharves on the bayou banks. They created a board of health to fight the problems of disease related to the swampy environment. Their drive to remain the gateway to Texas' agricultural heartland climaxed in 1841 with a city ordinance that established the Port of Houston.

By the time Texas entered the Union in 1845, Houston had proved it possessed the kind of staying power required for survival. It ranked third in population after Galveston and San Antonio. Buffalo Bayou had become the new state's most dependable waterway, with Houston as the depot where commerce transferred between water and road for distribution in or out. The city

■ *By the early twentieth century, a professional police force was protecting the growing city of Houston. Courtesy, Harris County Heritage Society*

owed its success in part to its location on that once swampy creek. But more important was the enterprise of its ambitious pioneers who transformed the bayou into an artery of commerce and marketed its advantages with a flair. Their style of development would run through the city's future years much as the the bayou itself rolled across its landscape.

Several factors of geography molded the development of Houston's economy and culture during its growth in the nineteenth century. To maintain its economic vitality, Houston recognized its role as the commercial center for an agricultural territory and Houstonians maintained their focus on building the transportation network that would serve the region. Road construction and aggressive lobbying for rail lines characterized the period.

Never content with the limited ability of Buffalo Bayou to handle seagoing vessels, city leaders continued to dream about the day when they could forge the bayou into a deepwater channel and truly promote their city as an ocean port. Until completion of the Houston Ship Channel in 1914, however, Houstonians had to accept their connection with Galveston as their route to the open sea. Throughout the century the two cities vied for commercial status, and it would take a catastrophic act of nature in 1900 to resolve the dispute.

Before looking at those developments, however, it's important to note two other factors that shaped Houston's character. Like the rest of Texas, young Houston was built at a cultural crossroads. Pioneers from the Deep South led the way. But Houston also represented the western frontier with all its implications of independence and a fresh start. While southern in tradition, nineteenth-century Houston was frontier in spirit, with an appreciation for rapid growth, leadership by merchants, commercial strength, and new ideas.

Besides this mingling of southern and frontier lifestyles, Houston also gained from a situation unique to Texas: the influence of the republican era. For a decade Texas functioned as an independent nation, with Houston one of its principal cities. Its residents viewed the United States as a rival rather than a parent. In the process, the republican era spawned a legacy of self sufficiency that surfaced in everything Texan, from attitude to the legendary Texas boast. And Houston, expressly established to become the Republic's primary city, reflected this Texas characteristic into the twentieth century.

As important as early development of Buffalo Bayou had been for Houston during the republican era, attraction of rail lines emerged as an equally significant event prior to the War Between the States. The competition pitted Houston against Galveston. Leaders in that island city promoted it as the obvious spot for a fanlike network of rail lines to terminate at Gulf wharves for delivery of cargo. Houston leaders once again rose to the occasion and recognized the desire of the national rail builders to incorporate the Texas network into the transcontinental system.

A trio of Houston merchants—Francis R. Lubbock, William Marsh Rice, and Thomas William House—toured the state in 1856 to lobby for their plan to make Texas railroads part of the transcontinental design, with Houston as the Texas hub. Their aggressive marketing efforts resulted in a legislative decision in Houston's favor, providing loans and land grants to private builders. It gave Houston a clear-cut victory over Galveston in their battle for interior transportation dominance and in some measure determined the future of the two cities.

But nature played the most decisive card in their rivalry. Economically stymied by the Union blockade of the 1860s, Galveston flourished following Reconstruction and came to be known as the "Wall Street of the Southwest." It showed every sign of becoming a major league center for banking and finance. By 1870 it had become the state's largest city and just 10 years later boasted a population of 22,000.

But on September 8—one day in 1900—that bright future collapsed with the worst natural disaster in U.S. history. A killer hurricane suddenly engulfed the island, killing between 6,000 and 8,000 people. No structure escaped damage as storm tides climbed higher than 15 feet. The physical damage proved to be a small part of the impact. Although it rebuilt with impressive perseverance, Galveston never recovered psychologically. It became a landmark for demonstrating the kind of destruction nature could wreak. And the storm showed national leaders the need to have a port upriver. The disaster led directly to federal financial help for Houston's dream of converting Buffalo Bayou into the Houston Ship Channel.

But for another reason, the timing of the 1900 storm could not have been more beneficial for Houston. It left the city's chief rival prostrate on the eve of the most pivotal event in the economic history of Texas: discovery of oil at Spindletop near Beaumont on January 10, 1901. Galveston was down for the count, but Houston stood primed and ready to claim a nickname—Energy Capital of the World—as Texas entered the industrial age with a bang.

The salt dome gusher drilled by Captain A.F. Lucas at Spindletop spawned the industry that provided Houston its most important source of commerce. It dwarfed earlier oil discoveries in the state and inspired energy-driven businesses, like railroads, to find new ways to exploit this apparently unlimited source of fuel. The oil rush transformed Texas from a rural economy into an industrial one, and Houston stood well positioned to take advantage of the change. Oil industry giants like Exxon, Texaco, Gulf, and Mobil trace their roots to the chain of discoveries on the Gulf Coast between Beaumont and Houston in those early days of the twentieth century. Later discoveries in East Texas propelled Dallas into prominence farther north.

By 1935, however, 24 percent of all known Texas oil reserves could be found within 100 miles of Houston, and 40 percent of all Texas petroleum moved through its port. Still tied to an extractive economy, Houston's leaders recognized the continuing importance of their transportation systems in serving the infant oil industry. Pipelines quickly linked the city to the nearby oilfields. And those leaders seized the opportunity to realize a dream as old as the city itself—creation of a deepwater link with the Gulf of Mexico.

In the last decades of the nineteenth century, Houston had chipped away at Buffalo Bayou with various dredging projects. In 1869 a group of prominent citizens had formed the Buffalo Bayou Ship Channel Company to improve the waterway. It charged users and contributed to dredging programs while lobbying for federal assistance. In 1874 Charles Morgan, a major Gulf Coast shipper, purchased the company and completed its work. Then he stretched a chain across one of the improvements, Morgan's Cut, and raised the toll. Although his monopoly at first appeared detrimental to channel traffic, it produced positive results when the federal government reacted in 1881 by purchasing the improvements.

Congressional representatives continued to seek funds for more improvements and won an appropriation of $1 million in the wake of the 1900 hurricane. By 1908 the bayou had been dredged to a depth of 18.5 feet, just seven short of the 25-foot depths then required for ocean vessels. But it would take more than a hurricane and the birth of the oil industry to squeeze all the necessary help for the project, and once again, human ingenuity played its role.

■ *Horace Baldwin Rice, Houston's mayor from 1896 to 1898 and from 1905 to 1913, helped develop the city's deepwater ship channel. Courtesy, Texas Room, Houston Public Library*

Unable to secure federal gifts for the final touch, two Houston leaders devised a plan that would have made the Allen brothers proud. Just as the founders had attracted the Republic's first capital with an economic development package, Mayor H. Baldwin Rice and U.S. Representative Thomas Ball secured a deepwater ship channel with a plan of their own. They suggested creation of a local navigation district that would control the channel, sell bonds, and match federal improvement funds dollar-for-dollar. It marked the first time that local interests anywhere had pledged such a substantial contribution in a cooperative effort with the federal government, and it got results.

Houston parlayed a $1.25-million bond issue in 1910 into the Houston Ship Channel, opened with great fanfare by President Woodrow Wilson in 1914. It had taken 78 years, but Houston had transformed its quiet little bayou into a canal, 25 feet deep, 60 feet wide, and 50 miles long. But the channel's turning basin did not extend as far as the city's founders had predicted. Harrisburg and the fork with Brays Bayou turned out to be the true extent of potential improvements, leaving Allen's Landing to become a sentimental landmark in downtown Houston where Main Street meets Buffalo Bayou. The Allens, however, would still be grinning. Their city had already absorbed its one-time rival Harrisburg and made Buffalo Bayou all its own. By 1930 Houston had become the nation's eighth largest port, enroute to its status today among the top three.

Marketed from 1911 as the city "where 17 railroads meet the sea" and armed with a deepwater ship channel, Houston feasted on the growth of the oil industry in the twentieth century. It welcomed imaginative entrepreneurs who created a network of spinoff businesses. They turned the city into a manufacturing center to complement its status as a transportation hub. Cameron Iron Works got its start when James Abercrombie developed a practical device for prevention of well blowouts. Howard R. Hughes launched Hughes Tool Co. on the invention of a drill bit, and his son, Howard R. Hughes, Jr., became one of the nation's most legendary eccentrics. Refineries and pipelines bred petroleum byproducts and creation of the world's largest petrochemical complex along the Houston Ship Channel. And always throughout its march to the present, Houston was propelled by a cast of ambitious and colorful individuals who followed in the city's tradition of building economic advantages rather than merely discovering them.

The city's foremost builder in the twentieth century was undoubtedly Jesse H. Jones, a financial wizard known worldwide as "Mr. Houston." Ironically, he wasn't an oilman, building his fortune instead from several industries: lumber, media, and banking. But until Jones' death in 1956, Houston belonged to him.

He moved to Houston in 1898 at the age of 24 after working for his uncle's East Texas lumber company. He displayed a talent for taking advantage of every opportunity to arise. He made $25,000 trading oil leases at Spindletop and became one of the founding stockholders in the Humble Oil Co., now Exxon. But those adventures remained his only direct links to the oil business. His real commercial loves were land and credit, and he used his Spindletop earnings to start a lumber company.

By 1905 he was building the city's first housing subdivisions, selling his $5,000 homes on unprecedented terms: with 25-year mortgages. He diversified into construction and finance, producing more than 30 major buildings in downtown Houston by the 1920s and launching the bank that would eventually become Texas Commerce Bank, still one of the state's premier institutions. He bought *The Houston Chronicle* in 1916 and turned that newspaper into the largest of the Southwest. Behind the scenes, Jones controlled Texas politics and had a hand in every important Houston development, from creation of the Ship Channel to establishment of Houston Endowment, one of the nation's most influential charitable foundations. It's no wonder his name can be found on a number of structures around town. He symbolized the kind of broadminded

HOUSTON NEGRO CHAMEBER of COMMERCE
L. H. SPIVEY, PRES.
O. K. MANNING, Exec SECY.

■ *During the first half of the twentieth century, the Houston Negro Chamber of Commerce provided members of the city's black business community with networking opportunities. Courtesy, Texas Room, Houston Public Library*

instinct that has brought Houston to where it stands as this century moves to a close.

Characterized by strongwilled, ambitious visionaries, Houston has moved another step toward solidifying its label as the gateway to the future. City leaders won't let the world forget that "Houston" was the first word spoken from the moon. As the energy industry matured, the city continued reaching for a new ambition, one stamped "Tomorrow," and they found it in the fledgling field of space commerce. Attracting the government's space program in the 1960s, the city is now positioned to blast off when the private sector embraces this industry with so much potential. And in the process, the city has won its third and possibly most impressive nickname of all. The Bayou City became the Energy Capital and now it's known worldwide as Space City, U.S.A.

Through more than 150 years of persistence, its leaders have created the nation's fourth largest city as a monument to contradiction. Houston is a major port—located 50 miles from the sea. It's the center of the energy industry but its list of largest corporations includes businesses that do everything from waste control to funeral home management. If the Allen brothers and their associates could return home today, they would be satisfied with the decisions they made in the 1840s and proud of the tradition they started. Indeed, an assessment from the *Texas Tri-Weekly Telegraph* in 1857 explains as much today:

There was a time when it was thought that San Felipe, Velasco and San Luis would become large towns. And why did they not? They were well situated but their owners lacked enterprise. Compare the two towns of Columbus and Houston. The one situated at the head of tidewater on the largest river in the state in the center of the richest planting section of the world—the other on a shallow bayou, naturally incapable of navigation to any extent, surrounded by post oak and pine barrens and boggy prairies—one has had all the advantage of situation, the other of an energetic people. Notwithstanding, Houston has become the greatest business emporium of the state; while Columbus, Brazoria and Velasco . . . are now back where they were 20 years ago.

■ *Thirsty locals down suds
in one of the city's pre-World
WarI breweries. Courtesy, Harris
County Heritage Society, Lit-
terst-Dixon Collection*

2

THE

ENERGY CITY

T wo dates in Texas history command great reverence in the Lone Star State: April 21, 1836 and January 10, 1901. The first date marks the Battle of San Jacinto, when the Texas revolution climaxed with the defeat of the Mexican forces under General Santa Anna. It's simple to understand the results of that event and how it influenced everything that followed, from the creation of the Texas Republic to the emergence of Texas as a state.

In contrast, the second date merely unlocks a cabinet of mystery for those who hold it holy. They certainly recognize it as the date of the Spindletop Mound oil discovery near Beaumont. They know that Texas historians characterize it as the beginning of the state's modern economic era. And they realize that after Spindletop, oil became the dominant natural resource, transforming Texas from a rural economy into an industrial one.

But even most of those Texans dependent on the oil economy probably don't understand the energy industry in all its dimensions. And the reason is simple: no other industry compares for complexity. The challenge of extracting oil from beneath the ground and turning it into a marketable product is a massive, global jigsaw puzzle of specialization. Each piece of the process requires its own peculiar techniques, many of them alien to those intimately familiar with the operations in another piece.

Oil itself is merely the patriarch of a family of industries. Two of its offspring—natural gas and petrochemicals—sprang to maturity in the 1980s, ready to enter the twenty-first century as the new champions of the energy world, while their tired old man faced retirement. Both the dates and the development of those offspring

■ *The Gulf of Mexico gains yet another new oil production platform. Photo by C. Bryan Jones*

have tremendous significance for Houston. It lays a much stronger claim to the title of gas capital or petrochemical hub than it ever did to similar labels when oil was king of the oilpatch.

To understand Houston's role in the evolving future of energy, however, one must first appreciate its role in the past. Thanks to the complex nature of the energy business, that past in Houston constitutes a dramatic and colorful tale. But it's not the story of a single business as might be found with steel in Pittsburgh or autos in Detroit. It is many stories of many businesses, all part of that energy puzzle described above. You can't find the energy industry in Houston because it's everywhere—from the Exxon and Pennzoil buildings downtown to the refineries along the Houston Ship Channel, from Transco Tower in the Galleria to Baker-Hughes, Inc., on the city's southeast side. All these aspects work together to make energy Houston's economic wheelhorse. And in order to understand Houston's energy past, one must try to unravel the energy puzzle itself.

"If a drilling contractor has 10 rigs working and one has to stop, he says he's in a bust," says Sam Fletcher, the veteran energy writer for *The Houston Post*, explaining the heart of the energy puzzle. "If another contractor has only five rigs working and he adds one, he'll say he's in a boom. Oil prices were higher in 1983 than they were in 1988 but oilmen were pessimistic because the price was going down. They were optimistic about the lower price in 1988 because they thought it was headed up. The business is all a matter of perception. It's where you're going, not where you are. And no one understands it all."

■ *Facing page: A worker opens a valve on "Christmas Tree"—a term for the set of valves atop a well that controls the flow of oil and/or gas. On the right stands a drilling rig. Photo by C. Bryan Jones*

■ *Below: This aerial view of Houston's oil refineries testifies to the city's contribution to the nation's oil wealth. Photo by James Blank*

THE ENERGY PUZZLE

There's never been much of a market for earrings made of oil. As a mineral, oil holds a different allure for prospectors than gold. An ounce of oil has considerably less value than an ounce of gold. But oil in great quantities has unleashed economic forces beyond our comprehension. Oil is a sticky, dirty mixture of organic compounds with carbon and hydrogen as basic ingredients. It's not pretty stuff. But it is the substance of power. It is energy. It has put the world on wheels and kept it there. An appreciation of that power fosters understanding of the late-twentieth-century phenomenon called Houston. Without a basic knowledge of oil, its power, and the complex industry required to develop it, Houston will remain a riddle too.

The experts believe oil formed when organic matter from ancient plant and animal remains lay buried beneath the earth under great pressure for millions of years. But no one knows for sure. The hydrocarbons that exist as the liquid oil dissolve into natural gas at greater depth under influence from the higher temperatures farther down. Sometimes oil and natural gas are found together. The ancient organisms that eventually became oil and gas deposits originally lived in shallow seas. Their burial grounds have become today's oil reservoirs, where they stay as captives of pressurized tombs far below the surface, awaiting release.

The energy industry is actually a chain of processes devoted to finding those tombs, releasing their contents, developing the results into a variety of products, and selling them to a wide range of customers: exploration, production, refining, and marketing. Many separate businesses are involved but oilmen generally break the industry into two specific sections. Visualizing production as an island, they consider exploration as the business "upstream"—the processes involved in getting oil to the production island. "Downstream," they say, come the branches of the energy river, where they transform the oil into products for customers who need them.

But today's oil industry divides into many more specializations. And Houston has a presence in all of them. Upstream, geologists study land surfaces for signs that oil reservoirs may be located below. Petroleum landmen research ownership of prospective properties before companies lease the surface areas from individuals who own them. Once the leases have been negotiated, geophysical companies provide the high-technology tools for pinpointing those reservoir locations. Computers can now analyze mountains of seismic data to determine the best place for an explorer to

A welder lets sparks fly while repairing an oil rig. Photo by C. Bryan Jones

■ *A trio of storage tanks holds some of the city's black gold. Photo by C. Bryan Jones*

sink a drill. And because it costs so much to do that, explorers are willing to invest heavily in these upstream industries to increase the chances that when they do dig into the ground, it will be in the right place.

Once that spot is found, it becomes an island of production where other specialists perform their roles in the chain. Drilling companies drill the wells. These companies own the rigs and employ the crews who will learn if the explorer's predictions are correct. They send pipe deep into the ground. When the pipe hits a reservoir, the pressure is released and oil comes to the top where it's ready for production. Oilfield equipment companies provide the variety of tools used by drilling companies to keep the rigs at work.

After the drillers find the reservoir and oil begins to flow, well servicing companies take over to keep the well in operation. Additional rigs penetrate the reservoir as a field becomes a producer. Natural gas is released as a byproduct. Before anyone can get paid, however, the oil and gas must move downstream where other groups of specialists change it into things that businesses and individuals can buy.

That's where refining plants use sophisticated heat processes to break the oil into simpler substances demanded by consumers, creating products like gasoline and the different grades of motor oil. Oil from different parts of the world responds differently to these processes and establishes the criteria for value. West Texas Intermediate Crude, Arabian Light, and Nigerian Light are examples of the most desirable types.

Natural gas can be sold without refinement, but it can't be delivered to customers as easily as oil products. While oil moves on ocean tankers, railcars, or trucks, gas must travel to market through pipeline systems, and that's a requirement with dynamic implications for Houston as home to the world's natural gas transportation industry.

Yes, a lot of businesses constitute the oil industry. No wonder it's a hard sector to pigeonhole. The Houston oil directory lists thousands of companies in dozens of different categories. Oil and gas employment in Houston stood at 170,200 in 1988, representing 11.9 percent of the work force. And that was down from a high of 279,700 in 1982 when it accounted for 18.1 percent of the city's workers.

But they don't all work at oil companies. Besides the basic businesses noted above—oilfield service to refining—a long list of entrepreneurial specialists have further enlivened the oilpatch community. The oil price crash of the 1980s, for example, sent hordes of geologists out on their own as the large companies cut payrolls by limiting exploration. Some have found other lines of work. But others have survived by becoming self-employed consultants. When oil prices recovered, these independent geologists found even greater opportunities because the oil companies had thinned their own ranks so severely they had to rely on outsiders for a service traditionally handled in-house.

At another level, oilfield blowout firefighters provide a colorful example of the kinds of specialists needed to keep the industry running. The legendary Red Adair built his reputation from a base in Houston, and second generation professionals like Boots & Coots have already started adding their chapters to the chronicle.

By and large, however, the oilpatch culture can be viewed like a gigantic ocean filled with a large variety of fish swimming around in much their own fashion. Several of those fish must be observed closely. The whales are the "major" oil companies who create huge waves whenever they move. Although large and commanding respect, they don't necessarily always rule the waters. Plenty of sharks in the form of "independent" oil companies are cruising around, ready to snatch a share of the action in their powerful jaws. Both the majors and the independents have played crucial roles in Houston's growth as an energy center, and it's important to appreciate their differences.

The term "major oil company" doesn't necessarily refer to size, although most are pretty large. They got that way, however, for another reason: integration. A major usually enjoys a strong in-house presence in all stages of the industry, upstream and down. Its refinery and chemical operations help stabilize a major or integrated oil company's profit picture despite fluctuations in the price of oil. When oil prices drop and profits decrease from exploration and production, a major can balance the bottom line with higher profits from refining and chemicals because the raw material for those operations—the oil itself—is cheaper. Independent oil companies, on the other hand, have traditionally been upstream operators focused on exploration and production. They view the majors as customers as well as competitors, and they have been leaders in finding oil reserves. They take a beating when oil prices fall, and that experience has prompted more diversification among independents. While the major companies like Exxon, Shell, and Texaco have certainly had their impact in Houston, it's actually the independents and wildcatters who have provided the personality of Houston's oilpatch character.

Houston did not rise to prominence in the oil industry because large pools of oil lie beneath the city. The industry is so diverse it's always needed nerve centers to coordinate the different functions. Houston has been one of those. But it did get its start and substantial growth from the fact that large reservoirs of oil existed nearby. That's why a salt dome near Beaumont called Spindletop demands more reverence as a historic landmark than most other sites in Houston itself.

SPINDLETOP, WILDCATTERS, AND HOUSTON

With a population of 27,000 in 1890, Houston ranked as only the 18th largest city of the South, smaller than Texas rivals like Galveston, Dallas, and San Antonio. But its rail and port connections had made it a transit hub for the timber industry of East Texas. By the turn of the century that lumber trade had created the foundation of wealth and culture, an infrastructure of banks, a port, and railheads that would serve as the magnet for the leaders of the new economic colossus that spewed from the ground at Spindletop in 1901. Although Beaumont stood closer to the initial discovery, Houston emerged as the place where the wheelers of this new industry gathered to deal.

Initially Spindletop oil was stored in four large tanks with Houston as the distribution center. Only briefly, however, did local interests maintain control over the companies who would come to dominate. The Texas Company—later known as Texaco—set up shop in 1908. In 1916 Houston welcomed the Gulf Company's creation. But oilfeld development required huge infusions of capital, and not even Houston's banking nucleus could provide enough. Behind Gulf, for example, stood the resources of Pittsburgh's Mellon family. Sooner or later, all Texas wildcatters had to look east for help. Those early relationships between little oil and big oil extend to the present. They help explain the ties and the conflicts at work in Houston today between different factions of the oil industry.

No better example exists than that of the experience of the Humble Oil and Refining Co., called by *Texas Monthly*'s Joseph Nocera, "the greatest Texas oil company there ever was." Finally absorbed into Standard Oil of Jersey in 1960, whatever remains of Humble is today a part of

■ *Refining plants use sophisticated heat processes to break the oil into simpler substances demanded by consumers. Photo by Jay W. Sharp*

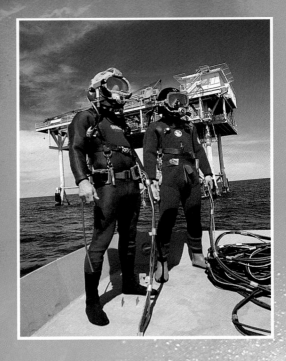

Exxon. Many consider Exxon's influential Houston office—Exxon Company U.S.A.—to be the modern vestige of Humble Oil, and indeed some local oilpatch veterans still refer to Exxon as Humble. Humble's founders enjoyed prominent roles in the creation of modern Houston, their individual destinies intertwined with that of the city. But they surrendered financial control in 1919—two years after Humble's birth in the boomtown north of Houston where oilfields had emerged in 1904—to Standard, selling half the company's stock for a whopping $17 million.

With the acquisition, Standard gained a toehold in Texas and won Humble's rich reserves. But more significantly, it forged the connection that has linked Houston forever with the so-called Big Oil companies headquartered in the East. That connection has actually been a pipeline of manpower that began when Standard acquired the oilmen who ran Humble. Consider Will Farish, Humble's first president. He finished his career as head of Standard. And all across the landscape of the major oil companies loom similar examples of leaders and innovators who passed through Houston en route to corporate glories back east. Global business decisions might have been made in New York, but the oilpatch operations were coordinated by experienced hands in Houston.

Although its official headquarters lie elsewhere, Big Oil maintains a powerful presence in Houston. In 1989 the USA Oil Industry Directory counted just six Houston-based firms described as large oil companies: The Coastal Corp., Conoco, Pennzoil, Shell Oil Co., Panhandle Eastern Corp., and Union Texas Petroleum. But that same year the world's largest oil company, $5.3-billion Exxon Corp. surprised the industry by announcing a relocation of corporate headquarters from New York to the Dallas area. Such a move should send shockwaves through the communities involved, but a look at the real employee numbers demonstrates the complexities of oilpatch diversification and Houston's link to a a giant like Exxon.

For New York the decision meant the relocation of only about 300 persons. Those persons, of course, included heavyweight decision makers. But a look at Exxon's status in Houston shows another side to that company's situation. With seven divisions headquartered in Houston, Exxon already had a presence of 12,500 employees there.

Exxon Company U.S.A. supervised all domestic operations from Houston, while other Exxon divisions controlled a range of activities: Exxon Shipping Co., Exxon Chemical Americas, Exxon Coal & Minerals Co., Exxon Production Research Co., Friendswood Development Co., and Exxon Pipeline Co. Houston has a similar relationship with Texaco, headquartered in White Plains, New York, but supervising domestic operations through Texaco U.S.A. in Houston.

Chevron is a latercomer, tracing its Houston connection to the city's offices of the old Gulf Oil Co., acquired by Chevron in the 1980s. Conoco, now a subsidiary of DuPont, has its headquarters in Houston. Mobil represents the only major with minor operations there.

Shell Oil offers an unusual example of Big Oil in Houston. It relocated its headquarters from New York to Houston in 1972, becoming the first major to actually headquarter there. Suddenly it seized status not only as Houston's largest public company but as the largest one in Texas.

■ *Facing page: Sport divers probe the eerie depths of inner space beneath an oil production platform. Photo by C. Bryan Jones*

■ *Facing page, inset: Commercial divers prepare to inspect a production platform in the Gulf. Photo by C. Bryan Jones*

■ *Ships tie up in the Port of Houston's turning basin.*

Psychologically, the move created tremendous impact because until then Houston and the entire state were considered more like colonial outposts of the majors rather than actual centers of empire. Then, in 1985, Shell's major shareholder, Europe's Royal Dutch-Shell Group, bought the rest of the company, instantly demoting it to the status of a privately held company within the Royal Dutch structure. Shell Oil remains stronger than ever, contributing to the city's business and social fabric as the largest oil company headquartered there. But it no longer appears on the list of Houston public companies, and for many the feeling has never been the same.

That rivalry between Big Oil, with its corporate anonymity, and Little Oil—or the independent entrepreneurial spirit—has characterized the city's oilpatch image throughout the twentieth century. Big Oil might have more money and, ultimately, more power, but it can't compete in another way with its little brother. The independents provide most of the character and color of this city's personality. Houston is actually the product of that different breed—those who stayed home and built the industry from the other side, independent of corporate bureaucracy. They generated much of the wealth and most of the eccentricity creating the oilpatch of legend. They were the wildcatters, the independent producers, and the oilfield service entrepreneurs whose companies reflect their personalities rather than the dark curtain of some corporate veil. With the notable exception of Tenneco Inc., the story of Houston's independent oil community development revolves around a parade of ambitious, forceful individuals who overshadowed their boards of directors and linked personal wealth from the oil industry to the growth of their home.

None of these independents had greater impact or better symbolizes the tie between Houston and oil money than Hugh Roy Cullen, known in oilpatch lore as the King of the Texas Wildcatters. Besides making and losing numerous fortunes during his early years, Cullen also gets credit for the foundation of generosity on which the University of Houston (UH) and the Texas Medical Center were built. Buildings and structures throughout the grounds of those institutions honor the name of the Cullen family, which remains influential and active to this day through its company Quintana Petroleum.

The son of a North Texas farmer, Cullen came to Houston in 1907 at the age of 26, after a career as an independent cotton trader. He admired the port project under way in Houston and began trading in Ship Channel properties. Through land transactions, Cullen learned about the oil business and caught oil fever. He trained himself in geology, studying formations in West Texas where he went briefly to learn about drilling.

He launched his first oil company in 1920. Back then, oil exploration was as much common sense as it was science, and opportunities existed for observant prospectors like Cullen, who could detect signs of oil below on the surface above. Despite some occasional setbacks, Cullen developed a reputation as someone with a nose for oil, and a fortune followed. He created Quintana Petroleum Company in 1938.

His philanthropic side emerged in 1937 when he donated $335,000 for construction of the first building on the UH campus. Still viewing himself as an uneducated working man, Cullen sympathized with the goals of the school: to provide educational opportunity for young people who could not afford to go away to college. Cullen's oil fever quickly turned into educational fever as the King of Wildcatters cemented the tie between oil wealth and community service. He took charge of the school's fundraising efforts with the result that Cullen money financed construction of nearly all campus buildings until it became a state university in 1963. With his spare change, Cullen made donations to the city's emerging hospital structure. The benchmark of his philanthropic career occurred in 1947 with creation of the Cullen Foundation as a charitable trust.

By the time of his death in 1957, Cullen had established the stereotype against which most Houston oil legends have been gauged. While his philanthropy and business talents speak for themselves, eccentricities emerged as byproduct of the wealth, and their notoriety created another side to the traditional wildcatter image. Politically ultraconservative, Cullen championed right wing causes that today would have placed him with the "lunatic fringe," according to an assessment by the *Houston Business Journal*. He once celebrated a UH football team victory over Baylor University by donating $2.3 million for a new engineering building. He announced formation of the Cullen Foundation with an endowment of $80 million worth of oil lands, then told reporters he'd decided on the spur of the moment to make a change: "We've decided to double it," he said quietly while the audience gasped.

Even in death, Cullen continues to haunt society columns through the adventures of descendants and heirs like the Baron Enrico Di Portanova, a jet-setting grandson who challenged the family's hold on what he contended was his share of Quintana. News stories about the probate court battles and gossip column coverage of "Baron Ricky" in his global travels have only kept the Cullen legend alive and added the modern touch to the myth of the Houston oil baron.

While Cullen was building a fortune as a wildcatter, other oilpatch pioneers were discovering alternative roads to wealth. They provided the foundation for Houston's dominance in those unheralded segments of the industry like oilfield services and etched their family names into the city's cultural tapestry. Howard Hughes, the reclusive billionaire who died in Houston in 1976, traced his fabulous wealth to his father's development of the Hughes Drill Bit, a tool that revolutionized oilfield drilling. The company spawned by that invention, now a part of Baker-Hughes, Inc., after a merger in the 1980s, remains headquartered in Houston. Both Hugheses—senior and junior—have their names enshrined on the company's honor wall where they are recognized as two of many Hughes Tool employees who enhanced that company's success with patented inventions over the years.

The controversial public side of oilpatch luminaries like Cullen and Hughes often contrasted sharply with the privacy and success of their business empires. Quintana and Baker-Hughes still stand at the top of their respective fields, but both founders are more fondly remembered for the extracurricular activities generated by their wealth. That sort of notoriety has been lower among the post-World War II generation of empire builders.

The modern oilpatch has sparked its share of mavericks, but their exploits have been more easily followed in the business sections of the local press than in the gossip columns. The new breed has been symbolized by scientific wildcatters like George Mitchell and Michel T. Halbouty who received their geology training in a university but used the same sort of two-fisted business ambition to create their companies. Still influential and active as oilmen, they get plenty of publicity but it's always related to business stands and decisions.

A well-rounded scholar, self-made millionaire, and influential policy maker, Halbouty emerged in the 1980s as a champion of Little Oil and the independents. Outraged by the wave of mergers reshaping the oil industry, he became an articulate spokesman for increased exploration, warning that the nation lay vulnerable to foreign oil powers. As an advisor to presidential commissions and an outspoken member of professional groups like the American Association of Petroleum Geologists, Halbouty thundered against government policies that, he believed, destroyed financial incentive for finding new reserves.

Born in 1909, he worked his way through Texas A&M University to earn that school's first master's degree in geology and parlayed his genius into Halbouty Energy Co. With a network of producing properties and smart Houston real estate acquisitions in the 1960s near Houston's Galleria area, Halbouty helped create the image of the new Houston oilman.

Cut from much the same no-nonsense mold and just 10 years younger than Halbouty, Mitchell also played a large role in transferring oil wealth back to the economic development of the entire region. Another A&M geology alum, Mitchell built Mitchell Energy Corp. from scratch in the 1960s, then diversified with spectacular success in the 1970s and 1980s. He created The Woodlands, a planned business and residential community some 50 miles north of Houston, and saw it grow into a little city of its own with a population of 27,000 by 1989.

Mitchell also helped create the Houston Area Research Center (HARC) as a consortium of educational institutions eager to develop Houston's prominence in technology. Indeed, it's hard to predict the field in which he'll be best remembered, despite the fact that his talents as a scientific wildcatter provided the start.

While Halbouty and Mitchell established a more mainstream tone for Houston oilmen of prominence in recent times, the city's oil community still counts its share of mavericks. Roy Huffington, founder of Huffington Oil, is a prime example. A dead ringer for the late actor John Wayne, Huffington moved his exploration operations to Indonesia in the 1960s as a protest against federal intervention in the oil industry. Vigorous into his 70s, the globetrotting Huffington remained active in Houston civic circles of the 1980s, juggling trips overseas with a variety of appearances back home. In the process, he became one of the few independents to successfully penetrate the overseas exploration market.

Much more visible on the national scale have been Oscar Wyatt, founder of The Coastal Corp., and J. Hugh Liedtke, the patriarch of Pennzoil, Inc. Both sat atop companies that, in the 1980s, should have become acquisition targets. Instead, those firms prowled as corporate predators, due in large part to the personalities of Wyatt and Liedtke. One veteran oilpatch analyst summed up the situation simply by noting, "Nobody anywhere wants to mess with either one of those guys."

Tough, unpredictable, outspoken, and ambitious, they built oilpatch empires by adding a dimension of business savvy to the stereotypical image of the wildcatter-as-prospector. Liedtke won international attention as the architect of Pennzoil's legal campaign against giant Texaco, collecting a multibillion-dollar settlement in a dispute over the acquisition of Getty Oil. Both created independent oil companies that have come closer than any to challenging for status as integrated majors.

While most independent oil companies have taken their image from a reflection of individuals who created them, Houston's largest public company offers a contrast. Tenneco Inc. unquestionably qualifies as an oilpatch maverick, but that reputation doesn't flow from the antics of a single individual at the helm. Growing from a natural gas transmission enterprise of the 1940s, Tenneco diversified *into* oil and gas exploration and then moved farther afield, acquiring insurance interests, an auto parts chain, and farm equipment manufacturers among other non-energy businesses. By the mid-1980s Tenneco was diversifying *out* of some of its investments, selling the insurance companies and, more important, its oil and gas production reserves. Describing itself as a conglomerate rather than an oil company, with J.E. Ketelsen, a former J.I. Case executive, at the helm, Tenneco was nonetheless impressing Wall Street by the end of the decade. Retaining its natural gas transmission company, Tenneco appeared well positioned for the new era about to dawn on the United States oil industry: the age of gas.

SURVIVAL: OILPATCH TO GASPATCH

A sea afloat with many odd fish, Houston's oil community endured a dramatic and painful transition in the 1980s when it led the city into a crisis unlike any it had experienced before. Intoxicated by greed in what seemed like a limitless chain of oil price increases in the late 1970s, companies all over the oilpatch expanded recklessly. Many financed growth with preposterous levels of debt. Oil money infiltrated every economic sector and created a boom marked as much by arrogance as prosperity. The Northeast shivered and complained about the high price of oil. From the oilpatch, however, came reports of bumper stickers that proclaimed: "Freeze a Yankee in the Dark."

Oil prices peaked at $35 per barrel in 1981, and Houston's oil-based economy started to crumble as the price took a downhill slide. Foreign powers, who had helped stimulate the boom by hoarding their oil in the 1970s, opened up the spigots and flooded the market. Just when Houston believed things couldn't get worse, along came 1986, when Saudi Arabia pumped even more of its high quality crude into the global system, sending oil prices below $10.

Just five years before, Houston had shimmered like a magnet in the Sunbelt, drawing workers from plants in the North and symbolizing internationally the power of runaway free enterprise. Almost as quickly, bankruptcy and foreclosure became the important cottage industries, providing jobs for untold numbers of lawyers, accountants, and court personnel. By 1986, three bankruptcy judges in Houston shared more than 21,000 cases as the number of business bankruptcies leaped 400 percent.

As staggering as those numbers were they couldn't match for shock value the identity of some of the victims. Former Texas governor John Connally topped the list of celebrity bankruptcies in 1987 when the oilpatch cancer infected his real estate empire. Connally's response, however, would come to symbolize the reaction of all of Houston to this serious economic threat. He took to the airwaves as pitchman for University Savings & Loan, urging his neighbors to be frugal. He rolled up his sleeves and auctioned off family heirlooms, vowing that he'd not surrender to financial ruin.

The prize example of how the oil price decline could destroy so quickly was provided by the rise and fall of Global Marine, Inc., an offshore drilling contractor. In 1977 the Houston-based firm had just a dozen vessels in its fleet, with assets valued at less than $50 million. By 1985 it had become one of the largest offshore drilling operators in the world, with its fleet of 35 units. Such rapid growth isn't cheap. Between 1979 and 1984 it spent $1.5 billion to add 28 mobile drilling rigs to the fleet. When oil prices cratered, those rigs went out of work, and Global Marine found itself sitting on $1.1 billion worth of debt with no way to make payments. So, in January of 1986, Global Marine with its 11 subsidiaries sought reorganization under Chapter 11 of the federal bankruptcy code.

There was to be a happy ending, however, for Global Marine, John Connally, and Houston

■ *Facing page: A pumper lifts oil from the well when the well does not flow by itself. Photo by C. Bryan Jones*

itself. Despite the suffering caused by the oilpatch recession, it provided many with an education in economic reality. Companies like Global Marine learned how to trim their operations, diversify, and keep debt in check. Companies large and small perished by the thousands, but Global demonstrated its will to survive and emerged from Chapter 11 in February 1989, wiping out some $700 million of its debt. Individuals like Connally learned to appreciate the opportunities still available in Houston. Thousands moved elsewhere or simply disappeared, but Connally emerged from Chapter 11 less than a year after beginning reorganization of $93 million worth of debt.

But the most significant lessons occurred on a community level. In the 1980s Houston learned how to live with its most precious economic resource. It recognized the importance of maintaining a tie to the energy sector while severing the umbilical cord of dependence upon it. Like their predecessors 150 years before who faced the relocation of Texas' capital to Austin, city leaders in the 1980s mapped a blueprint for survival. They created organizations like the Houston Economic Development Council to foster diversification, and Houston Proud to generate a spirit of togetherness that had never really existed in Houston before.

Until the 1980s, Houston had been repeatedly criticized as a city without a soul, one that lacked an important sense of community. Thus, the oil era's benchmark contribution may have come from its collapse rather than its development. The companies that emerged from the crisis were smarter and leaner. The individuals gained confidence and wisdom. And the city? It gained an entire new outlook and perhaps even a whole new economy from the struggle.

As it moved into the 1990s, Houston's energy community had been strengthened by its trials. It had consolidated and pruned out the quick-buck faction that had climbed aboard the energy bandwagon with little cash and less concern for long term growth. Energy had led Houston into a disastrous recession, but in the end, it also helped lead the way out. Oil companies learned new respect for their downstream operations. With oil prices low, refinery products and petrochemicals became more profitable. The crisis had forced economic diversification, and by 1989 the Texas comptroller's office declared the city "less dependent on the energy industry than ever before."

But another event of 1989 signaled greater changes ahead. In September of that year Baker Hughes announced that, for the first time ever, more rigs were drilling for natural gas than for oil. Texas Railroad Commissioner John Sharp hailed the announcement as a major shift in the energy industry and a historic milestone for Texas, noting the "rebirth of our state's energy industry." With more than 20 percent of the nation's remaining gas reserves and the 1990s looming as the decade of environmental concerns, Texas in general and Houston in particular appeared perfectly positioned to welcome an increased role for natural gas.

Beyond its location as a center for exploration and production, Houston offered something even more important to the energy industry with gas as the dominant commodity. It was unquestionably the headquarters for the natural gas pipeline industry. As home to companies like Enron, Transco, Panhandle Eastern, Coastal, and Tenneco, Houston could boast in an age of gas that, more than ever before, all roads to power pass through here.

"More oil and gas companies here are really gas producers," notes Victor A. Burk, managing director of oil and gas services for Arthur Andersen & Co. "The 1990s will be the decade of the environment with a lot more emphasis on gas. It's really stimulating for Houston. They can raise capital again for exploration."

From oilpatch to gaspatch Houston learned the value of maintaining its dominant industry while helping other sectors blast off for the future, too. And the ugly impression of the "Freeze a Yankee" slogans was overshadowed by the proliferation of telecopier prayers appearing in offices all over Houston in the waning days of the decade: "Dear Lord, please send us another oil boom. We promise not to screw this one up."

3

THE

SPACE CITY

W hen lovers gaze at the moon they turn mellow and hear violins. Unless, of course, they live in Houston. In that case, they turn ambitious and hear cash registers ringing.

It's a strange effect that comes from living where economic development leaders can honestly boast that their city's name was the first word spoken from the moon: "Houston, Tranquility Base here. The Eagle has landed." The moon holds as much power over Houston as it does on Gulf Coast tides. That's not to charge that Houstonians are any less romantic than people anywhere else. They just understand the economic importance of space commerce better because, in Houston, that infant industry is expected someday to have an impact on everyone there.

Indeed, over the years Houston has answered to a variety of nicknames. In the beginning it was a paper city. In later times it became the Bayou City. And for most of the twentieth century it's been the Energy City. But Houstonians who travel overseas know that foreigners recognize their home for its connection with space more than anything else. The Houston Police Department even decorates its uniforms with a patch that illustrates the path of satellites around the globe and identifies Houston by its nickname of the future: Space City.

The exact status of that future, however, remains a subject in debate. Until the 1980s space and its possibilities were government monopolies. Only the United States had a bankroll big enough and brainpower sharp enough to explore beyond the gravity of earth. Although Houston played a central role in that federal adventure, it still couldn't gauge with much ac-

■ *Johnson Space Center visitors are treated to close-up views of a variety of rockets. Photo by C. Bryan Jones*

curacy the financial impact of the revolution that began in the last decade when private entrepreneurs began to chisel off small slices of the industry and clamor for more. Staring into an unknown void of economic development, business leaders offered a wide range of estimates to cover the potential out there. They only know two things for sure. The impact in Houston has already been significant. And the prospects have no bounds.

Perhaps that's why Houston has enjoyed more than its share of imaginative entrepreneurs eager to exploit the space age. They've ranged from the arcane to the totally credible. And who's to call any of them dreamers? It's home to the world's first self-proclaimed space lawyer, Art Dula (as distinguished from spaced-out lawyers, a category in which Houston boasts a healthy supply as well). One of the city's savings institutions became the first to apply for a branch on the moon. One company, Space Services Inc., has discussed plans to handle burials in space while yet another firm, Lunar Industries, envisions the day when cement barges will load natural product on the moon and deliver it to construction sites on earth. Both Space Services and Lunar Industries are run by scientists with impressive credentials and great hopes for the future. Lunar Industries' William Agosto has a contract with NASA (National Aeronautics and Space Administration) that will have him intricately involved with the first moon base when it comes to pass, while Space Services, under the leadership of former astronaut Donald K. "Deke" Slayton, enjoys the reputation of being the first private firm to send a rocket into space. Dula has pioneered the field of space law, building his practice throughout the 1980s, collecting a client list and launching his own company, Space Commerce Corp.

To understand how such companies came to be and to accurately assess their prospects, it's first necessary to review the story of Houston's space connection and see where that link may lead. Like other sectors in Houston's development, space is more a triumph of leadership than coincidence. Politicians and ambitious business leaders make Houston's space history just as colorful as its past in energy or regional transportation. It's a tale that involves scientists, real estate developers, and the world's largest oil company. Houston's space industry is actually based in an independent-minded community 25 miles southeast of downtown. A marsh prairie at the edge of Clear Lake just off Galveston Bay seems an unlikely place to support the group of 10 small cities that have sprung to existence there since the 1960s. The explanation lies in a series of national political developments that occurred about a quarter of a century ago.

THE FEDERAL ADVENTURE

Shocked into the space race by Soviet space successes in the late 1950s, the United States wasted no time catching up. The first group of astronauts began making their own headlines, denting the heavens and providing proof that space exploration might actually be a possibility in the twentieth century. Shortly after Alan Shepard's successful suborbital flight on May 5, 1961, President John F. Kennedy added his endorsement with announcement of a lofty goal to land a man on the moon by the end of the decade. But the country needed a facility where that plan could be designed.

By July, NASA had drafted a list of the assets needed by communities eager to vie for the site of its proposed Manned Spacecraft Center. NASA sought a location with access to water transportation that was in the proximity of a military base, a commercial jet airport, and an established university specializing in science and space-related research. It wanted a place with a major telecommunications network, a pool of contractor and industrial support, adequate water supplies, a mild climate year-round, and room to build and grow. Houston didn't exactly have the best qualifications in each of these categories, but it did have four other assets that would prove more important: Congressmen Albert Thomas and Olin E. "Tiger" Teague, Vice President Lyndon B. Johnson, and the Humble Oil and Refining Co. (now Exxon Corp.).

In his 24th year in Congress, Thomas was a shrewd and gentlemanly politician who wore bow ties and had taken the rookie congressman JFK under his wing. As chairman of the House Appropriations subcommittee that monitored NASA's budget, Thomas packed considerable clout. Teague was a war hero whose Texas district included the Galveston Bay area, where the Johnson Space Center now stands. He also chaired the House Space Committee back then. Johnson, long a champion of the space program, chaired Kennedy's National Aeronautics and Space Council as vice president.

■ *Facing page: German payload specialists working for the Federal German Aerospace Research Establishment train for space flight in Houston's KC-135 or Zero-Gravity aircraft. Courtesy, Johnson Space Center*

■ *Below: The immensity of these rocket engines is apparent when viewed next to Johnson Space Center visitors. Photo by David S. Wadsworth/Image Finders*

JFK wanted the lab in Boston, but the Texas political lobby, sold on Houston, overcame the area's deficiencies by packaging a land deal that must have left the Allen brothers grinning from the grave. Just as the Allens had attracted the Texas capital with an offer of cheap land a century before, this generation of Texans persuaded Humble to donate 1,000 acres of rangeland near Ellington Air Force Base to Rice University, which in turn offered the property to NASA. The government announced Houston's selection on September 19, 1961.

Before anyone files Humble's gesture completely in the philanthropy drawer, however, a few things should be noted. By donating the land to Rice instead of directly to NASA, Humble got a big tax break. Humble also swapped another 600 acres to Rice for 100 acres of university property in Downtown Houston. And most significant for Humble's future prosperity, it retained ownership of the 31,000-acre parcel that became the cornerstone of Friendswood Development Corp., now one of Exxon's most profitable operating divisions.

Some developers feel blessed when they own land where the government builds a freeway interchange. If you're Exxon, you own the land around the government's space program. Their holdings marked the beginning of Clear Lake City, a master-planned community custom designed for families who would build the space industry. A company like Exxon always gets its payday but Houston and Rice got paydays, too. Thanks to Exxon, Houston is Space City. Rice sold its additional 600 acres there to the government for $2 million. And through its Exxon alliance, Rice became the initial research university for the manned space program, receiving a grant of $1.8 million to construct the Space Sciences Building and finance the new Department of Space Physics and Astronomy.

■ *Some of the comforts of home, including video tapes and books, travel with the space shuttle astronauts into outer space. Photo by Bob Rowan/ Progressive Image Photography*

Rockets would not launch from Houston nor would their construction occur there. No matter. As home to mission control, Houston seemed like the center of the universe. It anxiously welcomed the participants in a new industry with adventure as the theme and excitement as a byproduct.

NASA started moving into the newly completed facilities in 1963, and employees of big name private contractors paraded into the area. Lockheed arrived to support development of the launch escape system and McDonnell Douglas to provide the simulators. Rockwell came to build the Apollo Command and Service Modules while TRW coordinated data handling and trajectory analysis. Hamilton Standard, Bendix, IBM, Motorola, Grumman, and Ford Aerospace joined the community, each fulfilling a part of the mission that would see the government space program through its various phases, Mercury to Gemini to Apollo to the moon and beyond.

Houston's role as home to the Manned Spacecraft Center took shape somewhat resembling its nerve-center relationship to the oil industry. With astronaut training responsibilities moved to Houston in 1965, the space center became a campus, as well as a headquarters for development and mission control. With the relocation of astronauts and their families, Clear Lake became a hometown for the celebrities and heroes who would make the race for the moon. Developers smelled profit, and Exxon's Clear Lake City soon boasted nine smaller siblings: Webster, where the center actually stands; El Lago; Seabrook; Nassau Bay; League City; Kemah; Clear Lake Shores; Friendswood; and Taylor Lake Village.

All America thrilled to the datelines from Houston, its window on space. Gemini 6 through 12 included space walks, docking, and rendezvous in space. Apollo 1 sent the nation into mourning with the fire that erupted on the launch pad at Cape Kennedy, killing all three astronauts aboard. Unmanned missions of Apollo 2 through 6 reminded Americans of the dangers out there and of the need to proceed with caution. The successes of the manned Apollo flights 7 through 10 climaxed with orbits around the moon and proved the perseverance of the nation in pursuit of its ambitious goal. Apollo 11 cornered the largest global television audience in history when it landed astronauts Neil A. Armstrong and Edwin "Buzz" E. Aldrin, Jr., to actually walk on the moon, while astronaut Michael Collins orbited aboard the lunar command module. The worldwide fanfare was understandable and deserved. Could any event in all recorded history really compare with the achievement of travel to another world? Few could offer a contender.

In the wake of the accomplishment, however, new questions began to surface. What next? Where is this experience taking us? Was this just a neat little trick, or can we harness the power of spaceflight for more universal commercial applications? All these questions still cry for complete answers. But events in the years since Apollo 11 demonstrate that the young industry is drafting a response, and Houston remains intricately involved.

THE GOVERNMENT HANDS OFF TO PRIVATE ENTERPRISE

NASA followed its landmark Apollo 11 moon shot in the 1970s with more trips to the moon, Skylab, and an orbital rendezvous with the Russians. All the while, NASA and the nation seemed to be grappling with more definite questions of direction. Some critics openly wondered about the actual value of the space program, weighing its expense against the financial return. Houstonians could see the tremendous financial impact locally, but NASA was forced to justify its efforts with a continual presentation of spin-off technology—devices and procedures that transferred from the frontier of space into business or the home. In the two decades since man first walked on the moon, that legacy of advances has been impressive. Just listing some of them helps explain why private enterprise started itching for its opportunity in space.

The space program gave medicine lightweight, ultrasound, diagnostic instruments for monitoring heart functions externally; rechargeable cardiac pacemakers; enhancement of X-rays by computer processing; safer methods of breast cancer detection; and techniques for freezing white blood cells used in leukemia research.

It gave transportation the concept of computer designs for automobiles, truck chassis, and railroad car structures; adaptation of Lunar Rover drive controls for the handicapped; improved highway guard rails and road surfaces for increased safety; analyses of rail car wheel bearings to reduce future derailments; and techniques to improve rapid transit switch controls.

In energy and the environment, the space program gave us heat pipes to protect Alaska pipeline structural supports; furnace devices used to reclaim and recirculate waste heat; solar collector systems for homes; and hazardous-gas analyzers for measuring automobile emissions and air pollutants.

To the field of public safety, it gave improved breathing systems for firefighters; fireproof materials for clothes and home furnishings; ultrasound emergency warning devices for home, school, and public facilities; and lightweight pressure vessels for aircraft downed over water.

Besides opening up the heavens, NASA opened a brand new frontier of technological development. During the 1970s Houston and its Clear Lake suburb consolidated their hold on economic growth stemming from those advances. The Johnson Space Center (JSC) became one of the state's top tourist attractions, where visitors could share the experience of astronaut education, examine rocks from the moon, and relive great moments in its museum. Clear Lake became

Communications satellites send signals from space to satellite ground stations such as this one in Houston. Photo by Bob Rowan/ Progressive Image Photography

a recreational haven which now boasts more than 7,000 boat slips and 12 marinas. The University of Houston expanded into the area in 1975 creating the University of Houston-Clear Lake. It is one of only 14 upper level universities in the United States and is the fourth largest graduate school in Texas.

By the 1980s it became clear that government and private enterprise could indeed form an alliance. That's when the federal focus shifted and homed in on a new direction that would benefit both. The space shuttle program and plans for a space station marked the dawn of the age of reusable spacecraft. About the same time, another shift occurred that would significantly influence the direction of private space development in Houston. Early pioneers of the government space effort began retiring to second careers in the Houston area. Suddenly Houston's ambitious entrepreneurs had a powerful new asset to exploit in their own goals: experienced minds. Together those two developments moved Houston and the space industry to where they stand today—on the threshold of commercialization.

Of the many firms to emerge in Houston's fledgling space commerce community of the 1980s, three have commanded the most attention and seem to embody the alliance of entrepreneurs with NASA alums: Space Services Inc. (SSI), Space Industries, Inc. (SII), and Eagle Engineering. Each operates in a special niche of the space field and illustrates the different dimensions blossoming as business reaches for the stars.

SSI burst into national visibility in 1982 when it became the first private firm to successfully launch a rocket. It views its business future as space transportation: delivery of cargoes like satellites into orbit from earth. SSI made history in March 1989 by becoming the first private company to be paid for taking cargo into space. Blasting off from White Sands, New Mexico, it sent a 73-foot rocket to an altitude of 200 miles, where a parachute opened, allowing a 650-pound payload capsule with six materials-processing experiments to float back to earth. NASA, through its Consort research program, paid SSI $1 million to expose the experiments, designed to investigate the manner in which liquids and metals mix when heated.

"We want to do this every day," said SSI's founder, David Hannah, Jr., at the completion of that mission. A millionaire Houston real estate developer, Hannah became a space buff in 1976 when he read an article in *Smithsonian* about the prospects for colonies in space. He lobbied President Jimmy Carter and helped create the Space Foundation in 1979 with a group of fellow Houstonians eager to reassert their city's role in the future of space. He attracted investors and dabbled with the dream of launching a rocket.

Those dreams turned to nightmares in August 1981 when SSI's first attempt exploded on its Matagorda Island launch pad, devouring $1.2 million worth of investors' money. Undaunted, Hannah turned to NASA for help and, in the process, discovered someone with something more valuable than money to invest in SSI. Donald L. "Deke" Slayton was retiring from his long career as an astronaut and flight specialist. Looking only for a consultant, Hannah landed Slayton as a top executive. Slayton suggested significant changes in fuel type and rocket design while adding credibility to the company. SSI also linked up with Eagle Engineering for that young

■ *A replica of the battleship*
Texas, *now one of Houston's*
tourist attractions, was original-
ly featured in a parade celebrat-
ing the formal dedication of the
Houston Ship Channel on
November 10, 1914. Photo by C.
Bryan Jones

company's contribution. In 1990 SSI faced widely publicized financial difficulties that threatened its future and underscored the scale of investment required to make commercial space business a reality. Regardless of SSI's future, however, its past guarantees the company a place of honor in the industry's development.

Eagle had been founded by Owen Morris and fellow engineers who named the company after the historic moonlanding vehicle. The company ranks as the prominent prototype for NASA engineers striking out on their own. While most of its work remains aerospace related, Eagle has also branched into projects for analysis of medical, petrochemical, and automotive products, further demonstrating the versatility of space science expertise.

While SSI and Eagle were at work on their plans, the son of a Houston oil baron was anxiously explaining his dreams to another retired NASA legend. That alliance between oilpatch heir James D. Callaway and Maxime A. Faget resulted in the founding of SII in 1982. SII has designed and will operate the Industrial Space Facility as the first permanent, man-tended commercial space facility developed for research. Hailed by some as the father of manned spaceflight, Faget had been chief of manned spacecraft design from Mercury through Gemini and Apollo and into the shuttle era. A legendary space engineer, Faget received the first annual Rotary National Award for Space Achievement in 1987. He, in turn, recruited astronaut-physicist Joseph P. Allen who achieved national prominence in the 1980s with his spacewalks retrieving satellites.

While SSI focused on transportation, SII plans construction and deployment of actual space industrial facilities. SII so impressed NASA with its plans that the government agreed in 1985 to defer collection of its launch fee until after SII's orbiting facility starts generating revenue. That's the equivalent of a $250-million advance.

None of these private endeavors should be confused with the big plum for space development, construction of the U.S. Space Station. SII's facility would serve as an adjunct to this project, but it could hardly compete with the scope of the government's plans for the multibillion-dollar project. With much of the planning coordinated from Houston, the space station also means a larger role in the future for companies there.

Vulnerable to the whims of politics, however, government planning for space remains unpredictable, and the decisions of Congress can derail even the most specific blueprints for expansion. Even more unpredictable is the aspect of disaster. Its impact was clearly demonstrated in 1986 when the shuttle *Challenger* exploded after takeoff. So close to the entire space program and its participants, Houston went into mourning over the tragedy which effectively put the nation's entire space effort on hold for more than two years. In an ironic way, the *Challenger* tragedy has demonstrated the nation's resolve toward space. The investigations into the cause and the debate over solutions only strengthened the whole space program, preparing it for more ambitious adventures in the 1990s.

HOUSTON, SPACE, AND THE FUTURE

For Houston's space entrepreneurs operating today, space commerce resembles the oil industry of 150 years ago. Early oil pioneers in Pennsylvania knew they had discovered a source of energy with tremendous potential. But oil had to create its own markets. Until Spindletop demonstrated the true abundance of the commodity and until Detroit responded with mass production of a vehicle to use it, the oil industry was merely one of potential rather than reality. As time wore on, the industry discovered more ways to insert its products into modern life.

And so it goes with today's primitive space commerce efforts. The space business pioneers know that Houston has enjoyed the benefits of space spinoff. And they're quick to list the ways that today's industries can use space to improve their products. Until they can remain on the moon or on manmade satellites like the space station for long periods of time, however, those entrepreneurs can't really predict what kinds of new products or services might stem from the effort.

"So far, the growth of space commerce has been very slow," says Bill Huffstetler, manager of the New Initiatives Office for the Johnson Space Center and the space program's link to private enterprise. "The demand hasn't existed. When we start going back to the moon and to Mars on a long range, integrated pro-

■ *An aesthetically pleasing fountain and waterscape offer a peaceful respite from the daily business activities of downtown. Photo by Bob Rowan/ Progressive Image Photography*

gram we'll learn more. And the only way to make it is with the private sector involved. So far, the guys in Houston have been the most innovative. Deke and Faget have good ideas. Houston's space community is very innovative and dedicated. They know the trials and tribulations because of their service in the federal space program. Houston has the most realistic set of people in space commerce anywhere in the United States."

So what do those "realistic" space entrepreneurs have in mind? For starters they've been measuring the potential out there from all angles. William Agosto of Lunar Industries says space will become a source of cheap energy, and his reasoning makes a lot of sense. Thanks to the low gravitational pull of the moon, engineers could travel there and construct a massive solar-powered furnace, then launch it back toward earth. That goal would be impossible from down here. But Agosto and his fellow pioneers have other, more immediate targets in mind.

In the first real analysis of space commerce and its impact, the Space Business Research Center through NASA and the University of Houston-Clear Lake published a report in 1988 detailing the markets and prospects for business ventures. The report noted: "The world's newest industry—currently centered in the United States—already has surpassed many of the oldest and largest industries in the country. Despite its infancy, the space industry is now one of the key industries nationwide in volume . . . The $14.1 billion U.S. space industry is a blend of public and private activity with the federal government buying the bulk of shipments with $9 billion in deliveries."

Houston's share of that impact has been immense. In 1987, for example, the space center itself contributed $786 million to Houston's economy, a figure representing about a quarter of the center's total budget. Most of the money flows directly to JSC and contractor employees as salaries and wages. But secondary effects like businesses with indirect ties to NASA add over $900 million more to the local picture.

The industry itself can be divided into four markets, each distinct but dependent on at least one of the others. Space transportation is the largest single sector. It involves the manufacture of launch vehicles plus related products and services. Payloads are predominantly satellites, and their operations constitute the second identifiable market—communications satellites. That market includes the satellites themselves, ground stations for receipt of their signals, and service income from leasing satellite transponders for audio, video, or data communication channels. Remote sensing emerges as the third major space market. It involves all the potential applications of satellite photographs and digital images for weather and crop forecasting, oil and mineral exploration, and other businesses that need the big picture. The final market remains embryonic, but it is the one most attractive to Houston's entrepreneurial community: microgravity materials processing.

The vacuum of space offers manufacturers the chance to do things they can't do on earth. They can produce perfect crystals, pure pharmaceuticals, and alloys for commercially feasible superconductors or more powerful computers. By 1989 only one product had been manufactured in space for commercial sale: 10-micrometer latex spheres, made on five different shuttle flights between November 1981 and February 1984. A total of 89 units had been sold for gross revenues of $56,000. SII's industrial space facility is designed to exploit these opportunities as a technological stepping stone for the space station. And SSI is developing a craft similar to a Mercury space capsule that will carry experiments for such manufacturers into orbit.

For impatient Houstonians, the time between man's first stroll on the moon and the construction of industrial plants in space still seems too long. But true space believers like to cite America's experiences in the early nineteenth century to place the time lag in proper perspective. They note that it took John Jacob Astor 30 years after the Lewis and Clark expedition to create America's first native fortune from the fur trade of the Rocky Mountains. It's only been two decades since "Houston" became the first word spoken from the moon. They're betting that connection will only have greater implications in the years to come.

4

THE

MEDICAL CITY

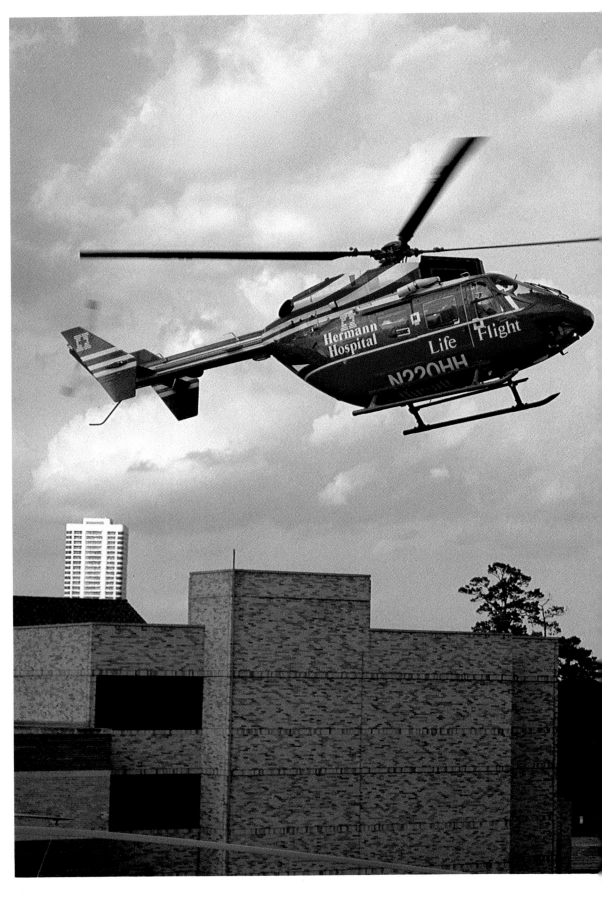

W ell aware of Houston's international reputation in energy and space, outsiders often express surprise when told the identity of the city's single largest employer. It's not an oil company, nor is it the Johnson Space Center. With more than 50,000 full- and part-time employees, the Texas Medical Center (TMC) dwarfs businesses and public institutions alike. Add the center's formidable inpatient population—240,000 in 1988—and it's clear that the Texas Medical Center ranks as a community unto itself.

Economically and culturally, the presence of the TMC has played an enormous role in Houston. Located just south of the city's central business district, the Texas Medical Center stands as a core for a health services industry with impact well beyond the center's 546-acre complex of 41 member institutions. Acknowledged as one of the world's top treatment locations for the most devastating ailments, particularly cancer and heart disease, the TMC attracts patients from all over the globe, filling nearby hotels with relatives and supporters, while emerging as a significant player in the international service sector. Its focus on the cutting edge of medical treatment has rippled into the cutting edge of research to spawn yet another important growth industry for Houston: The city launched more than 50 biotechnology firms in the 1980s. At the same time, TMC stands among the nation's most influential medical education sites as home to Baylor College of Medicine and the University of Texas Health Science Center.

Medicine in Houston posts important numbers in different fields: business, economic development, culture, image, and education. But most

■ *Hermann Hospital's Life Flight Helicopter has contributed to the hospital's reputation as a well-respected trauma care center. Photo by Bob Rowan/ Progressive Image Photography*

■ *The Texas Medical Center has played an enormous technological and cultural role in Houston's development. Photo by James Blank*

■ *The Del Oro Institute for Rehabilitation prepares patients to confront commonplace tasks and experience real-life situations with its "Easy Street" simulated environment. Photo by C. Bryan Jones*

important, Houston the medical city appears to be just hitting top stride as the nation closes out the twentieth century. Its best years still lie ahead, creating in Houston yet another gateway to the future that easily rivals prospects in energy or space.

Indeed, statistics from the 1980s underscore the impression that growth in the TMC is just getting started. Funded research in TMC, mostly for cancer, heart disease, and molecular medicine, rose from $105 million to $229 million between 1986 and 1988. Patient visits had risen to 2.3 million in 1988 from 2 million two years before. Each day in 1988 the center welcomed 107,000 persons, including patients, visitors, students, faculty, and staff. And, while Houston reeled in the mid-1980s from the oilpatch recession, the TMC seemed unaffected. New construction stopped all over the city except in TMC where some $3.5 billion worth of expansions and additions rose from the ground.

But statistics tell just one side of the medical story in Houston. Like oil and space, medicine has been a dramatic and glamorous business. Much the product of oilpatch philanthropy, Houston's medical industry has spawned its share of colorful characters and provocative events. Few can think of heart surgery without recalling the rivalry and contributions of Michael DeBakey and Denton Cooley, men who becme celebrities on an international level due to their work in Houston. In 1954 DeBakey became the first to employ a dacron graft to bypass an aneurysm in just one of many history-making achievements that kept his face on the cover of magazines like *Time*. And it was on Cooley's operating table in 1969 that Haskell Karp made history by surviving 63 hours with an artificial heart and drawing the international spotlight to the medical center. In the field of immunology, Houston's "Bubble Boy," identified only as "David," captured the imagination of a generation by living all 12 years of his life inside a sterile, plastic bubble.

The city's timing has been perfect. As Nicholas Lemann noted in a 1979 article for *Texas Monthly*, the development of the Salk vaccine in the 1950s marked a turning point in American medicine, away from a preoccupation with acute ailments into the era of chronic diseases like cancer and heart problems. It's an era that offered all the elements of heroic theater, pitting dedicated medical crusaders against invisible bugs as ancient as life itself. Houston researchers have helped write the first chapters of human history's next great adventure and mystery tale. That yarn won't be complete until the horror of cancer and heart attacks are eliminated from our plans for the future. It's certain that Houston will play a prominent role all the way to the end.

TEXAS MEDICAL CENTER—A LEGACY OF OIL AND COTTON

It would be a serious mistake to think that all of Houston's medical enterprise is generated in the Texas Medical Center. More than 102 hospitals with 22,370 beds serve the 15-county area surrounding Houston, and 51 of those lie within the city limits.

Several large systems have evolved, like the Memorial Care hospitals. Research has outlets outside the TMC, too, notably at St. Joseph's Hospital in Downtown Houston, where cancer advances have occurred. But the core of Houston's prominence in international medicine and its launchpad for the future in that field remains headquartered at Main Street and Holcombe Boulevard where the Texas Medical Center stands, a hub of excitement and activity. The story of

Houston's medical past, as well as its future, can be found there.

Curiously enough it was cotton, not oil, that provided the major Houston fortune that formed the foundation of the city's medical industry through creation of the Texas Medical Center. But land and oil wealth played their parts as well. And it was two heirless, unusual Houstonians who got things started with a lot of help, once again, from farsighted city leaders with an open mind toward economic development.

One cornerstone of medical philanthropy arrived in 1914 when George Hermann, a legendary eccentric, became upon his death the greatest public benefactor the city had ever known.

He left the bulk of his estate, then valued at $2.6 million, for the construction and maintenance of what would become Houston's first charity hospital, Hermann Hospital. A Houston native born in 1843 to Swiss immigrants, Hermann had parlayed his sharp mind into enormous land wealth. He operated a wood and saw mill on acreage south of the city where Houstonians dumped their garbage.

By the turn of the century, fellow Houstonians were aware of his unconventional ways. A Confederate veteran and confirmed bachelor, his penny-pinching habits had created their own aura. He once threatened a lawsuit in a dispute over $2.75. Although a millionaire, he sailed second class when traveling to Europe, and at the time of his death he was renting a room in the home of a friend. He had traded two mules and a wagon for 30 acres of land near Humble where oil was discovered, but he always viewed himself as a cowboy and was buried with his boots on.

But Hermann had endured an experience in New York that helps explain the focus of his generosity. While visiting up north he had become ill and collapsed on a sidewalk, landing later in a large charity hospital where the level of cruel, indifferent treatment horrified him. He vowed that he would create for his native city a charity hospital where such atrocities would never occur.

■ *Designated one of the nation's first three comprehensive cancer centers, the M.D. Anderson Cancer Center has pioneered anti-cancer drugs and treatments. Photo by Bob Rowan/ Progressive Image Photography*

Ironically, he died in Baltimore seeking treatment for stomach cancer—a treatment that was unavailable at home in Houston.

But Hermann's estate generated the city's first important attempt at providing modern medical care. Unfortunately, in 1914, Houstonians were ill prepared to smoothly handle such a large gift, and the story of the Hermann estate has been one laced with scandal. It took 11 years to get the hospital open, a six-story structure about four miles south of downtown on the southern edge of Hermann Park, another George Hermann bequest. Indeed, the controversy over proper use of estate funds for care of the poor has lingered into the 1980s when indictments and jail terms ensnarled several prominent individuals associated with the trust.

Nevertheless, Hermann Hospital remains an important medical facility. It has pioneered the frontiers of emergency care through an alliance with the University of Texas and development of Hermann's world-renowned Life Flight Helicopter service. Originally constructed beyond the urban boundaries of Houston at the end of the trolley tracks, Hermann Hospital saw the city sweep past its location, absorbing it into what now constitutes Houston's downtown. Its palatial Moorish architecture anchors the northeast corner of what has become the Texas Medical Center.

While Hermann's oilpatch generosity and his hospital have served as a cornerstone for this complex, the top measure of credit for TMC as a concept belongs to the cotton wealth empire of Monroe Dunway Anderson. One of the center's key landmarks, M.D. Anderson Hospital has become synonymous internationally with cancer treatment and research. Before the hospital was built, however, Anderson had built a fortune in Houston as founder of the world's largest cotton company, Anderson, Clayton & Company. Anderson's $19-million legacy upon his death in 1939 formed the foundation and launched the debate that would lead in 1946 to dedication of the Texas Medical Center, Inc.

Anderson's story is one to make Horatio Alger proud. Born in 1873 in Jackson, Tennessee, Anderson was the son of a Presbyterian minister who had spent two years in a Union prison camp and returned home to organize a bank. But the father died in 1878 leaving his widow with eight children, including Monroe. As an elementary school student he joined a friend in starting a small laundry to help with the family finances. After eighth grade graduation, the young Anderson became an assistant cashier in a Jackson bank and earned a reputation for frugality.

By the time he was 31 he had accumulated enough to invest $9,000 in a venture with a boyhood friend, Will Clayton, organizing the company in 1904 in Oklahoma City. Initially the firm bought cotton from growers in Oklahoma and Texas, selling to mills in Europe. The company expanded, and by 1908 Anderson was in Houston opening an office there. Eight years later, headquarters relocated to Houston, drawn by the city's port expansions. Over the years the company expanded into ginning services and cottonseed oil mills, eventually becoming the world's

■ *The University of Texas' M.D. Anderson Cancer Center offers a ray of hope for many cancer patients. Photo by Bob Rowan/ Progressive Image Photography*

largest single buyer, storer, seller, and shipper of raw cotton.

Despite his wealth, Anderson led a simple life. A close friend once told reporters: "To him the spending of money except for a useful purpose was distasteful, clear evidence of lack of breeding." He lived in hotels and boarding houses, taking Sunday dinners at his brother's home where nieces and nephews filled the familial void in the life of this confirmed bachelor.

In the mid-1930s Anderson's health began to fail. Lacking heirs and eager to preserve his wealth for significant purposes, he established the M.D. Anderson Foundation in 1936 with an endowment of $300,000. When he died three years later, Anderson's $19-million estate ranked as the largest ever for Texas. His trustees then began to consider meaningful ways to distribute the money. There's little doubt that Anderson would applaud the results if he could return and review their response.

Prominent attorneys who helped create the powerhouse law firm now known as Fulbright & Jaworski, John H. Freeman and William B. Bates first toyed with the idea of establishing a white collar hospital. They noted that the very rich had plenty of money for medical expenses and the very poor could get it free. But the folks in the middle had nowhere to turn.

With their attention already focused on a medical outlet for the Anderson fortune, the trustees noted that the Texas Legislature had appropriated $500,000 to build a state-owned cancer hospital and research facility under operation of the University of Texas. Acting in the city's best heritage of economic development, they crafted another one of those classic Houston propositions, not unlike the actions of the founding Allen brothers in attracting the Republic's first capital or those of city leaders in the 1960s vying for the space center. They abandoned their white collar hospital plans and offered the university a site in Houston plus another $500,000 to establish what would be called M.D. Anderson Hospital.

As they grew more enthusiastic about their plans for a medical use of Anderson's money, Freeman and Bates developed a friendship with someone destined to really inflate their dreams. Dr. Ernst William Bertner was the house doctor at the Rice Hotel. He became acquainted with Freeman, who lived on the same floor of the hotel, and encouraged the trustees, believing they could build a medical center in Houston that would one day rival the Mayo Clinic, with $100 million worth of buildings.

Inspired by Bertner's visions, the trustees moved quickly. In 1943 they bought a 134-acre tract of land south of Hermann Park. Then they began recruiting medical schools and other hospitals to join Hermann and M.D. Anderson in the neighborhood. Desperately seeking a top-flight medical school to enhance the reputation of the complex, they wooed Baylor University's medical school away from Dallas. They offered Baylor a site, a million dollars for a new building, and another million for research.

Free land and additional $500,000 grants attracted other facilities into the parade: UT built its dental school there, Methodist Hos-

■ *The Texas Heart Institute, created around the heart surgery work of Denton Cooley, is located beneath the 950-bed St. Luke's Episcopal Hospital and Texas Children's Hospital, where 38 medical and surgical subspecialty services treat the whole spectrum of childhood illnesses. Photo by Bob Rowan/ Progressive Image Photography*

pital moved from an old building downtown and St. Luke's Episcopal Hospital was built. They persuaded Hermann Hospital to use $500,000 of Anderson's money to finance a new wing facing the Medical Center. By the end of World War II Houston had the foundation in place for an exciting new industry that has continued to grow dramatically through good times and bad. Besides the facilities, the center has attracted a long list of legendary surgeons and researchers—the people who actually made TMC into the world-class complex of today.

The major institutions of the TMC can be classified in four different categories: general care hospitals, specialized hospitals, educational facilities, and public health buildings. It's worth taking the time to understand the role of each institution within its area.

General care hospitals include Ben Taub General Hospital, the principal hospital facility of the Harris County Hospital District. It is the city's primary provider for indigent care and serves as the major emergency medical center in the area. Like Ben Taub, Hermann Hospital enjoys a reputation for trauma care through its Life Flight Helicopter program. The primary teaching hospital for the University of Texas Health Science Center at Houston, Hermann was the city's fourth largest hospital in the 1980s with more than 900 beds. St. Luke's Episcopal Hospital ranked slightly larger with more than 950 beds and has been associated with the heart surgery work of Denton Cooley. But the Methodist Hospital, with more than 1,500 beds and 5,600 employees, easily ranks as the largest of the TMC general hospitals, and has been closely associated with the work of Michael DeBakey. Methodist is the primary private teaching facility for Baylor College of Medicine.

From among the specialty institutions, the University of Texas System Cancer Center-M.D. Anderson Cancer Center employs nearly 1,000 more personnel than Methodist, but it has just little more than 500 beds. In 1971 it was designated as one of the first three comprehensive cancer centers in the nation, a place where innovative surgeons pioneered modern anti-cancer drugs

■ *Hermann Hospital is housed in this palatial Moorish-style building at the northeast corner of what is now the Texas Medical Center. With more than 900 beds, Hermann was the city's fourth-largest hospital in the 1980s. Photo by Bob Rowan/ Progressive Image Photography*

■ *Right: This attractive atrium-like interior belongs to Methodist Hospital, the largest of the TMC general hospitals. Photo by Bob Rowan/ Progressive Image Photography*

■ *Below: Baylor College of Medicine, of which the Cullen building is part, is the only private medical school in the Southwest. Photo by Bob Rowan/ Progressive Image Photography*

and developed the prototype of the Cobalt 60 unit to make radiotherapy a viable treatment option. M.D. Anderson has become a world unto itself, the last oasis of hope for anyone battling any variety of what has become mankind's most frightening medical enemy. A tour of the facility and visits with its patients open doors to observations of life and death unavailable anywhere else—unless it would be across the parking lot at another TMC specialty facility called Texas Children's Hospital, where 38 medical and surgical subspecialty services can treat the entire spectrum of childhood illnesses.

Texas Children's benefits from more than $20.6 million worth of research annually as the primary pediatric teaching hospital of Baylor College of Medicine. And Baylor operates the nation's only Children's Nutrition Research Center, in cooperation with Texas Children's Hospital, for the U.S. Department of Agriculture. In 1988 the hospital handled more than 148,000 outpatient visits. It was here that immunology research led to the case of David the "Bubble Boy," who died February 22, 1984, leaving a legacy of important lessons and making his doctor, William T. Shearer, an international figure.

Another important specialty facility is the Texas Heart Institute which was created around Cooley and is located beneath St. Luke's and Texas Children's. Dedicated in 1972, it symbolizes the break that occurred between Cooley and DeBakey, who represent the first generation of celebrity physicians to bring fame to Houston's complex. DeBakey came earlier than Cooley, arriving in 1948 to head Baylor's department of surgery. An ambitious workaholic, he became, according to *Texas Monthly*'s Lemann, "a figure of great complexity—certainly the most powerful man at the Texas Medical Center, arguably the most famous doctor in the world . . . He established what has become the tone of the Medical Center—big plans, fast growth, advanced surgery, lots of publicity."

Cooley was the most promising in a group of young surgeons recruited to Baylor by DeBakey in the 1950s. As their careers in heart surgery progressed it was only natural that the two world-class egos would clash. DeBakey remained a phenomenon into his late 80s during the 1980s, keeping Baylor and Methodist at the top in heart treatment and personally handling 50 or more surgeries per week at times. Meanwhile, Cooley was enhancing the reputation of the Texas Heart Institute, a facility carefully designed as the world's largest cardiovascular surgery service. Its multiple operating rooms and Cooley's image have made open heart surgery a regular event, averaging 30 or more operations per day.

Besides those premier specialty centers, the TMC also hosts The Institute for Rehabilitation and Research (TIRR), where programs focus on the handicapped and on spinal cord injuries; the hospice at the Texas Medical Center, which provides physical, emotional, and spiritual care to the terminally ill; and Shriner's Hospital for Crippled Children, which specializes in pediatric orthopedics.

In the academic arena, the presence of Baylor College of Medicine and the University of Texas Health Science Center at Houston gives the TMC two of the nation's most respected medical schools. The Southwest's only private medical school, Baylor is no longer affiliated with Baylor University in Waco. In 1988 Baylor counted 1,814 students, compared to 2,837 enrolled at UT's Health Science Center.

The UT medical school came to Houston in 1970 after leadership at Hermann Hospital aggressively promoted its creation in the legislature. The Hermann trustees realized that Hermann needed a university affiliation to maintain its prominence in the medical center where Methodist, St. Luke's, and M.D. Anderson had employed their academic ties with Baylor to establish international recognition. The UT Health Science Center has added a wide range of disciplines to round out the school's initial medical educational specialties. Its divisions include Dental Branch, Continuing Education, the Speech and Hearing Institute, a graduate school of Biomedical Sciences,

■ *A young patient at Memorial City Medical Center undergoes Magnetic Resonance Imaging, a procedure used to examine many parts of the body. MRI often provides information not available otherwise or obtainable only by more invasive procedures. Photo by C. Bryan Jones*

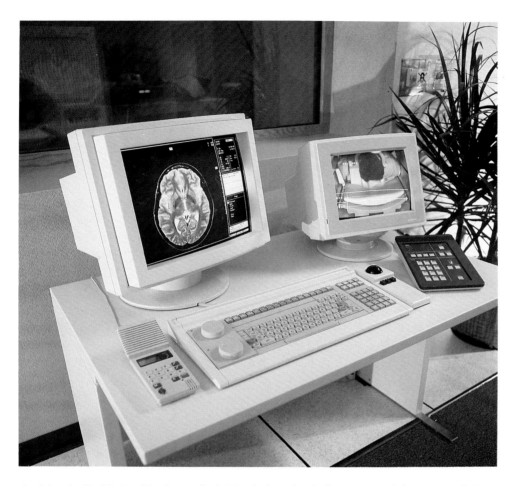

■ *Magnetic Resonance Imaging can depict various conditions in the brain, the spine, the heart, and pelvic structures. Photo by C. Bryan Jones*

the School of Public Health, the Medical School, the School of Nursing, and the School of Allied Sciences. Between them, the two major medical schools spend more than $300 million annually on their operations.

Besides those two major medical schools, Houston's TMC academic sector also hosts the Houston Academy of Medicine and its Texas Medical Center Library, one of the nation's largest medical libraries; Houston Community College for Health Careers, where more than 1,000 students prepare for employment in many levels of the industry; the Institute of Religion, which conducts graduate education and research in pastoral ministry, religion, and medical ethics; the Prairie View A&M University College of Nursing, which offers a four-year bachelor of science degree in nursing; Texas Women's University-Houston Center, which provides health care education for both undergraduate men and women, with programs in occupational therapy, nursing, nutrition, and health care administration; and the University of Houston College of Pharmacy, which has a five-story campus at the TMC.

In the public health arena, TMC is home to the City of Houston Department of Public Health, the Harris County Medical Society, and the Texas Medical Center Inc. Also in the neighborhood—just across Holcombe Boulevard—is Houston's second largest hospital, the Houston Veteran's Affairs Medical Center, with more than 1,000 beds and 2,500 employees.

During the first decade after World War II, Houston's TMC was establishing itself. It recruited surgeons like DeBakey and Cooley to build the bedrock of a medical mother lode. In the 1960s it pioneered treatments in heart and cancer care, enhancing its reputation. In the 1970s, with the addition of UT to its medical academic community, TMC began to influence advances in so many different directions no single volume could chronicle them all. And, just as it did with the government's space program, in the 1980s the private sector started cultivating its ties to the medical research under way at Houston's TMC. From those early financial seeds sown back in the 1940s has grown a complex and vital hedge of medical technology and enterprise, poised for unlimited blossoming in the years ahead.

MEDICAL BATTLES ON MULTIPLE FRONTS

Fueled by the investment community's relentless search for promising ventures and the state's need for economic diversification, Houston's dimension as the medical city hit full throttle as it entered the last decade of the twentieth century. Rooted in the research activities of the TMC, a vibrant biotechnology industry sprang from the ground and spread across Houston's landscape. Advances and opportunities emerged from every direction and the community stood primed for the future.

One significant development occurred in Austin, when the legislature approved 11 bills in 1987 to enhance technology transfer and stimulate investment in high risk fields. The move attracted an increasingly more sophisticated type of investor into the Texas biotechnology fields. Perhaps more important, it enabled public university researchers to start participating in the profits from their discoveries. With TMC well in place, the changing temper of the times appeared destined to benefit Houston.

"We're basically starting a new industry here in Houston," said Bill Doty, director of M.D. Anderson's Office of Technology Development, in 1989. He likes to compare today's environment with that of earlier years when M.D. Anderson developed its Cobalt 60 radiation treatment. Through licensing agreements and commercial development, that breakthrough would have meant millions for the facility, which would have recycled those dollars into further research efforts. Instead, it passed into the public domain. In the same vein, brilliant academics often moved into the private sector where their efforts earned bigger salaries.

State law left the various institutions to devise their own methods for bridging the gap between researchers and investors. By the end of the 1980s, they were well on their way.

Baylor, a private institution, got off to a head start by launching BCM Technologies Inc. (BCMT) in 1984. Created as the business development arm of Baylor, it is a wholly owned for profit subsidiary of the school. Its mission is to actively establish new commercial ventures based on inventions of Baylor researchers. By the end of the decade, Baylor-negotiated royalty agreements totaled just $500,000, but that figure was expected to grow to $1 million by the mid-1990s, allowing BCMT to reach the break-even point.

BCMT's contribution to Houston's medical economy can be seen in the eight small biotechnology firms launched during its first five years of operation. The BCMT roster includes Houston Biotechnology Inc., started in October 1985 to provide bioprocessing and genetic engineering for eye and neurological disorders. It expects to see $50 million in revenues by the mid-1990s. Another example is Xenos Medical Systems Inc., established in March 1987 to provide multiwire gamma camera low radiation X-rays, with expectations for $50 million in revenues by 1995. Another of the BCMT offspring is Triplex Pharmaceutical Corp., founded in June 1989 to produce DNA-altering pharmaceuticals, with expectations of $50 million in revenues by the end of the century.

The UT Health Science Center counted two promising young firms in its fold. LifeCell Corp. produces a tissue-freezing machine that preserves microscopic biological materials such as tissues, bacteria, and blood cells for biological researchers and manufacturers. Until the machine was developed in 1986 by a UT team, researchers had to add preservatives that would change the tissue's properties or freeze it, creating ice crystals that would cause damage. In 1988 LifeCell sold $1.2 million worth of its "cryofixation" devices and was expecting annual revenues to hit the

$15-million range by the mid-1990s. Ampholife Technologies Inc. emerged in 1989 as a UT sibling for high-speed production of cancer drugs, with prospects for $60 million in revenues by the end of the century. Ampholife markets a system that separates and purifies proteins for laboratory research.

At the same time M.D. Anderson had spun off two little companies. Argus Pharmaceuticals Inc. was created in 1987 to produce a tumor killing drug pioneered by researchers there. And Molecular Diagnostic Associates, Inc., was born in 1988 to provide a wide range of laboratory services.

The 1980s also witnessed the creation of several Houston venture-fund enterprises established to ferret out creations from the city's medical research community. Oil wealth played a role in making them possible, with George Mitchell's Mitchell Energy & Development getting into the act. Formation of the Woodlands Venture Partners expanded the medical research community's boundaries beyond Houston and into Mitchell's Woodlands project where it funded five new technology companies.

By the end of the 1980s, a new generation of superstar surgeons was at work pushing the efforts of DeBakey and Cooley into the twenty-first century. Heart and lung transplants, genetic research, and high-tech cancer treatments kept Houston's reputation growing as the medical city. And a ripple of exciting advances was spreading across the city from its initial outpost in the

■ *Programs for spinal cord injury patients are the focus of the Institute for Rehabilitation and Research. Photo by Bob Rowan/ Progressive Image Photography*

5

THE

INTERNATIONAL CITY

On August 20, 1976, a 27-year-old Vietnamese telephone systems troubleshooter in the fishing village of Qui Nhon told his mother he was going out for breakfast. The mother looked up with a sigh. Thanh Ngoc Nguyen was her baby, the youngest of 10 children reared in a lifetime of warfare. Their country had been overrun, their neighbors imprisoned. Just months before, her husband had died. Then, as Thanh and his wife left the house in South Vietnam, the woman sensed something more than breakfast was afoot. She would be proven correct. Her son was vanishing from her life. He had planned it that way.

Before Thanh's father had died, he had taken his son aside and discussed the future. He reviewed the young man's life—technical school training which brought employment from the government of South Vietnam, his flight through the jungles after conquest by North Vietnam, four months in a prison work camp, and finally the frustration of being unable to work under the new regime. The father's advice seemed clear. Thanh's brothers were older, their lives already burdened with children. They could not escape. Thanh had only his wife.

"Go anywhere to find your life and have freedom," the father had told his son. He held out a handful of gold coins. Just 10 months earlier he had used five of his coins to bribe a guard and win Thanh's release. Now, he wanted the rest of his secret treasure to finance a much grander escape. He wouldn't live long enough to bid his son farewell five months later or to see his wife question why her son never returned from breakfast. But he would be remembered at each

■ *The growing cultural diversity of Houston's population has brought change to all facets of community life, including the city's houses of worship. Photo by C. Bryan Jones*

step of Thanh's journey as the refugee moved along the path cleared by that handful of gold. Thanh left in a 15-foot boat with his wife, 17 friends, and the clothes on his back. Even those paltry possessions would eventually be burned as a smoke pyre to attract ships as the boat drifted over the waves in the South China Sea. Rescued by Red Chinese seamen, they finally landed in Hong Kong where the International Rescue Committee pondered their fate. By March 15, 1977, they'd been placed on a plane bound for Houston.

Thanh started life in Houston with less than most of the people born there. Assigned an apartment in public housing, he got a job in a car wash, then parlayed his electronics training into a position with a local burglar alarm company. He enrolled in the Houston Community College refugee program, learning English as a second language and mechanical design. Drafting and machine shop jobs followed, and Thanh saved everything he could. He became a draftsman at Houston's Hughes Tool Co., moonlighted as a burglar-alarm service technician and invested his savings in a video rental firm. By 1984 Thanh was able to earn $105,000 from his various enterprises and smile with pride at the sight of his picture in *Money* magazine as an example of an immigrant Vietnamese "moneymaker."

Thanh's story is just one of many dramatic tales that have unfolded over the years in Houston. But it does illustrate a central aspect of business and culture there. From its birth as a paper city, Houston had been portrayed also as a gateway for foreign immigration into the Southwest. Texas, after all, was a province of Mexico. Galveston Island ranked throughout the nineteenth century as the Ellis Island of the South.

As Houston's port developed so did its reputation as an international business center. As Houston became the energy city, its oilpatch experts circled the globe introducing their technology and hometown habits to people all over the world. As space city, Houston has captured the imagination of nations far and wide while welcoming their top minds into its scientific community. Houston the medical city often resembles the United Nations complex of New York, with its mixture of languages and attire as visitors move about the Texas Medical Center seeking unique treatments for a variety of life threatening afflictions.

■ *The variety of Houston's businesses increases as the city's population diversifies. A 1988 study revealed that Houston ranked second behind Dallas in Asian-owned businesses, with 84.9 Asian-owned businesses for every 1,000 Asian-American residents. Photo by C. Bryan Jones*

In addition to all its other labels, Houston certainly must be called an international city. Thanh represented only one ethnic group. But his story and the motives that fueled it can be found all over Houston's business and cultural landscape. In its ethnic diversity, Houston clearly stands out from other cities in the Southwest. Asians, Europeans, Africans, and Hispanics have all enjoyed an impact there. And, in the years ahead, as the globe continues to shrink through advances in communications and transportation, Houston's international background should provide one more important link to the future.

The statistics reveal some intriguing facts about this city more often symbolized by oil rigs than a melting pot. But those two icons would appear to have much in common. At the end of the decade, Houston ranked third in the number of foreign offices, fifth in foreign consulates, and sixth in international air passengers. According to a private study in 1988, Houston ranked second behind Dallas in Asian business ownership, with 84.9 Asian-owned businesses for every 1,000 Asian-American residents. The 1986 "Houston International Business Directory" listed 623 firms from 51 nations represented there. Another 574 domestic firms from Houston boasted representation in 108 foreign lands. And it counted an additional 766 firms or organizations in Houston with no branches or offices abroad, but involved in international business.

Houston led the South and Southwest as a center for international finance with 53 foreign banks and 15 of the specially chartered Edge Act corporations that allow some foreign banks to engage exclusively in international finance and transactions. With consular offices from 53 foreign governments in the city, Houston's consular corps easily ranked as the largest in the South. The city counted trade, investment, and tourism offices for 28 foreign governments, plus 29 active foreign chambers of commerce and trade associations. More than half the cargo passing through the Port of Houston represents foreign trade, with enough in 1988 to rank the port first in the nation for foreign tonnage.

From a population of less than one hundred in 1975, the Indochinese had grown to more than 50,000 by the mid-1980s, and Asian Houstonians overall numbered more than 130,000, up from just 32,335 in the 1980 census. In 1987 Texas A&M University estimated that the region's Hispanics accounted for 17 percent of the population and its blacks, 18 percent. The Texas Department of Health projected that by 1999 minorities will be a majority in Harris County, with Hispanics and blacks representing more than 52 percent of the population. By then Hispanics are expected to outnumber blacks 1.9 million to 743,000.

The explosive growth of minorities in Houston merely follows a pattern established during the community's pioneer days. Census records from 1850 count more European than American-born Houstonians. Chinese immigrants built railroads there in the 1870s. A historical marker on NASA Road 1 commemorates the site of Salibara Farm where Japanese immigrants taught Texans the art of rice cultivation at the turn of the century.

In a detailed study of the city's ethnic origins, Rice University in 1984 identified four basic categories within its international population: foreigners, immigrants, American ethnics, and the assimilated. Foreigners are those who are visiting temporarily or living there while maintaining foreign citizenship. Immigrants represent the newcomers who have abandoned their homelands for economic or lifestyle opportunities available in Houston. American ethnics are those immigrants from other cities in the United States who bring with them the customs and identity inherited from previous generations. And, the assimilated include those ethnic groups who display international roots despite losing many ties to their old country, like the Cajuns with their spicy blend of French, Indian, and Spanish ancestry.

The study, entitled "The Ethnic Groups of Houston," also noted three important trends with regard to Houston's ethnic population: diversity, increased intensity, and pluralism. Diversity had surfaced in the variety of city restaurants, church services, publications, and media. The intensity emerged as the city's ethnic groups demonstrated signs of increased interest in maintaining their international heritage. And the pluralism has been evident in their desires to build businesses within the economic structure of their adopted homeland.

HISPANIC HOUSTON

No other ethnic group offers quite the prospect for economic and cultural impact in the United States of the twenty-first century as the Hispanics. That's all the more true in Houston. But no other ethnic group offers the same degree of mystery about its identity. Depending on the author, an analysis may limit Hispanics to those of Mexican-American heritage or lump well-educated immigrants from Cuba with poverty-stricken refugees from Central America. Population

estimates may reflect American-born and naturalized citizens or add in the untold thousands of undocumented aliens who have crossed the easily accessible Texas border and vanished into the city's industrial underground. The only agreement about Hispanic Houston concerns the community's prospects for the future: It is clearly headed for influential, even majority status, with prominent leaders in all walks of life.

By the mid-1980s, Houston's Hispanic population was officially estimated at half a million, with many experts chortling about its failure to include 75,000 to 150,000 Salvadoran refugees alone. Hispanics were known to account for 36 percent of the total enrollment of the Houston Independent School District. And they had certainly made their mark in the city's political arena. In business, 16 Houston-area companies ranked among the nation's top 500 Hispanic firms according to the June 1989 issue of *Hispanic Business* magazine. The 67-county Houston-area market included more than 700,000 Hispanics in 1989, making it the nation's seventh largest.

But economic leaders in the late 1980s harbored other reasons for cultivating Houston's reputation in Hispanic affairs. Eager to participate in the emerging opportunities of the global economy, port and trade officials recognized Latin America as a natural marketplace for their overtures. Promoting Houston as the gateway to Latin markets, they focused on businesses and industry south of the border. The Port of Houston opened its first foreign field office in 1988, selecting Caracas, Venezuela, as the location. With millions of consumers, cheap labor, and valuable raw materials, the emerging economies of Latin America from Mexico to Chile loomed as

virgin partners for Houston's international ambitions. Thus Houston leaders have been aggressively emphasizing the city's historic ties to the Latin culture and the presence of a vibrant Hispanic business community.

Those ties, however, may not be as obvious as they would seem. Despite Houston's proximity to Mexico, it wasn't until the twentieth century that the city began to attract Hispanic residents in large numbers. Given the history of hostilities between the United States and Mexico in the nineteenth century, that should not seem too unusual. But that background of hostility only heightened the tensions of racial prejudice. As the first waves of Mexican immigrants fled their nation's violent revolutionary period of the early twentieth century and swept into Houston, they found employment in the city's industrial sections along the ship channel. They congregated in barrios on the city's east side, and they faced some of the same social barriers confronting Houston's black community.

"Dark skinned Mexican-Americans were treated just like black Houstonians," notes Joe Feagin in *Free Enterprise City*. "Many suffered discrimination in housing and employment; they were largely excluded from political participation. Mexican-American children were punished for speaking Spanish in school. Most attempts to combat the blatant discrimination were unsuccessful until the 1950s and 1960s."

Despite the atmosphere of discrimination, Hispanics continued to migrate to Houston. First they came in search of economic opportunities. Then, with the growth of the Hispanic community in Houston, they came seeking each other. The last 25 years has seen vast improvements in

■ *The Tenneco fountain becomes an impromptu shower for one young resident. Photo by C. Bryan Jones*

opportunities for Hispanics in Houston and the emergence of important political leaders. Leonel Castillo, who served as city controller in the 1970s, won appointment by President Jimmy Carter in 1977 to head the Immigration and Naturalization Service. His unsuccessful bid for mayor in 1979 generated much interest. Meanwhile, Houston Hispanics have moved out of the barrios and spread across the city.

In 1989 the city supported four Spanish-language weekly newspapers, each with circulation above 37,000, plus three Spanish radio stations and two Hispanic cable T.V. stations. Its Hispanic Chamber of Commerce was actively organizing commercial interests. And the Hispanic business community enjoyed its share of success stories.

Foremost among those was the saga of Donald Bonham and his Fiesta Mart, Inc., chain, an enterprise that actually fed upon the whole spectrum of Houston's international nature. Unique in all of Texas, Fiesta was launched by Bonham in 1972, catering to Hispanics in Houston's inner city. After founding his own chain of grocery stores in South Texas in the 1960s, Bonham and his family had lived in Santiago, Chile, where he served as a consultant to the Chilean government to improve food distribution there.

Returning to Texas and locating in Houston, Bonham duplicated the Hispanic theme mart concept just in time to profit from the explosion of ethnic identity there. In the 1980s his stores expanded rapidly across the city, numbering more than a dozen by the end of the decade and offering consumers of most any race or nationality a chance to savor experiences and products from their native lands. Typical was the 110,000-square-foot bazaar in Southwest Houston opened in 1983 featuring everything from exotic or gourmet foods to a currency exchange and package delivery service to Mexico and El Salvador. Fiesta ranked fourth in market share among Houston groceries, with $350 million in annual revenues.

Critics still complained that the city lacked proper Hispanic representation at high levels of business and community leadership. But it was clear by the end of the decade that Houston's Hispanic community had crossed several significant economic and political plateaus. Hispanic entrepreneurs were making their mark in a variety of endeavors. One example was Alexander G. Arroyos, who had started Dynamic Warehousing in 1967 as a one-man operation while working for another company. In 1989 his company recorded $19.6 million in sales and earned the number 99 spot on the list of top 500 Hispanic-owned businesses in the country according to *Hispanic Business* magazine.

In all, Houston had 16 of the top 500—companies that provided a wide range of products and services: Barrios Technology Inc., McLean Cargo Specialists, South Coast Drywall, Mariana Properties, North American Trade, Del Rey Chemical International, World Commerce Forwarding, Emily Investments, Tejas Office Products, Ortiz Brothers Insulation, Tamex-Thomas Inc., Gilram Supply Inc., National Export Crating, and TAG Electric Co.

Meanwhile, other Hispanics were rising through the ranks of professional careers like the law and medicine. At Houston's large institutional law firms, among the more powerful in the country, a number of Hispanic attorneys had risen to the partnership level by the end of the decade. One example was Doris Rodriguez, promoted to partner at Andrews & Kurth in 1987 after more than seven years in the firm's banking section. She attended the University of Houston law school at night for four years while maintaining a job as a financial management analyst for the Department of Housing and Urban Development. Her father had migrated to Houston from Mexico in 1945. Lacking a formal education, he nevertheless understood the advantages of an education and always made sure his family lived close to the best schools available in his adopted homeland.

As the city headed into the 1990s, its cultural fabric was filled with similar examples of foreign newcomers overcoming the obstacles of immigration to thrive and add their special touch to an international city. Hispanics represented a large share, but they were only one portion.

THE ASIAN CONNECTION

While they can't match the impact of Hispanics in terms of numbers, Asians emerged in the 1980s as the second ethnic group to build considerable influence. Although they could be found settling in many parts of the city's suburban neighborhoods, Asians had established the beginning of a small "Chinatown" district in Houston's downtown. It was nothing to rival those on the West Coast, but it was something new to Houston.

At the same time, the police were forced to learn more about the Asian culture in their efforts to combat crimes stemming from gangs rooted in the homeland. Meanwhile, Asian names began appearing more frequently on lists of scholarship winners from the city's public high schools and among the newspaper articles about prominent scientific contributions to the community. Politics remained elusive but other signs clearly showed that Asians had surfaced as important contributors to Houston's reputation as an international city. It seemed only a matter of time before city council or the legislature would include delegates with names like Nguyen or Chen.

Like the Hispanics, Asians are too often lumped into a single group without recognition of differences between specific cultures. Houston's Asian populations also must be seen in light of their different backgrounds. Each segment boasts its own history and niche in the city's international community.

For the Chinese, 1980 marked the centennial of the first Chinese to live in Houston. In 1870, crowds of curious Houstonians watched with interest as 250 Chinese laborers arrived on their way to jobs building Texas railroads. By 1880 the census report noted the presence of seven Chinese residents among the city's population.

The Chinese families live in every part of the city, but the small commercial Chinatown along Chartes Street on the eastern edge of downtown has created a loosely knit association of Chinese merchants. Although the area had failed to become a magnet for Chinese commercial development, its prospects looked better for the 1990s. Its surrounding atmosphere of aging warehouses was rapidly changing as corporate leaders advanced their building plans in its direction and with construction of the George R. Brown Convention Center nearby. In the early years, Chinese Houstonians tended to come from poorer families and entered the commercial trades upon their arrival. But it was higher status professionals from Taiwan and mainland China who fueled the explosive growth of the 1970s and have now combined with earlier generations to form a distinct community.

Consider two Chinese Houstonians who rose to national prominence in science and art during the 1980s. Dr. Paul Chu, a Chinese-born physicist reared in Taiwan, very nearly claimed a Nobel Prize in 1987 for his breakthrough work in the space age field of superconductivity as a research professor at the University of Houston. Officials at that university already credit Chu with elevating its international reputation into that of a true research facility, versus its old image as a community college for the Houston area. The State of Texas and the Houston Economic Development Council (HEDC) worked with UH in creating a special facility for Chu's superconductivity team, in an effort to derail a campaign by Stanford University to lure him away in 1988.

His work continued into the 1990s, forming the foundation of what economic development leaders hope will become a bold new industry headquartered in Houston in the twenty-first century. Superconductor research involves the manipulation and mixing of exotic chemical compounds to create material that conducts electricity without resistance. Its applications appear limitless, and if Houston goes on to seize a crucial role in that field, it will owe its importance to one of its Asian immigrants. In 1987 the *Houston Business Journal* labeled Chu "The man who just might change the world."

While Chu was working in his lab in 1981, a 20-year-old Chinese exchange student named Li Cunxin was creating an international furor with his secret marriage to an American ballet student and subsequent refusal to return to China. Li had become an internationally acclaimed ballet dancer and in the years after that crisis remained with the Houston Ballet, eventually becoming a principal dancer. The whole city cheered in 1986 when Li stood among 4,200 other immigrants as part of the largest naturalization ceremony ever held in Texas and became a citizen.

Houston's Indochinese population represents a more recent and revolutionary phenomenon. By and large they are the product of disruption in their homelands of Cambodia, Laos, and Vietnam. As such, they've come to Houston with a different kind of background than those of other immigrant communities, which grew slowly. Houston served as one of several primary American destinations for three separate waves of Indochinese immigration.

The first and smallest influx occurred before the fall of Saigon in April 1975, and it consisted of students, professionals, war brides, and officials on temporary assignment to the United States. The second wave came in the aftermath of the collapse of anticommunist forces. These refugees were young, half of them under the age of 18. Two-thirds came from urban environments and were better educated than most immigrants. More than half were reasonably fluent in English, and they turned out to be extremely ambitious. The last wave began in 1977 as those Indochinese who had remained in their homelands grew more disenchanted with the new regimes. These refugees faced the roughest road to freedom and arrived like Thanh Ngoc Nguyen, with survival instincts well honed. California attracted the largest part of this third wave, but Texas ranked second.

In less than a decade, Houston had welcomed nearly 20,000 Indochinese immigrants. A number of local organizations developed programs to assist with assimilation, notably Catholic Charities, the YMCA, and the International Rescue Committee. The Harris County Refugee Council was founded to coordinate the various programs.

■ Houston has nearly 30 institutions of higher education, including Houston International University, a testament to the city's rapidly diversifying population. Photo by Bob Rowan/ Progressive Image Photography

By 1985 Houston's Indochinese community had become the nation's second largest, trailing only Los Angeles, and the reasons were many. For one thing, Houston had loomed as the largest metropolitan area closest to one of the major refugee arrival centers at Fort Chaffee, Arkansas. Considering, too, the city's semitropical climate and its abundance of employment opportunities at the turn of the decade, Houston seems a natural destination for this group of immigrants. Houston's Indochinese can be found working at any number of jobs, physicians to trash collectors. Most hold blue collar or service positions thanks to training programs created by the Houston Community College system.

Ambitious, frugal, and eager to take advantage of opportunities in Houston, many of the Indochinese have become home owners. The Rice University study notes that the Indochinese housing situation reveals two significant characteristics about that community that will undoubtedly be reflected in other areas as its Houston influence increases. First, independence surfaces as a dominant goal among Houston's Indochinese, who view home ownership as more important than congregation in an ethnic ghetto. As a result, no ghetto has been established and they can be found living comfortably anywhere around Houston. The entrepreneurial instinct prompted creation of many private businesses and development of a Vietnamese commercial center on the fringes of the city's downtown. A survey for the Rice study discovered that Houston's Indochinese harbored ambitious goals for their children, with a focus on engineering and medicine. As that second generation of Indochinese immigrants matures toward leadership positions in the 1990s, it will certainly have a prominent role in the city's future.

The third group of Asian Houstonians exerts influence well beyond its numbers. The Japanese enjoy a rich tradition of business ties to this port city and constitute a vital part of its international image. The earliest Japanese immigrants came at the turn of the century to become rice farmers in the agricultural regions surrounding Houston. With world-class development of the Port of Houston, however, Japan and its business enterprises quickly outstripped its rice farmers for impact.

After World War II, as Japan gained international prominence in economic circles, that connection grew even more dramatically. Houston's port served as Japan's gateway to Texas and the nation's heartland. In the last quarter century exports to Japan through the port leaped sixfold as imports increased from less than $25 million in 1960 to more than $1.6 billion by 1980. Throughout the 1980s Japan vied with Saudi Arabia for status as the city's top trading partner, boasting a diversified mixture of goods from imported autos and steel to exports of petrochemicals and machinery.

All this economic activity has created a Japanese community of a higher class but transient in nature. With more than 100 Japanese firms operating offices in Houston, the city is host to several thousand temporary Japanese residents: business executives, doctors, government officials, students and their families. In addition, the city ranks as a major stopping point for those well-traveled Japanese tourists. These business-oriented and temporary Japanese Houstonians have not become as well integrated as other members of the Japanese community who have taken permanent residence there over the years. Some descend from those early agricultural immigrants while others arrived in a wave of immigration to the American Southwest after World War II. All told they form another important dimension to Houston's Asian sector.

GLOBAL OUTLOOK

Of course, Houston's international community has not been limited to Hispanics and Asians. Thanks to global industries like energy and space it has drawn heavily from all parts of the world. By the end of the 1980s foreign investors and Houston business leaders were embracing each other with an intensity guaranteed to build even stronger ties in the future. As Texas awakened to the opportunities beyond its borders, Houston—with the state's largest port and most cosmopolitan background—loomed as the Southwest's doorway to the world.

HOUSTON'S BLACK COMMUNITY

They don't add another foreign influence to Houston's population mix. But members of the city's black community do represent a significant portion of its ethnic identity. According to *The Houston Post*, in 1990 the city's black population numbered 538,834, or about 31 percent of the total. A black had served as Houston's chief of police for most of the 1980s before moving on in 1990 to accept the same position in New York City. Some of its most prominent and articulate political voices on national and state levels were black. *American Demographics* magazine had ranked the city third in the nation for its number of black-owned businesses per capita with 12,206. The city's black press was thriving. One of the city's most remarkable downtown structures is a beautiful black church—Antioch Baptist—which sits among the gleaming skyscrapers, its neon "Jesus Saves" a constant reminder of cultural diversity in the South's largest metropolis.

Despite all those pluses, however, Houston entered the 1990s like other southern cities, facing the dilemma of racial questions developing in a new era that could not be ignored. It was clear that blacks had moved into leadership positions across the city's governing landscape. It was clear they had contributed to the culture that had made Houston unique. But it was also clear, according to research by *The Houston Post* and other local observers, that the city and its black community were poised to face new challenges in the years ahead. *The Post* concluded that there exists what it called "Two black Houstons" —one consisting of a middle class and another where struggle for economic equality remained the dominant theme. And it cited experts who predicted that the new technological age would only widen the gap between the two.

"Black Houston has improved over the years. There was a time it was extremely rare to find a black man in suit and tie downtown," the newspaper quoted Lorenzo Thomas, an English professor at the University of Houston. "Today, I see that there are serious problems facing the community. At the same time that employment opportunities have expanded for blacks we still have far too many people who are not getting in a place to take advantage of the opportunity. And we have detrimental things like drugs and crime facing the community."

Rice University sociologist Stephen Klineberg added his thoughts: "We've moved away from an economy where all you needed was a strong arm and a willingness to work to get a job. It's clear the rising tide doesn't lift all boats any more. It only makes life better for those who have education to qualify for new jobs in the technological age."

Joe R. Feagin noted in his book about Houston, *Free Enterprise City:* "Much of the wealth of white Houstonians and other south Texans, not just in the past but also in the present, is ultimately rooted in uncompensated slave labor or poorly compensated free black labor. Houston is a southern city, historically part of the plantation south and this is an important part of the racial culture or mind of the city."

Nevertheless, the city could reflect on its history as a multicultural community and its open-minded, frontier attitude toward newcomers as a reason to boast that blacks, just

■ *MacGregor Park is among the city's more than 250 parks, most of which offer facilities for sports and recreation. Photo by C. Bryan Jones*

like the city's other ethnic minority groups, enjoyed opportunities greater than those available in many other places.

Blacks have been a part of Texas history since the beginning. They accompanied the Spanish explorers, and free blacks flocked to the region as a refuge while Mexico controlled the government. As colonists from the states increased their numbers, however, the black slave population increased, too. Blacks and Mexican prisoners-of-war actually cleared the land for the original Houston townsite in the summer of 1836. Urban slavery became common as towns blossomed in the young republic, and by 1860 Houston counted a population of 1,000 black slaves. Houston and Galveston were important centers for the slave trade in those years before the War Between the States, and one of Houston's landmark downtown locations—Old Market Square—retains part of its name and mystique from its reputation as a site for slave auctions.

Cary D. Wintz, in *The Ethnic Groups of Houston*, explains that Houston witnessed its first massive influx of blacks after the end of the War Between the States: "The flood of blacks into the city was not welcomed by city officials or the majority of the citizens." But the author notes that blacks played a "surprisingly active role in local politics in the years following the Civil War."

Nonetheless, the legacy of segregation remains in Houston—like everywhere else in the South—the dominant factor affecting the city's black community today. Black Houston was built in a segregated environment, and Wintz notes the construction occurred in haphazard fashion, partly by law and partly by custom. Houston never enacted a complete code of laws to regulate black behavior, and it had no ordinance segregating residential areas. Still, blacks tended to congregate in specific areas that have come to be defined today as black neighborhoods.

At the same time, Feagin points out, Houston was the first Texas city with an organized chapter of the Ku Klux Klan. He says that residential segregation was rigidly enforced through deed restrictions. He notes the occurrence of some residential desegregation in the 1970s but says that in the late 1980s "three quarters of black Houstonians resided in predominantly black areas. Houston's black communities are generally segregated and distinctive. Most of Houston's black population remains concentrated in the Fourth Ward and in a broad belt on the eastern side of the city."

But the ease with which integration occurred in Houston compared to other locations in the South stands as yet another symbol of the city's entrepreneurial attitude. Its leaders realized that an image of prejudice could only hurt the city's development. Some might criticize the motivation as lacking the humanitarian spirit, but they still must acknowledge the results. Feagin chronicled the major integration developments, noting that a series of suits and well-placed black protests forced abolition of racial barriers at the municipal golf courses (1950), the public library (1953), city buses (1954), public schools (1960 and 1966), restaurants (1960) and most other public facilities (1960-1963). The longest desegregation court battle occurred over school desegregation but, by and large, Houston moved peacefully into the new era.

In an article for *The Houston Chronicle* in April 1990, Thomas R. Cole, an associate professor of medical humanities at the University of Texas Medical Branch in Galveston, noted the differences and recalled the efforts of Mayor Lewis Cutrer who established a biracial committee in 1960 to study the issues and make recommendations. Cole wrote:

Remarkably, integration came to Houston without serious violence or loss of life. White businessmen, civic leaders and politicians decided early that Houston would not go the way of Selma, Little Rock or Birmingham. The students remained level headed and received wise advice from an older generation of black businessmen and professionals. By the mid-'60s, the civil rights agenda had moved on to new venues. Many veterans of the movement grew up and enjoyed the fruits of integration.

In its research on black Houston, *The Houston Post* in February 1990 reported some intriguing statistics. It found that 11.1 percent of the city's black work force was unemployed in July 1989, down 4.6 percent from 1988, but charged that blacks were more than twice as likely as whites to be unemployed. The paper also noted: "Many blacks who have achieved middle class status live outside Loop 610 in subdivisions with spacious modern homes with modern conveniences. These middle class blacks live in stark contrast to those struggling from check to check, subsisting in substandard housing pervasive in the Third, Fourth and Fifth ward areas."

Contrasting those stark statistics, however, is the impact of Houston's black chief of police in the 1980s, Lee P. Brown. While other blacks like the late U.S. Representative Mickey Leland left their mark in the political arena, Brown may well be remembered in the long run as the one who forged unbreakable ties between the black community and Houston's predominantly white business establishment. Functioning as he did in such an important and controversial administrative post, Brown won the support of that sector and undoubtedly enhanced the level of respect toward members of his race. When the nation's largest city enticed Brown away in late 1989, Houston's business community admitted it hated to see him go.

When Mayor Kathy Whitmire tabbed Brown in 1982 to become Houston's sixth chief in as many years, it represented a bold move on two counts. Here was a black man taking the helm of a department marred by accusations of racism and brutality. Moreover, Brown was an outsider from Atlanta, the first Houston chief in 42 years who had not come from the ranks of the department. With a doctorate in criminology from Berkeley, Brown added the influence of academic preparation to the unlikely combination of credentials that made him the city's top cop. Many predicted problems, but it quickly became apparent that the black chief was a political asset to the mayor who appointed him. Opponents never tried to make him a campaign issue in any of the four elections that followed his appointment. And *Time* magazine offered its assessment of Brown's contribution in a 1985 report on black police chiefs:

Using community outreach techniques he pioneered in Atlanta, Brown made the department responsive for the first time to business and other community groups. He reorganized the demoralized top echelon of the department into an efficient management team and has won over line officers by supporting their demand for overtime pay and other benefits. The soft-spoken chief is not shy about his accomplishments. "I'd give myself an A," he says. That seems about right. When Houston power brokers gathered for lunch a year ago and his name came up, everyone at the table gave him the same grade.

Although he's gone, Brown leaves a legacy of racial cooperation in one area that always ranks near the top of challenging city issues—crime. He showed the city that race need not be an obstacle in accomplishing significant goals. And his tenure must be acknowledged as a major turning point for Houston's black community.

Another plus for that community has been the continuing success of its newspapers: the *Houston Defender, The Houston Informer,* and the *Houston Forward Times.* Each boasts its own personality, but they've all received accolades for performing the role as a focal point for black community awareness. The *Defender,* founded in 1930, has won 21 national awards since 1984, more than all other black Texas newspapers combined. Its founder, C.F. Richardson, was called the "mouthpiece of the Southwest," and his early editorial stands won him a beating from the Ku Klux Klan.

The Houston Informer ranks as the third oldest black contemporary newspaper in the nation. It was created before the turn of the century through a merger between Houston's first black newspaper, the *Texas Freeman,* and *The Houston Informer.* Its modern editor and publisher, George McElroy, has enjoyed a national reputation as a journalist and spokesman for the black community. In an interview in 1990, the 67-year-old McElroy described the current outlook of the black

■ *Our Lady of Guadalupe School has been educating Houston's Hispanics for almost a century. Photo by C. Bryan Jones*

press in Houston: "Before integration, blacks needed more guidance so we were more militant in giving our viewpoint. But today, they're better read. Now we just hold up the mirror and show people what's going on. They make their own decisions."

With a circulation of 30,000, the *Forward Times* ranks as the largest black weekly in the Southwest.

Thanks to Houston's booming economy, the city became a fertile location for cultivation of black entrepreneurs in the 1980s, according to William O'Hare, a contributing editor at *American Demographics* magazine. Using data from the U.S. Census Bureau's "Survey of Minority-Owned Business Enterprises," O'Hare counted the number of black-owned businesses in the 48 U.S. metropolitan areas with black populations of at least 100,000. It was in that 1987 project that Houston emerged as the nation's third largest center for black businesses per capita, trailing only Los Angeles and San Francisco. In analyzing his findings, O'Hare noted that average black Houstonians had 12.3 years of education, a relatively high level. He cited the growth of black businesses as evidence of a "healthy, growing economic climate" in Houston.

As the 1980s drew to a close, however, social observers in Houston were emphasizing the need for the city's black community to get serious about education. Said Rice University's Klineberg: "Education is not just a nice thing to have anymore. Education is an absolute essential prerequisite for getting on the first rung of the social ladder."

If they are to continue their progress in the 1990s, Klineberg said, Houston's blacks must ensure the proper education of their children to prepare them to compete in the technological age dawning everywhere along the city's horizon.

6

THE

PHYSICAL CITY

Most Houstonians would never admit it. But their Sunbelt city owes a great deal to that industrial haven of the Frostbelt—Detroit. The call of the frontier and the yearning for expansion fueled Houston's birth. Farsighted leaders provided an economic foundation with construction of a port more than 50 miles from the open sea. And the presence of large oil reserves in the region allowed Houston to create an industry around what's become our most vital natural resource. Without Detroit's creation of the auto business, however, that natural resource might never have achieved such a level of prominence. And without the automobile, Houston's geographic development would have produced a very different city, indeed.

The city's area is vast. It covers 579.58 square miles, ranking it ahead of the nation's three most populous cities in area. The city limits reach into three different counties: Harris, Fort Bend, and Montgomery. That commanding size can be a source of awe but that alone does not make the city geographically unique. It's similar to other western rivals in spreading out across the landscape of the twentieth century. After all, the concepts of wide open spaces with room to grow emerged as the strongest magnets beckoning new companies and people to locations all over the West.

But Houston has had some influences upon its physical growth that make it truly unique. To really understand the city as a place and appreciate the contribution of its architecture, one must first consider the role of highways and zoning in shading its growth. Only then does the pattern of life in Houston begin to make sense.

■ *Downtown office towers exemplifying Postmodern business architecture provide an appropriate backdrop for two Houston businessmen engaged in conversation. Photo by Bill Ross/ West Light*

Comics during Houston's booming 1970s used to joke about the city's most important roadway, Interstate 610. Newcomers would arrive, get on 610 and learn hours later that they had moved to a city where the main thoroughfare runs in a circle. After passing the Astrodome several times they'd sheepishly look for an exit. That's why Houstonians call 610 "The Loop." For stand-up comics, the circular configuration emerged as a symbol of the city's hectic psyche. Everybody on main street driving in a circle as fast they can go. For anyone eager to understand the city, however, The Loop becomes as basic a landmark as rivers or other natural boundaries somewhere else. Houstonians describe the city's geographic divisions with The Loop as a primary reference point. Houston may cover 579.58 square miles, but if you are there, you can only be in one of two places: inside The Loop, or out.

Viewed from above and compared to a wheel, with The Loop as its rim, Houston suddenly makes sense. In the very center acting as a hub is Houston's relatively small "downtown" or central business district. And running across the city like spokes through the hub are the other major freeways that link this city with the rest of the country. A series of recent construction projects have added to that network without complicating the wheel-like pattern. Farther out in every direction a second rim has been developing with construction of the Beltway 8 projects: a series of toll roads and state highways circling the city in what's becoming known as the Outer Loop.

With its secondary roadways and streets, Houston's highway system has formed the boundary lines for a wide variety of neighborhoods and activity centers. Harris County includes part or all of some 32 independently incorporated cities. But inside The Loop or out, Houston's actual city limits embrace them all, surrounding many smaller communities and influencing the others. Bayous and the Ship Channel may separate some of the areas, but bridges and tunnels make them all a part of the place known as Houston.

Joe R. Feagin in *Free Enterprise City* calls it one of the city's great historic ironies that "this auto-centered metropolis first rose to economic greatness on the foundation of rail transport." Houstonians do love their cars, however, and each new development in the city's highway structure has opened new territory for business and residential pioneers. Houston's automobile orientation was ordained right after World War II when the Texas Highway Commission launched a major construction program with a large slice of its expenditures earmarked for the Bayou City.

By the 1980s the city had attracted more than three-quarters of a billion dollars of highway funding on 210 miles of freeways. To a great extent, the areas outside The Loop enjoyed the fruits of the boom of suburban residential development that swept the entire country after World War II. But one other factor unique to Houston's physical growth must be considered to put things in proper perspective. That factor is zoning, or in Houston's case, the lack of it.

Houston stands unique among major U.S. cities in that it has had no traditional zoning laws to govern real estate development. The issue has always been controversial, and several times in Houston's past certain groups have mounted lobbying efforts to get a zoning system in place. The situation has prompted criticism from some national experts on urban development who cite

■ Facing page: Energy firms, financial-sector companies, and the legal profession occupy most of the office buildings that compose the downtown skyline. Photo by Larry Lee/ West Light

■ An auto-centered metropolis, Houston had received more than three-quarters of a billion dollars of highway funding on 210 miles of freeways by the 1980s. Photo by Bob Rowan/ Progressive Image Photography

the lack of zoning as one reason to label Houston a wide open city. On the other hand, critics of zoning laws point to Houston as an example of a city where other natural pressures have had the same effect as zoning ordinances might. They say deed restrictions and market values of the land have rationed land use on their own, creating a city similar in physical appearance to other cities with a farflung geography. The zoning debate aside, Feagin argues that the city's antizoning bias has had specific impact, and he suggests three reasons why the bias exists.

"The lengthy struggle over zoning highlights a number of features of Houston's political-economic history," writes Feagin. "First, it reveals the depth of the conservative laissez-faire philosophy among the city's leaders, even when that philosophy interferes with other interests of the leadership such as protecting elite residential neighborhoods from commercial encroachments . . . Second, the failure to implement zoning accents the power of the real estate and development capitalists in the city, for these interests have traditionally been the most consistently opposed to zoning. Third, Houston represents the nearly unique failure to implement professional planning in a principal Sunbelt metropolis."

As a result, in Feagin's opinion, Houston has "more commercial strip development along major arterial streets than in zoned cities. And the lack of zoning has meant a larger than average number of oddly mixed land uses: massage parlors are built across the street from churches, and office towers are erected in the backyards of wealthy suburbanites."

Without zoning, Houston developers have avoided much of the red tape that can bog project development schedules. They have needed only a few months to launch complex structures while counterparts in other locations must study zoning regulations for years before breaking ground. Feagin believes the lack of zoning has facilitated the growth of 18 separate business activity centers in Houston. Several of these might be considered "downtown" in their own right if located anywhere else. But any serious tour of this place called Houston must begin with the neighborhood acknowledged by everyone as the city's authentic downtown, the central business district at the hub of Houston's wheel-and-spoke highway network. Unlike other modern cities that have grown by gobbling the regional landscape, Houston has not surrendered its downtown in the process but strengthened it as the heart and brains of its commercial and cultural existence.

DOWNTOWN HOUSTON

It rises from the prairie like some manmade mountain range visible to motorists at almost every point in an excursion around The Loop. Downtown Houston covers a grand total of just 1.5 square miles, or about 300 blocks, bounded by I-10 on the north, U.S. 59 on the east, and the curve made by I-45 on the west and south as it winds through the area. With more than 170,000 workers, compared to 2,000 residents, Downtown Houston ranks as the single largest employment center in the southwestern United States. It is home to the city's largest, most powerful companies. Other local business activity centers may think they are challenging this pocket of power for prestige, but anyone who keeps those skyscrapers in sight while circumnavigating The Loop realizes they can only be pretenders.

Downtown Houston harbors the centers of government at City Hall and the Harris County Administration Building. Federal and state courthouses administer justice for the region here. An impressive arts district beckons residents to the ballet, theater, and symphony. The George R. Brown Convention Center is a world-class facility, competing with only the upper echelon for gatherings as large as the national political conclaves that bring recognition as well as millions of outside dollars into the economy. And Downtown Houston is home to the business leaders who have made the city the commercial titan of the Southwest with the mixture of architecture that's been cited often as symbolic of the new age in corporate construction. Some say it's the city against which other cities must measure their architectural development, functioning as a lab for

the nation's foremost designers during the last 20 years in their experimentation with what's now known as the "Postmodern" style.

"Houston has a freewheeling pop architecture which breaks rules constantly but always for a reason," observed Paul Goldberger, architecture critic for *The New York Times,* in 1985. "It is a city that has grown enormously in the last decade with very little in the way of a past history to get its architecture moving in any particular stylistic direction or a present set of legal restrictions to constrain it."

His predecessor at *The Times,* Ada Louis Huxtable, had noted, "Houston is *the* city of the second half of the twentieth century."

Houston City Magazine described its hometown skyline like this:

In the distance, the skyline of the nation's fourth largest metropolis resembles a modern-day Xanadu, America's own Emerald City. The shapes and styles that are outlined against the sky suggest a futuristic place, one likely to be found in a science fiction novel. A 56-story edifice sporting tiered gables festooned with spires rising by steps and a skin made of a handsome, rough red granite is the first structure that catches the eye. Next to this Gothic, cathedralike building are strikingly interesting structures: a pencil-thin, 75-story, five-sided granite tower resembling a high-tech spindle and a structure of 71 floors clad in emerald green glass with elegant stainless steel pinstripes that looks like the tallest Dunhill lighter in America.

Sound inviting? There is an explanation for all this variety. But it's important first to note that Houston's downtown is a comment on a way of life as well as modern business architecture. Except for the Wortham Center and its neighboring arts complex, most of these buildings exist for commerce. Wheeling and dealing on a grand scale in the daytime, the residents of this 9-to-5 environment flee elsewhere when the work day is done.

A phenomenon of very recent history, Downtown Houston emerges as the nation's most stunning example of Postmodern business architecture. A survey of the city's 25 largest office towers finds all but five located in Downtown Houston, with the eldest being One Shell Plaza, completed in 1970. What's more, 15 of the buildings on that list weren't completed until sometime in the 1980s.

In the early years of this century, Houston's downtown skyline followed the fortunes of cotton companies and fledgling oil enterprises. Construction of the 37-story Gulf Building in 1929 gave Houston the tallest structure west of the Mississippi at that time. Since much of the downtown construction activity has occurred to accommodate energy companies, their needs have been reflected in the result. They require large amounts of space for their various administrative activities. Feagin notes that by the mid-1980s about 61 percent of the office space downtown was devoted to the energy business, with banks, law firms, and accounting firms taking another 30 percent. Downtown Houston housed 33 corporations with offices employing more than 1,000 people. An extensive tunnel system connects many of the downtown buildings and gives executives speedy pedestrian access to each other.

In the last two decades, the development of Downtown Houston offered American architecture an unprecedented opportunity for experimentation and growth. Because they have been hailed as turning points in modern American business architecture, some of Houston's downtown structures demand a closer look.

It was here, in the 1970s and 1980s, that an internationally known architect and a local developer proved two things. First, that aesthetics and decoration could have a role in the creation of a commercial office building. And second, that business could profit from the combination. The result is a concentration of late twentieth-century architecture unparalleled anywhere in the world.

Local observer Douglas Kilburn, writing in *Houston City Magazine* in 1984, offered his prediction: "So vast is the display and so pure is it that there is little doubt that when the future wants to study late twentieth century architecture, Houston is where it will come." And the road toward appreciating the impact of Downtown Houston begins with an examination of the careers of two men most responsible: a Houston developer named Gerald Hines and the legendary New York architect Philip Johnson.

HINES, JOHNSON, AND PENNZOIL PLACE

"The kind of architecture that is in Houston could only have happened in Houston. Other cities don't have that kind of daring," noted Johnson in 1984. By then, the 78-year-old architect—one of the most influential in the world—was able to look back on the city where he had left his mark all over six miles of skyline. He had seen his theories come full circle there as part of a productive alliance with Hines, a Houstonian who has also risen to international prominence from humble origins.

"He is one of America's two or three master builders. More than anyone else, Hines is responsible for the pace-setting, upscale architecture that has changed the look not only of Houston but also of so many other American skylines in the late 20th Century," says Ann Holmes, arts critic of *The Houston Chronicle*.

With offices in 34 cities, Hines counts the development and management of at least 380 projects among his accomplishments, more than 78 million square feet of building. *Forbes* magazine says he has constructed more than any other builder in the nation. As head of Houston-based Gerald D. Hines Interests, Hines has said he doesn't have a favorite among his buildings, calling them his children. But there have been some moments in his career in Houston that stand apart both for him and for American architecture. His personal story is one of those truly Houstonian sagas of entrepreneurial drive.

■ *Facing page: Historic buildings in Sam Houston Park and contemporary skyscrapers share Downtown Houston, providing a contrast between the old and the new city. Photo by Bob Rowan/ Progressive Image Photography*

■ *Pennzoil Place looms over the Wortham Center and its neighboring arts complex. Photo by C. Bryan Jones*

Hines launched his development career inauspiciously enough in 1953 with a $16,000 investment, converting a small frame house into an office building on the edge of downtown Houston. A native of Gary, Indiana, Hines held an engineering degree from Purdue University and had migrated to Houston in 1948 to work for an air conditioning company. By the mid-1950s, however, he'd recognized the opportunities in Houston real estate and turned his speculatory sideline into the company that now bears his name. Today, his name is probably best known in association with development of The Galleria and Transco Tower—world-class projects outside Downtown Houston. But his stamp on the downtown really dates from the late 1960s when Hines won the first plum of his career—development of One Shell Plaza, completed in 1970 as the new home for Shell Oil Co. in its move from New York.

At the time, Houston's architectural community was beginning to feel pressures from outside architects who had landed several important design contracts. They'd upset the local connections and introduced the International Style of construction, in which decoration can have no role, form must follow function, and most buildings resemble boxes with rows of windows. The locals viewed the arrival of the San Francisco firm of Skidmore, Owings & Merrill as an invasion when hometown corporations Tenneco and First City National Bank employed them to create new buildings, which marked the first impressive steps toward changing the city's skyline in the 1960s.

Hines had been close to the local community, too, as *Texas Monthly*'s Nicholas Lemann recounts, in smaller construction projects outside the downtown. But when it came time for construction of One Shell—at 50 stories, the tallest building in the state at that time—Hines turned also to Skidmore. The result was a structure recognized as innovative. A reinforced concrete framework with a skin of Italian travertine marble, One Shell bellies outward at the base and reveals subtle, complex curves that mark the start of a departure from the completely rectangular appearance that distinguished International Style from the Postmodern era about to dawn in Downtown Houston. One Shell at 900 Louisiana Street remains a landmark among the city's structures, ranking number nine on the list of the largest office buildings, with 1,228,173 square feet. And it's been a commercial success for Hines Interests, sparking a sister structure in Two Shell Plaza just across the street. Those triumphs were merely the salad, however, before the main course, which arrived in 1975 just two blocks away at 711 Louisiana, the address of Pennzoil Place.

Predictably, the impetus for dramatic innovation in Houston architecture came from an oilman, in this case the strong-willed J. Hugh Liedtke. In the 1980s he won international recognition by leading his Pennzoil Co. to victory in that controversial lawsuit against Texaco. A decade earlier, however, the Pennzoil chairman was building something more permanent than a court case against an oilpatch rival. His company—once associated with George Bush in the President's early years—had prospered and grown, and by the 1970s Liedtke believed it deserved a monumental residence. He hired Hines to develop it and insisted that Pennzoil Place be distinctive from the boxlike structures sprouting elsewhere in the country.

Pennzoil Place posed other challenges, too. It would house not only Pennzoil but Pennzoil's sister, Zapata Corp., and each wanted an independent identity. When Liedtke decreed more pizzazz in the preliminary plans displayed by Hines and his designer from One Shell, Hines turned to Johnson for help.

Johnson was not exactly a stranger to the Bayou City. A late bloomer to the profession, he had enrolled at Harvard University's school of architecture in 1940 at the age of 34. Blessed with inherited wealth, he had traveled in Europe and served as curator of New York's Museum of Modern Art before choosing a career. He could afford to be selective about his contracts and, in the 1950s and 1960s, established a reputation for the International Style. In 1949 he'd designed a home in Houston for Mr. and Mrs. John de Menil of the Schlumberger oil well service company, and later he'd returned to do the campus of the University of St. Thomas.

■ *Designed by I.M. Pei and Partners and built by Gerald Hines, Texas Commerce Tower is the city's tallest building. Its 60th-floor skylobby is one of the nation's premier observation points. Photo by C. Bryan Jones*

In the years between those Houston experiences and the Pennzoil opportunity, he had polished his reputation but softened some of his ideas. Johnson and his partner John Burgee tackled the Pennzoil dilemma with an open mind. They suggested two trapezoidal, steel-frame buildings 10 feet apart, with angular tops and a glassed-in plaza between them. Liedtke applauded. Then Hines added a concept that sealed the new merger between attractive architecture and American business.

"There remained the question of how to make sure that even the new Philip Johnson would not be extravagant and send Hines careening into bankruptcy," wrote *Texas Monthly*'s Lemann in a 1982 account of the events. "Hines's solution led to the second reason the Pennzoil building changed American architecture: he figured out how to build the work of Philip Johnson without its costing too much while at the same time making a profit from Johnson's reputation and talent. Johnson would submit his designs to Hines, and Hines would submit them to his business people who would figure out in a systematic fashion how much they would cost. With a little imagination and some give and take, compromises could be reached."

The alliance produced a previously unknown result, as Pennzoil Place attracted critical acclaim plus tenant demand that forced Hines to add two floors during construction. Huxtable visited for *The New York Times* calling Pennzoil Place both "an important building" and a "profitable investment." Together, Hines and Johnson worked to build other Downtown Houston landmarks reflecting the style that's become known as Postmodern.

Of course, Hines has not been the only developer of note in Downtown Houston. It would also be wrong to conclude that local architects got shut out completely by national names from New York and San Francisco. But Hines and Johnson have had the most dramatic impact. Kenneth Schnitzer with his Century Development Corp. made his mark in the Allen Center complex and more prominently with the 1983 construction of Allied Bank Plaza, a 71-story building now called First Interstate Plaza. The banking turmoil of the late 1980s prompted a number of name changes on the roster of buildings all over town. For anyone eager to match the downtown buildings with their original names, developers, and architects, here's a thumbnail sketch:

The Tenneco Building at 1010 Milam is historically significant as the structure that, when completed in 1963, ranked as the cornerstone of a new era in the city's downtown architecture. In developing its new building, Tenneco picked San Francisco's Skidmore, Owings & Merrill as architect, much to the chagrin of local designers who considered Downtown Houston as their own turf. The building introduced the International Style of architecture to the city's skyline and offers a classic example for comparison with the later style that has made the city famous—Postmodern.

First Interstate Bank Plaza at 1000 Louisiana is Houston's most spacious office building. Developed by Schnitzer and Century as Allied Bank Plaza in 1982, it was designed by the national firm of Skidmore, Owings & Merrill. Its tower is covered in blue-green reflective glass. The flat sides of the building align with neighboring structures, but two quarter circles, offset and juxtaposed, shroud one side and distinguish its form. It is home to Union Pacific Resources, the law firm of Butler & Binion, and First Interstate Bank.

Texas Commerce Tower at 800 Travis is Houston's tallest building. Completed in 1981 by Hines, it was designed by New York's I.M. Pei & Partners as a sleek, pentagonal concrete tube with a granite skin. The tower rises 1,049 feet from the street, and its five-sided configuration offers stunning views of the entire Houston area. Its skylobby on the 60th floor is open to the public and provides what's been described as one of the premier observation points in America. It is home for Texas Commerce Bank and the law firm of Andrews & Kurth.

Pennzoil Place at 711 Louisiana is the city's fourth largest office building. Completed in 1975 by Hines and Johnson, it launched a new era of American architecture and ranks as the most influential piece in the city's skyline. It is home to Pennzoil, Zapata Corp., the Houston offices of Arthur Andersen, and the law firm of Bracewell & Patterson.

First City Tower at 1001 Fannin ranks fifth in square footage. Finished in 1981, it's been called the local architectural community's "revenge" by *Texas Monthly* because it was designed by Houston's S.I. Morris 20 years after developer First City National Bank sidestepped him for Skidmore in construction of its first office building. Top tenants include First City, Houston's largest law firm of Vinson & Elkins, and Cooper Industries, Inc.

NCNB of Texas at 700 Louisiana challenges Pennzoil Place as the most unorthodox skyscraper in Downtown Houston. Completed in 1983 as RepublicBank Center, it marked the second collaboration downtown by Hines and Johnson, one in which they clearly demonstrated they had indeed broken the shackles of the International Style. NCNB ranks sixth in square footage, but its 56 stories dwarf Pennzoil Place across the street. Most remarkable is the Gothic effect of its many prickly spires on three steeply pitched rooflines with gabled ends. It hosts NCNB of Texas bank, Houston's office of Peat, Marwick, Main & Co., and the brokerage firm of Rotan Mosely.

1100 Louisiana—recently called Interfirst Plaza—was completed in 1980 as First International

■ *An eye-catching, brightly colored sculpture at 1100 Louisiana stands in sharp contrast to the office buildings surrounding it. Photo by Bob Rowan/ Progressive Image Photography*

Plaza by Hines with Skidmore as the architect. The structure's pink tower offers a delicate glow from afar, but closer inspection reveals an intricate design that mixes pink reflective glass with flame-cut Texas pink granite. 1100 Louisiana houses Tenneco Inc., Huffington Inc., and the Houston offices of Coopers & Lybrand.

The Enron Building at 1400 Smith ranks eighth in size among Houston office buildings. A creation of Schnitzer's Century Development and Houston's Lloyd Jones Brewer & Associates, it was completed in 1984 and houses Enron Corp. An oval cylinder, its tower rises up to terminate with a simple rolled parapet, with a line of white neon illuminating its peak at night.

One Shell Plaza at 900 Louisiana remains a landmark because of its association with Hines and with Shell Oil Co. It ranks ninth among Houston office buildings. Designed by Skidmore and completed in 1971, it marked a major beachhead in the invasion of Houston by national architectural firms. It is home to Shell Oil and the law firm of Baker & Botts.

Chevron Tower at 1301 McKinney was known as Gulf Tower upon completion in 1983. The merger frenzy of the 1980s sealed the fate of developer Gulf Oil Corp. and gave the new name to that corporation's new owner. It ranks 10th in size and represents the architectural design of another prominent Houston firm, CRSS Inc. A pair of triangles set back-to-back create a diamond shape and as many as 10 corner offices on a single floor. The Chevron Tower achieves a silvery tone with alternating bands of polished gray Italian granite and silver reflective glass tipped with aluminum. The facade's light gray color reduces heat absorption and energy costs. It's home to Gulf's successor, Chevron USA Inc., and the law firm of Fulbright & Jaworski.

Downtown is more than just its buildings. And Houston is more than just its downtown. But a look at the people who created the city's most prominent suburban development—The Galleria—only underscores its relationship with downtown: Both are, in many ways, the offspring of Gerald Hines.

THE GALLERIA

Although it's located just outside The Loop, Houston's Galleria area has developed a mystique of its own. The neighborhood takes its name from the world-class shopping center developed by none other than Gerald Hines. It is also home to Houston's third largest office building and the nation's tallest suburban skyscraper—Transco Tower—another example of the collaboration between Hines and Johnson. Hines adopted the name Galleria for his retail project at the corner of The Loop and Westheimer Boulevard, but it has since grown to cover a wider range of business and residential territory. In recent years the Hines Interests have been careful to warn some businesses that they can't attach the Galleria label to their names without distinguishing it from The Galleria in some way. The chamber of commerce for the district cautiously calls itself the Galleria Area chamber. Hines, of course, is only trying to protect a valuable identity, but the issue itself demonstrates a reality of Houston: the Galleria is a community larger than Hines must have envisioned when he launched it 20 years ago.

Known variously over the years as the Magic Circle, City Post Oak, and most recently, Uptown Houston, the community Houstonians recognize as the Galleria Area employs more than 78,000 people and has a daytime population of 220,000 shoppers, hotel occupants, and office building visitors. Home to 3,543 separate companies, with 18,161,520 square feet of office space, it covers 1,600 acres on the city's near west side. The area ranks as the third largest business center in Texas—surpassed only by the downtowns of Dallas and Houston—and 13th largest in the nation. It contains $1.5 billion worth of improved property. The total amount of lease space exceeds that of downtown Denver or the entire city of Minneapolis. Its heart is The Galleria—the retail center that gave life to the district—and its story begins with Hines.

To call The Galleria a shopping mall is to call Madison Square Garden a gym. A 52-acre multiuse center, the 900,000-square-foot retail area caters to the city's elite, with shops and merchandise available nowhere else. Amenities include restaurants, clubs, four movie theaters, and an Olympic-size ice skating rink. The complex also has two Westin hotels, which have enabled The Galleria to establish a reputation as an important small-to-mid-size convention and meeting center. Hines opened the first phase in 1970 and slowly expanded while the property in the area assumed an identity of its own.

But the major new landmark there was another Hines contribution, the breathtaking 64-story Transco Tower. Completed in 1983, it immediately gave The Galleria a claim to challenge Downtown Houston as an architectural showplace. The design is a throwback to the early 1900s, honoring the age of setback skyscrapers like the Empire State Building. Transco even has a spotlight on its roof to call attention to its design at nighttime. Major tenants include Transco Energy and Hines Interests.

■ *The Galleria's Olympic-size ice rink may be the training ground for future Olympic skaters. Photo by Bob Rowan/ Progressive Image Photography*

THE AIRPORTS

Railroads and highways opened the path for business growth in the nineteenth and twentieth centuries. But airport development will undoubtedly emerge as the linchpin for growth in the twenty-first. Thus, Houston's two airport complexes loom as business activity centers destined to make their mark on the city's geography. Already, Houston's major airport complex, Houston Intercontinental Airport, some 20 miles north of Downtown Houston, has spawned creation of a business and residential center that may one day rival the Galleria area. Meanwhile, the timely rehabilitation of the city's vintage airport, William P. Hobby Airport, has provided a new engine to keep commerce churning in Downtown Houston.

Houston's aviation history began in 1937 when the city bought a private airfield owned by the W.T. Carter Lumber Company south of what is now The Loop. Originally named Houston Municipal Airport, the new public facility became the base of operations for the early aviation exploits of Howard R. Hughes, Jr., a native Houstonian who was personally responsible for many improvements to the airport. The airport briefly bore Hughes' name until city fathers learned that facilities named for living persons could not qualify for federal funds. They changed it back to "municipal" and then in 1954 changed the name to Houston International Airport in recognition of the Pan American connection with Mexico City.

In 1967 the city renamed its airport after William P. Hobby, a Houstonian who had served as Texas governor from 1917 to 1920. His widow, Oveta Culp Hobby, was one of Houston's leading citizens, active into the 1980s as a media executive through ownership of *The Houston Post* daily newspaper and the city's NBC affiliate television station, KPRC-TV (Channel 2). Their son, William P. Hobby, Jr., served as Texas lieutenant governor from 1973 to 1991. But the airport bearing the Hobby name suffered a short-lived identity crisis almost as soon as the change was made. Construction had already been under way since 1962 on the facility destined to steal its role.

Seventeen years earlier federal officials had advised the city to scout for a new airport site to relieve congestion and allow for growth. A group of Houston oilmen and business leaders quietly purchased a 300-acre tract of land in the far northeastern corner of the county, and in 1960 sold it to the city for $1.86 million—a figure that represented the cost plus interest. They called their holding company Jet Era Ranch Co., and the land they held for the city became the roots for what is now Houston Intercontinental Airport.

Built for $110 million, the first phase of Intercontinental opened on June 8, 1969, when all scheduled airline operations officially shifted from Hobby. With 80,000 visitors at the opening ceremonies, the occasion was touted as the most important day in Houston's history since the Houston Ship Channel opened in 1914.

Naturally the wide open spaces surrounding the new airport attracted development, and IAH has expanded explosively in its two decades of life. It now ranks as the nation's second largest airport in terms of size, covering 8,000 acres, with more than 12,000 parking spaces. The airport boasts four terminal buildings and handles more than 15 million passengers each year. It is a base of operations for 23 major airlines, including Continental which headquarters in Houston.

Continental's acquisition in the early 1980s by Houston's Texas Air Corp. and relocation to Houston prompted one of the most dramatic business sagas of the decade. With his decision to take the airline into bankruptcy and successfully restructure its financial standing, Texas Air's Frank Lorenzo carved himself a niche in the Texas business hall of fame. While he made enemies among labor and pilot organizations, Lorenzo also made history by bringing Continental back to prominence. Along with the airline, IAH soared to new heights, becoming a major international hub for Continental.

And what of poor little Hobby on the city's south side? It was to rise again, thanks to the entrepreneurial efforts of another feisty Texas air carrier, Southwest Airlines. Although Southwest calls Dallas home, in the late 1970s the airline returned Hobby to the big leagues with its creative approach to seizing control of the Lone Star State's commuter service. Southwest inaugurated shuttle services by filling open slots at smaller fields, notably Love in Dallas and Hobby in Houston. With stewardesses clad in hot pants, and free drinks for all aboard, Southwest made its mark in those hectic boom times, providing executives an entertaining way to travel and serving them at airports more convenient to downtown locations. Between 1974 and 1988, passengers through Hobby increased from 695,972 to 7.7 million, as Southwest continued to thrive and other airlines returned to the close-in location.

THE PROVINCES

As the 1980s ground to a close, Houston could best be described as a federation of activity centers that might qualify as important cities in their own right. Beyond the downtown, the Galleria, and the airport clusters, distinctive business and residential neighborhoods had gained power in some farflung locations. Chambers of commerce had sprouted all over Harris County to represent commercial interests in specific locations.

To the northwest, the opening of U.S. 290 as the Northwest Freeway brought transportation to a blossoming location. Compaq Computer headquartered there as one of Houston's most remarkable high-tech success stories. To the west, there was enough development that serious talk of yet another airport created a controversy.

Farther north, in Montgomery County beyond Intercontinental Airport, the planned community launched in 1974 by oil millionaire George Mitchell had become one the nation's impressive development success yarns. Criticized as naive for his dreams in the 1970s, Mitchell turned

The Woodlands into an investment worth $1.4 billion, with commercial and residential properties attracting a population of 11,000 by 1990. Home to Mitchell's company, Mitchell Energy and Development, The Woodlands had also attracted the Houston Area Research Center (HARC) and some budding biotechnology firms. It was being hailed as one of the nation's most promising new communities by publications like *Fortune* and *Money*.

Meanwhile, Exxon Corp.'s real estate division, Friendswood Development Corp., was leaving its imprint in the south through creation of Clear Lake City near the Johnson Space Center and other projects beyond The Loop. Newcomers were discovering older residential sections as well. Close to Downtown Houston, neighborhoods like the Montrose, West University Place, and the old Houston Heights experienced revivals. River Oaks, with its rows of million dollar mansions overlooking Buffalo Bayou just west of downtown, remained the city's most posh address as the neighborhood that Houston's social and business elite called home.

The result is a sprawling, wandering, growing creation: a community of many looks and faces. From its downtown capital of modern architecture to its growth in the provinces, Houston looks the part of a city heading powerfully toward the future in many important directions.

■ *Downtown Houston has emerged as the nation's most stunning example of Postmodern business architecture. Right photo by Bob Rowan/Progressive Image Photography. Facing page photo by Chuck O'Rear*

THE

ACADEMIC CITY

When Houston launched the Houston Economic Development Council (HEDC) in 1984, that fledgling organization wasted no time focusing on an issue of paramount importance to any city with heavyweight plans for the future: higher education. The presence of a solid academic community and environment emerges as prerequisite for growth. As economic development leaders assessed Houston's situation in that regard, they realized it enjoys a number of strengths that form a foundation for a reputation for educational excellence. They also realized the importance of a commitment to keeping that foundation firm.

Counting its number of higher education institutions, Houston could never compare with locations like Boston, Philadelphia, or San Francisco. As a city in the South, however, it stands out in higher education for several reasons. It's the home not only to a large, public university system with three separate campuses in the area but also to a private school that ranks among the best in the country. Both schools are members of the Southwest Conference and bring big-league college athletics to the area. One school produced a Heisman Trophy winner in football as recently as 1989. Houston benefits from the presence of several smaller universities, too, and one of the nation's pioneering black institutions, which has surfaced in recent years as a symbol of ethnic pride. In short, the Houston area offers much variety in higher education. And on some levels it competes nationwide in attracting outstanding scholars to the city.

"The higher education mixture in Houston

■ *Rice University, which is listed in Barron's Guide to the Most Prestigious Colleges and ranked "most competitive," is located about four miles from Downtown Houston. Photo by C. Bryan Jones*

■ *Right: Students of the eight-acre University of Houston-Downtown enjoy a lively volleyball game. The school, founded in 1974, offers undergraduate degrees in the arts, sciences, business, and technology. Photo by Marc Gladdin*

■ *Facing page: Rice University founder William Marsh Rice, who earned a fortune as a cotton merchant and later, as a railroad, banking, and real estate magnate, established a trust for the creation of a university "dedicated to the advancement of art, literature, and science." This statue of Rice sits atop his ashes in the campus quadrangle. Photo by Jay W. Sharp*

is great for students," says Richard Van Horn, a former president of the University of Houston, who left in 1989 to become president of the University of Oklahoma. "That kind of diversity is wonderful for the city. You can find every kind of higher education experience you can imagine."

Not all top educators share that view. Rice University President George Rupp charges without much elaboration that "Houston is unusual in how small a range of higher education is available."

One explanation for his complaint can be found in a respected guide book, the 16th edition of *Barron's Profiles of American Colleges,* published in 1988. It ranks the nation's colleges according to six degrees of admission competition, from "Most Competitive" to "Noncompetitive." While Houston is represented by Rice in the top group, its largest public institution, UH, ranked in the fourth grouping— Competitive schools. The small University of St. Thomas emerged as Houston's only entry between those two, with a spot in the third grouping— Very competitive. Although UH ranks equally with the largest number of state schools, the short range of alternatives in the top three categories may have sent a number of Houstonians packing for the University of Texas-Austin or Texas A&M University.

But there are plenty of indications that UH is gaining on those competitors and will no doubt be listed among the big leagues very shortly. Meanwhile, there's no doubt that college-bound high school students can find a wide variety of colleges sprinkled around those edges.

Indeed, there's a colorful crazyquilt of collegiate experience covering Houston's higher education landscape, with exciting developments occurring on every patch. Individual institutions must be viewed in the context of their neighbors for the impact to be fully appreciated. Here's a look at the pieces that constitute the jigsaw puzzle of higher education in Houston.

UNIVERSITY OF HOUSTON

Rice may be the city's oldest university and its most prestigious, but any survey of Houston's collegiate landscape should start with the city's namesake institution. And it's important to understand right away that the University of Houston should not be confused with its sister institutions—Downtown or Clear Lake. Despite their ties to the UH system, those universities demand an independent identity. For a while in the 1980s the system struggled with labels for its primary campus, calling itself UH-University Park and then UH-Central Campus. But that's now been simplified. When you talk about the University of Houston these days you're talking about the 540-acre campus located on Cullen Boulevard just three miles south of the central business district. And that place is far removed from the school once known around town as "Cougar High."

The school was founded in 1927 as Houston Junior College. In 1934 it officially became the University of Houston with the help of donations from legendary Houston oilman Hugh Roy

Cullen. Although Cullen had left school after the fifth grade, he wanted his city to have a college that would serve working men and women and educate their children. Cullen's initial goals are not too far removed from those of current economic development leaders. They want UH to be the kind of top-notch research institution that will help them attract industries with research needs to the city. At the same time, they want it to be the kind of broad-based institution that will offer the children of newcomers an opportunity for a quality college education.

UH gets more respect now both nationally and at home where city leaders realize the role a broad-based public research facility must play in economic development. *Barron's Profiles of American Colleges* labels it a competitive institution in regard to admissions, a category placing it among most state universities but just below Texas competitors like the University of Texas-Austin or Texas A&M University. The university has made great strides toward finding an identity and displaying a personality.

By 1989, UH was enrolling nearly 30,000 students, 10,000 of those in graduate school and half the population attending school full time. Offering undergraduate degrees in more than 125 different fields plus graduate degrees in 114 master's fields and 53 doctoral tracks, UH boasted more than $55 million in endowments. Engineering, drama, and business administration had emerged as showcase programs, and a stable of celebrity professors had come on board: Pulitzer prize winning playwright Edward Albee, mathematics whiz Gary Wheeler, and "Mr. Banking" Paul Horvitz. Its honors program had tripled between 1984 and 1988 to include more than 800 students.

■ *Law students of the University of Houston attend classes in this stately building located on the 540-acre campus. Photo by C. Bryan Jones*

But UH's wide inventory of course offerings and growing acclaim as a research facility make it too vast to pigeonhole. Indeed, there is something there for almost anyone, except those who get nervous about large classes and need frequent attention from instructors. Nevertheless, UH still fights a local image stemming from its history as a commuter school for housewives and other part-time students. During those years critics dubbed it "Cougar High" in reference to the university's mascot and its reputation as "just another high school." UH leaders wince at those references today and they have every right to object. Their university is rapidly becoming an institution of great significance to the city.

UH has stated that its goal is to be an educational institution capable of producing Houston's leaders of tomorrow, and it wants to be a major research facility that can attract development to the community. Its major breakthrough in research has been the superconductivity work of Dr. Paul Chu, a project that earned him a National Medal of Science and consideration for the Nobel Prize. Business leaders were quick to create a special facility for superconductivity research when other schools tried to lure Chu away in the late 1980s. His successes in that frontier field rank as a turning point for UH in its research image. External research grants increased from $13 million in 1983 to $40 million in 1988. UH attracted more than 50 National Merit Scholars in each of those years, compared to just six back in 1983. Van Horn liked to call those improvements the "Chu effect."

■ *The oldest buildings on the Rice campus display a wealth of architectural detail. Photo by Bob Rowan/ Progressive Image Photography*

Van Horn's departure in 1989 marked the end of an era at UH. Van Horn had come from Carnegie Mellon University in Pittsburgh in 1983, and his tenure at UH was viewed as a time of great progress. In leaving the school, Van Horn predicted it would reach $100 million in research grants by the year 2000. He also noted a reason why UH is well positioned to work with its city in blazing important new educational paths toward the future. UH is the only large public institution in Texas with a major research capacity in an urban area. UH and the Houston economy desperately need each other. With full realization of that need, it appears the days of "Cougar High" have been left in the dust.

RICE UNIVERSITY

Calling Rice University one of Houston's schools is like listing the Mona Lisa among European paintings. Rice, with 4,000 students, is an unusual, special place even on a national scale. And its location in Houston lends more recognition to the city than vice versa. Rice has a story all its own. It's a national institution that has transcended the home town. In that regard, Rice offers Houston high school students an Ivy League equivalent in their own backyard. But only a handful can qualify.

From its founding in 1891 with a $5-million endowment from cotton baron William Marsh Rice, Houston's oldest university has been difficult to categorize. It charged no tuition until 1965, and even now the cost is half what a student would find at a comparable university. Ask Rice admissions counselors for the minimum achievement level required for admittance and they'll smile that there is none. They'll look at anyone with a high school degree. But competition is so fierce that a whopping 70 percent of the freshmen hail from the top five percent of their respective classes, and a third scored high enough on entrance tests to be National Merit Scholars.

An interview is mandatory and the school's admissions committee has a reputation for focusing on applicants with rounded interests. What do they want? The answer is intentionally left vague. One 1968 applicant from New York impressed Rice by sending a tape of original music performed by his combo. Isn't it refreshing to imagine a committee of straight-laced academics grooving to a prospect's bebop as part of his college admission test? Of course, his SAT score of 1,340 didn't hurt, either.

Of 4,406 applicants in 1988 only 1,329 were accepted, with 611 entering the university. Texans predominate with 311, but there's a wide geographic mix, including foreign students. Renowned for engineering programs, Rice attracts as many liberal arts majors. *U.S. News & World Report* has repeatedly ranked Rice among the nation's top 10 colleges and universities in its annual survey, officially placing it in a sphere with institutions like Harvard and Stanford.

Despite a one-billion-dollar endowment that ranked Rice fourth in the country, the university entered the 1990s with ambitious fund-raising goals. It realizes the challenge will be to maintain adequate funding for the high caliber of research needed to keep it in the vanguard. Rice remains satisfied with its size, enrolling about 4,000 annually and planning to maintain that level in the foreseeable future. Its leaders view growth in terms of improved quality rather than a larger student population. As a private school, however, its sources of funding are limited to what it can raise, and leaders there are well aware of the large amount of tax dollars moving into public institutions like UH.

These contradictions make for a campus with an exotic blend of high intellect and diverse backgrounds. A picturesque 300-acre academic park bordered by 4,000 trees and hedges, Rice generates a sense of community associated more with a traditional university in a small town than the urban world that actually surrounds it. Undergraduates live on campus, and everyone is assigned to one of eight social colleges that serve not only as dormitories but as primary centers for life. The campus even has its own hangout in Willy's Pub.

Beyond the achievements of its environment today, Rice enjoys one of the most colorful histories of any university in the country. The story of its nineteenth century benefactor, William Marsh Rice, and the legacy that established the university is the stuff of high drama, with Rice's murder at the center of the plot. The crime even included what today sounds like a comic twist as police were able to prove that, indeed, the butler did it.

A New England native, Rice had migrated to Houston in 1839 at age 22 and spent the rest of the century accumulating a fortune in cotton, importing, exporting, shipping, railroads, and real estate. After the death of his wife in 1863, Rice left Houston and never again lived there with any degree of permanence. But in 1891, he visited associates there and told them of his intentions to found the William M. Rice Institute for the Advancement of Literature, Science and Art. He invited his friends to serve as the first board of trustees but wanted no publicity, demanding that nothing be built until after his death.

In the next few years he quietly transferred portions of his estate to the institute, including real estate holdings in Texas and Louisiana. The first signs of intrigue occurred with the death of his second wife in 1896. She had written a secret will leaving half the Rice estate to relatives and charities. Suspecting collusion among some of his wife's relatives, Rice contested her will and claimed status as a resident of New York, where Texas community property rights would not apply. Before that dispute could be resolved, however, Rice became a murder victim in 1900 at the age of 84, when a servant placed a chloroform-soaked sponge on the old man's face as he slept.

The murder investigation revealed details of an intricate plot implicating an attorney employed by beneficiaries of Rice's late wife. *Collier's Weekly* carried the story of the murder investigation by New York Police Chief Arthur A. Carey, who told of chasing the hearse in an effort to delay cre-

mation of the victim and allow an autopsy. The attorney was eventually convicted of murder, scheduled for execution in the electric chair, and subsequently pardoned in 1912—about the same time the school was to finally open its doors.

But the murder victim and the city where he built a fortune have an impressive legacy in that world-class university which bears his name. In 1930 his ashes were moved to the campus and buried under the huge statue of him, which dominates the campus quadrangle. Some even say they've seen his ghost wandering among the furniture in the historic founder's room, which served as headquarters in 1990 for the Economic Summit of Industrialized Nations.

TEXAS SOUTHERN UNIVERSITY

While Rice University sets a fund-raising goal of $200 million without taking a deep breath, Texas Southern University crosses its fingers and hopes it can raise $5 million for its needs. Inadequate finances have been just one of the hurdles facing this institution, which can claim its own special tradition among Houston universities. But William H. Harris, upon being appointed president in 1988, declared TSU to be "at a major turning point."

He vowed, "We intend to make sure people understand that TSU is a complex university that people in Texas might choose, not just for blacks."

Coming to TSU from Paine College, Harris brought a reputation as a fund-raising specialist, and he quickly put that background to work at TSU by organizing an annual campaign. He was well aware of the image problems he inherited, with a management vacuum, poor academic showings, and declining enrollment contributing their blows.

At the root of any TSU revival, however, will be another side to its image—as the symbol of black progress in Houston. More than 2,000 blacks enrolled when it opened in 1947 as the Texas State College for Negroes. As Houston's "Black University," TSU enjoyed the advantage of automatically attracting top students and instructors from the black community. It survived and thrived despite second-class treatment from the legislature on funding needs.

Now it receives its appropriate share of the state's higher education dollars, but the new era of racial equality has had its drawbacks, too. Other schools have recruited their share of promising black students, placing TSU in a new era of competition. Meanwhile, admitted Harris, the additional public funds available only since 1983 still could not instantly erase the legacy of years of financial neglect. As a result, Houston's black community has rallied around TSU.

As a result, in the late 1980s TSU developed an image for attracting two types of students. One is the group with few other options. As an open admissions school, TSU requires only a high school degree. It provides an opportunity for late bloomers or those held back by economic circumstances and in that regard alone fulfills an important role in the city's higher education mixture. But TSU has also earned the interest of a second group best described as a growing group of middle class black youngsters in search of a black experience and eager to strengthen the institution that has provided their city with so many of its black leaders. In the long run, this resurgence of pride in TSU as a symbol may be its salvation.

Harris agreed: "This image is extremely important. We make that point clearly and often."

Enrollment had risen to 8,766 by 1989, a 16 percent increase since 1986. An improved marketing effort deserves most of the credit. The university's leadership has vowed to challenge what Harris called the misconception that TSU, as an open admissions school, draws the unqualified. Instead, it's a place in Houston where everyone has a chance.

"We get freshmen from across the gamut, from the brightest to some who have had difficulties in high school," he said. "We have structured a curriculum to meet the needs of those who have done well while focusing on the needs of students who need more time. A lot in the latter categories will end up among the best."

■ *Facing page: The rich and finely detailed architecture of buildings on the Rice University campus makes this Houston educational institution an aesthetically pleasing academic environment. Photo by Jay W. Sharp*

UNIVERSITY OF ST. THOMAS

What a pleasant surprise awaits at this city's most unheralded college campus—the 12 city blocks in the Montrose area that comprise the University of St. Thomas. Ten minutes from the central business district, near the museum and medical centers, it is the city's only Roman Catholic institution, founded in 1847. Barrons rates the school "very competitive," making it the city's only university in a league with the University of Texas-Austin and Texas A&M University. It's easily Houston's best kept collegiate secret.

But Joseph H. McFadden, who became president in 1988 vowed to change that. The first layman to head the university, he said: "Our biggest challenge is to make the public aware of what we have to offer. Those who know it, think well of it but a lot of people just don't know what we do."

U.S. News & World Report included St. Thomas among its list of the nation's five most selective universities for schools of its size—1,661 in 1989. The university limits its advertising to a couple of short announcements in Houston newspapers during registration. But lately it's been attracting national coverage.

With many classes conducted in older houses, the charming campus stands in sharp contrast to the hustle and bustle inside Houston's skyline which perches above it. A liberal arts university with no collegiate athletic program, it attracts 64 percent of its students from the Houston area and the average age of undergraduates is 20—a figure that sets it somewhat apart from the commuter image of other Houston schools except Rice University. In 1987,

■ *The Crooker Student Center is among the University of St. Thomas' campus buildings, which, along with the campus grounds, occupy 12 city blocks. Photo by C. Bryan Jones*

69 percent of the freshman class ranked in the top fifth of their high school classes. The school's graduate business program attracts a larger share of older Houstonians attending part-time.

McFadden says the school needs to better identify the areas it would like to be known for and develop a complete professional fund-raising program. He'd also like to see enrollment grow to 2,000.

The students enrolled at St. Thomas enjoy several advantages. With a student-faculty ratio of 11:1 they receive personal treatment. The school's location, close to museums and the central business district, offers the chance for convenient cultural enrichment and access to the business community. St. Thomas has developed a reputation for several showcase programs. International studies offers an undergraduate degree program. The school has a nationally renowned storm research center. It benefits from cooperative efforts with the University of Houston and Notre Dame University on engineering degrees. And it offers a unique general philosophy doctorate called Thomistic Studies.

HOUSTON BAPTIST UNIVERSITY

Suburbs used to be places where city workers lived. Now they have a life of their own and are places where residents can shop, work, and even get a college education. In Houston, that last suburban opportunity has been provided by Houston Baptist University since l963. Controlled by the Southern Baptist Convention, this l58-acre campus in southwest Houston near Sharpstown Center attracts primarily a commuter population with an average age of 27. Ranked by Barron's in 1988 among the state's "less competitive" schools, HBU boasts an outstanding record among its pre-med and nursing students.

"The typical person on our campus would call it a small, independent institution," said Doug Hodo, president and CEO of HBU. "Our personality is that of a compact campus characterized by a broad spectrum of students who come from a cross section of cultures."

HBU's showcase programs include pre-med, nursing, and science studies that attract students on the undergraduate level, with 80 percent later accepted into medical schools. In 1989 HBU boasted a student enrollment of 2,483 and an impressive $28 million in endowments. Typical students arrive with an average SAT score of 1050-1100. A large majority come from a radius of 25 miles. A number of students enter HBU after completing community college credits. HBU is second in size only to Baylor among the seven Baptist schools in Texas.

Prudent land purchases prior to its founding have given HBU an impressive financial foundation. It was born from concern that Southeast Texas lacked a Baptist college. A committee started with the purchase of 390 acres of fallow rice land from Frank Sharp, the man who developed Houston's Sharpstown area and Sharpstown Retail Center on the city's southwest side in the 1960s. That acreage has blossomed into the school and other significant holdings that provide financial strength for HBU. Some 270 scholarships are fueled by church donations and other sources.

HBU expects growth of 4-8 percent in the 1990s, bringing enrollment to an "ideal" level of 3,200 or 3,400. HBU has enhanced its campus life with a successful and active collegiate athletics program, pinpointing sports in which it can be competitive despite its smaller size. The school's basketball and gymnastics teams have given it a national reputation.

After 25 years, HBU has sprinkled the Houston area generously with successful graduates operating businesses and contributing to the community. But the school offers a contrast to the buttondown, career orientation in its general interest graduate degree program. It takes a lot of pride in noting that a 75-year-old woman in 1988 acquired a master's degree there in what the school calls "love of learning" studies—a master of liberal arts for noncareer-base students.

UNIVERSITY OF HOUSTON-DOWNTOWN

With its open admissions policy, the University of Houston-Downtown operates in direct competition with Texas Southern University. While TSU boasts tradition and symbolizes the minority community, UH-Downtown represents a more recent theme in higher education. Opened in 1974, it is a city school with the appeal of city life and a curriculum tailored to the needs of the

■ *The state-controlled University of Houston-Downtown is located in the city on an eight-acre campus that, in addition to classrooms, includes a library, learning resource center, art gallery, and theater. Photo by Bob Rowan/ Progressive Image Photography*

central business district. But that's not to say it lacks innovation.

With all classes in one downtown building, it is convenient. More important, UH-Downtown has assembled some specialty degree programs designed to give students an avenue into the economic sectors that offer opportunities in Houston. It offers degrees in real estate, criminal justice, purchasing, and materials management, as well as engineering technology for support training in the oilpatch. It was designed as an undergraduate university to serve career entry students and preprofessionals. Most observers say it's doing exactly that.

"There's no question we fill a basic niche," said Manuel T. Pacheco after his appointment as president in 1988. "We designed our programs with input from the business community."

Despite its historic location near Allen's Landing in the old Merchants and Manufacturers Building, UH-Downtown may have suffered from its lack of tradition and charm. While TSU boasts a distinctive campus life, UH-Downtown stands as fast food's answer to higher education: Go to work, grab a class, and get on with your life. Under the leadership of Pacheco's predecessor, Alex Schilt, the building was restored and a solid academic program established.

"We view the open admissions policy as a positive," said Pacheco. "It allows people already launched on other careers to pursue a new field. We get students who are well prepared. Our hallmark is that we look at quality in terms of what we do with them."

UH-Downtown attracts students who need smaller or convenient classes. Most are already working, and the school's younger morning population surrenders to an older crowd for the evenings. The average age is 27, and the ethnic diversity adds its own dimension. It enrolled 7,065 in 1989.

Attending college in a high-rise may not be everyone's idea of the ideal university experience. But some of the school's insiders say this school holds plenty of surprises for those who would ignore it.

One instructor compared the school with "San Francisco State in the 1950s." The open admissions policy finds a lot of people who fall through the cracks. UH-Downtown is clearly the wild card in Houston's higher education deck.

UNIVERSITY OF HOUSTON-CLEAR LAKE

If its sister institution downtown ranks as a phenomenon of the business district, then the University of Houston-Clear Lake emerges as a hybrid of a different sort. Located outside the city's mainstream population center, UH-CL is all seriousness about its mission. It even limits enrollment to those students who hold an associate degree from a two year college or 54 semester credit hours with an average grade of "C" or higher. Party-loving freshmen or sophomores need not apply at UH-CL. The offspring of a large public institution that caters to everyone, UH-CL has tried to position itself directly in the path of Houston's high technology future.

"The key words here are corporate or professional. Our average age is 32 and half our students are graduate students. We are no-nonsense and career oriented," says UH-CL President Thomas Stauffer. "We're known by everyone as an institution that treats students like adults. Only a small percentage of our students are undeclared majors."

Most of the school's undergraduates come from eight regional community colleges, but the graduate students come from all over the world. UH-CL has focused on neighborhood resources to enhance its image. And the most notable resource in its neighborhood remains the Johnson Space Center. The school has tied into the space program anywhere it can manage to do so. Unfortunately, it was barred from offering engineering degrees—a factor that can only limit its appeal in a neighborhood that boasts 15,000 members of that profession.

Nevertheless, its pioneering efforts in computer technology and use of JSC resources whenever possible bode well for the future. One prime example is the school's Research Institute for

Computing and Information Systems (RICIS), established in 1986 to merge JSC and local industry with UH-CL computer research efforts. RICIS tackles specific computer research queries in concert with JSC expertise. In the process, students are exposed to new techniques and the university's image is enhanced.

But the high-tech approach isn't limited to computer studies at UH-CL. It also offers an unusual physical education program directed by Gene Coleman, who has served as "coordinator of player performance research" for the Houston Astros. In the high-tech atmosphere of UH-CL, Coleman is not a physical education instructor but a professor of human sciences. His school is called the Human Performance Institute and it employs an array of computerized equipment to produce fitness experts rather than coaches. Much of his fitness research has been conducted with JSC in its astronaut fitness work, and the school has attracted grants to further its growth in this area.

UH-CL set enrollment records all through the late 1980s, boasting a student population of 7,011 in 1989. It offers 40 undergraduate degree options and 37 fields for graduate students.

■ *The University of Houston-Clear Lake, located outside the city's center of population, offers students undergraduate degrees in 40 areas of study. Photo by Jay W. Sharp*

COMMUNITY COLLEGES

Even with its 28,449 students, UH did not rank in 1989 as Houston's largest campus. That distinction went instead to the Houston Community College System, with more than 33,000 attending classes under its supervision. Add its numbers to those of the area's other community colleges and you find more than 66,000 enrolled locally in those basic programs. The strength of the city's community college network is just one more indication of its diversity in higher education. Students attend these schools so they can better prepare for college careers or carve out a vocational path for their lives. These schools offer a wide range of certifications for occupations and two-year associate degrees at a number of convenient locations. They play an ever-expanding role in Houston's higher education picture, giving many students a foundation for transfer to one of the universities in the area.

Houston Community College is the largest of the districts. Other colleges include San Jacinto College, which has enrolled more than 17,000, North Harris County College District with nearly 14,000 students, and Lee College in Baytown boasting another 5,000. All the systems have some distinguishing characteristics but their trifecta of purpose remains the same:

* Provide transfer credits for students who want to continue their education with more focus at a four-year school.
* Offer occupational education for students who want to enter the work force.
* Coordinate continuing education programs for adults who need to enhance their skills.

With such a wide range of purposes, it's easy to see how these community colleges have tackled a difficult task. For some classes they must provide faculty capable of teaching college courses, while others need specific vocational expertise. And they've got to make all these divergent students and teachers feel at home.

Houston Community College was founded in l971, with 32 sites in the Houston, Spring

■ North Harris County College is a community college offering students three campuses from which to choose. Photo by C. Bryan Jones

■ *San Jacinto College is well known for its winning basketball team and its vocational course offerings, ranging from truck driving to underwater welding. Photo by C. Bryan Jones*

Branch, Cypress-Fairbanks, and Stafford school districts. It has a large central campus downtown and offers a well-known program in automated manufacturing and robotics. About one-third of the student body is poised for academic transfer to four-year schools.

San Jacinto College may be best known for its basketball team which annually ranks among the top in junior college hoops. Success of the "SanJac Runnin' Ravens" has prompted coverage of the school by some prestigious national publications. Beyond its athletic endeavors, the school is well known for vocational courses like truck driving and underwater welding.

North Harris County College is a 15-year-old system with three campuses serving New Caney, Humble, Aldine, Spring, and Tomball school districts. Positioned in one of the area's strongest growth sections, the campus is host to a Small Business Development Center and works closely with area businesses to develop training programs. Those connections help everyone associated with the school.

Lee College in Baytown is the area's oldest community college, dating from 1934 when it launched classes at Robert E. Lee High School. Serving the Goose Creek Consolidated School District, Lee boasts a 37-acre campus and is noted for its program for hearing-impaired students and as one of the first community colleges in the nation to offer computer writing labs.

Add in the impact from a number of specialty and professional schools and Houston might be mistaken for a college town. Medical schools like Baylor and the University of Texas dominate the Texas Medical Center. South Texas College of Law has become an important factor in the legal community of the entire Southwest. And Houston International University offers two basic four-year degrees through evening studies. All told, in 1989 the Greater Houston Area counted a student population of nearly 140,000 persons attending the various colleges or universities there.

■ *These students at Lee College in Baytown unwind with a game of tennis. Photo by C. Bryan Jones*

THE

CULTURAL CITY

W hen her husband first announced the transfer, she compared it with news of the end of the world. She'd lived in New York all her life but now, in the early 1980s, she was moving to Houston, Texas. She could only imagine the kinds of things that would pass for art in a place like that. Violins? Start calling them fiddles. Fancy dinners? Better develop a taste for barbecue. All the radio stations would be playing country and western music. Whatever would they do for a social life?

Today, you're likely to find her at The Galleria trying on cowboy hats. She'll don an evening gown later and attend a performance of the Houston Ballet. Then she'll stop for a nightcap at a genuine honky tonk, maybe dance the Cotton-Eyed Joe and brag about her volunteer work with the Houston Livestock Show & Rodeo.

She is really no one in particular. But she is a composite of someone known by many Houstonians who welcomed a population of newcomers as a by-product of the economic growth enjoyed by Houston since World War II. And she symbolizes something that is unique to Houston's culture. Its stylish and affluent domestic immigrants have had as much impact as ethnic newcomers from foreign lands. The city has polished its country and western tradition as the foundation for a new world of activity and entertainment. The result is an eccentric mix of cultural adventure that offers something for everyone. Because business development demanded it, for example, Houston has become the only city in the nation besides New York and San Francisco to maintain internationally recognized companies in the four major performing arts: opera,

■ *Young entertainers take to the stage at Hermann Park.*
Photo by Jay W. Sharp

ballet, symphony, and repertory theater. It also annually holds the nation's premier rodeo and livestock show. And don't forget about the Astrodome—in many minds it remains the Eighth Wonder of the World for historical reasons well worth recalling. Even the city's professional sports franchises seem to boast personalities and dynamics all their own. Houstonians can play at many types of games, clad in everything from tuxedos to Levis, and still feel right at home.

THE LAND OF THE URBAN COWBOY

When the legendary Gilley's Club closed its doors in 1989, its demise came in a way that stunned die-hard fans of the cowboy culture: by judge's decree, to end a squabble between its entrepreneurial partners.

"Six to ten years ago," wrote the late Bob Claypool, eloquently characterizing the shock in a column for *The Houston Post*, "if you'd asked me where Gilley's Last Stand would take place, I'd have conjured up visions of the muddy, unpaved Gilley's Club parking lot, with two big lube-pit bubbas, bellies straining against pearl button-snaps, down in that mud, heaving and ho-ing, throwing beefy forearms into each other's meaty faces and trying to keep from drowning in one of those murderous rain-filled chuckholes. That's what should have happened. It seems more manly . . . many such battles have taken place there over the years."

You can't go to Gilley's anymore, but it is one of those peculiarly Houston places that will live forever. Fans of the late movies on television can catch the image often in reruns of *Urban Cowboy* with John Travolta and Debra Winger. Much of the movie was filmed in 1979 in the Pasadena nightspot established in 1971 when struggling singer Mickey Gilley teamed with a former Shell Chemical Co. welder named Sherwood Cryer to create the world's largest honky tonk. Others can read a copy of Claypool's book about the place, *Saturday Night at Gilley's*. Either way, students of Houston's cultural life won't be merely rehashing nostalgia. The memory of Gilley's Club and the continuing annual success of the Houston Livestock Show and Rodeo represent the two most important reminders of exactly how close the Old West remains to anyone who lives in Houston.

In its heyday, Gilley's became as famous as any Houston landmark. A typical night in the mid-1980s would include as many tourists as locals, and the attraction wasn't limited to blue-collar refinery workers like the hero depicted by Travolta in the movie. His fling in the film with an aristocratic oilpatch debutante was not too farfetched. Gilley's Club and the cowboy mystique it symbolized drew from River Oaks as well as Pasadena. One of the most telling photos ever to run in *The Houston Post*, for example, shows socialite Lynn Wyatt—a regular on the city's best dressed lists—enjoying a wild ride on one of the mechanical bulls. In addition to the huge dance floor and fights in the parking lot, those bulls offered patrons one more way to prove their western worth as they paid to simulate the kind of experience a real bull rider gets competing at a rodeo.

With its ancillary enterprises—a record studio, beer, souvenirs, and even a brief stint as a boxing arena—Gilley's became a multimillion-dollar business success tale. Along the way, Mickey Gilley became one of the nation's top C&W performers. But it all came crashing down in 1988 after a jury awarded Gilley $17 million and forbade use of his name on the club in response to his lawsuit against 17-year-partner Cryer. A judge ordered it closed in 1989 to protect the assets still in dispute. As long as there is a Houston, however, there will always be honky tonks in the tradition of Gilley's. Its saga is the standard against which the urban cowboy myth will always be measured.

If Gilley's demise appears somewhat sad, its counterpart in designing Houston's cowboy mystique—the Houston Livestock Show & Rodeo—appears quite capable of bringing that tradition to new heights in the years ahead. An annual nonprofit event, it's the equivalent of New Orleans'

Mardi Gras. It's also an important year-round business for the professionals who manage the production, and its impact on the Houston economy figures in at well over $200 million per year. But its impact goes well beyond the financial boost it provides every year. Entertainment and education surface as prominent benefactors, too.

The event began in 1931 as a livestock exhibition and auction, adding the rodeo in 1937. The Houston Livestock Show & Rodeo itself lasts just two weeks each February or March when the Astrohall facility beside the Astrodome is transformed into the world's largest barn, complete with stalls for everything from chickens to cattle. One week of the livestock show focuses on professional breeders. But the second week is devoted to the youngsters—teens who come from all over the Southwest to park their campers in the Astrodome parking lot, show the product of their agricultural labors, and compete for prizes.

Throughout this two week period, the Astrodome next door becomes the world's most important rodeo arena as the nation's real cowboys compete for big money prizes riding bulls and busting broncos. The rodeo rides daily and an important part of the attraction is a musical headliner to perform at each session. The Houston show attracts the biggest names in country & western as well as popular music, and rodeo dates are viewed more as concert events than cowboy entertainment. Recent rodeo headliners have included singers and groups as diverse as George Strait and Chicago. In 1990 the show even added a new twist with Bill Cosby offering a comedy routine. Sideline activities include barbecue cooking contests and a carnival. Visitors can spend a couple of hours prowling the stalls in the livestock arena or shopping at the booths, which might offer anything from the latest style in belt buckles to the latest technology in feeding cattle.

All over town Houstonians are urged to "Go Texan" in the tradition of a popular promotional campaign launched in the 1950s. Executives routinely show up for work wearing Stetsons, and at some businesses it's considered unpatriotic to wear anything but cowboy garb.

More than 6,500 Houstonians from all walks of life volunteer for service on 60 special organizational committees. The competition for these prestigious positions has become so fierce that members risk losing their seats if they fail to work hard. They receive commemorative badges for their efforts, and many of the awards have become valuable collector's items.

In the week leading up to the start of each show, several groups of true western fans take off from work to participate in authentic Old West trail rides, camping out on horseback and finally arriving in Memorial Park for a nostalgic rendezvous.

In the process, the Houston show has collected some impressive statistics, particularly where its educational contributions are concerned. Revenues cover operating expenses, with net profits dedicated to academic charities. It ranks as the world's largest donor of agricultural scholarships. The show's first scholarship, totaling $2,000, was presented in 1957. Since then, the show has given more than 2,200 scholarships, worth about $16 million, to graduates who have pursued careers as diverse as veterinarians, state senators, bankers, lobbyists, and professors.

But all the educational contributions don't come directly in the form of scholarships. For those who don't win scholarships, the stakes of the show can still be high. An auction climaxes each junior exhibition week and historically has attracted Houston's society crowd in their best duds to throw some big bucks at those prize-winning chickens, hogs, and steers.

The show's grand champion steer usually emerges as the big money winner, with celebrities battling to outbid each other. In 1990, for example, retired convenience store executive Le Roy Melcher paid a record $180,000, outbidding retail furniture entrepreneur Jim "Mattress Mac" McIngvale who wore a bright gold Gallery Furniture T-shirt with his "Save You Money" advertising slogan emblazoned across the chest. The money went to an 18-year-old 4-H'er from the Abilene area who was expected to use some of the proceeds for educational purposes. The Saturday morning auction of the junior grand champion steer is always quite a show in itself, but the rest of the livestock raised and sold also amounts to a tidy sum for the young breeders who usually set it aside for college assistance.

Adding it all together, the Houston Livestock Show & Rodeo tallies some impressive superlatives. In 1990 the 58th annual show drew a record total of 784,483 for the 18 rodeo performances, with overall attendance at 1.32 million, verifying its strength as the city's single most important tourist attraction. Economic observers like to cite the show's economic statistics as a barometer for the city's economic health and they got a treat in 1990. Sales for junior livestock totaled $2.7 million, creating the highest total livestock sales figures since 1981's $6.2 million during the peak of the oilpatch boom. The 802 professional cowboys competing at the 1990 rodeo divided a purse of $358,919.

THE FINE ARTS GO TEXAN

With its roots firmly planted in western soil, the tree of Houston's cultural life has somehow managed to become a hybrid. Without losing that cowboy flavor, it's added branches that look unmistakably like something a New Yorker might understand: the symphony, the ballet, the opera, theater, and impressive art museums. Indeed, New Yorkers should understand them because they are in many ways a reflection of their influence.

The battle for acceptance on a world-class level has been a well-documented element of Texan and Houstonian ambition ever since oil money made this land the financial equal and commercial partner of moguls in the Northeast. Their independent spirit and eccentric displays notwithstanding, Houstonians have battled to demonstrate an appreciation for the fine arts ever since the beginning. They haven't always been successful in overcoming that Wild West image. But the fact remains that fine arts patronage is an often overlooked portion of the city's cultural personality. And the community has invested on a grand scale to make sure that part of its image can start getting its measure of respect.

It would be wrong to imply that Houston only discovered real culture in the last quarter century. Historian David G. McComb notes that pioneering Houstonians displayed an interest in cultural development. They formed the Philosophical Society of Texas in 1837. They launched the Houston Lyceum in 1854 to sponsor lectures, debates, and musical programs. And throughout its history the city has repeatedly seen patrons come forth to enhance its reputation as a place responsive to the fine performing arts.

But the true turning point for the city's cultural image occurred May 10, 1987, when it unveiled the $70-million Wortham Center as a performing arts complex downtown after 10 years of planning and fundraising. The opening prompted former Texas governor John Connally, a member of the Wortham Theater Foundation Board of Trustees, to ponder comparisons with the famous Kennedy Center in the nation's capital. He told reporters that the Wortham "will remake the city of Houston in the way the Kennedy Center changed the cultural tone of the city of Washington." Beyond the building's artistic impact, however, stands another reason to celebrate its existence. The complicated fundraising effort that made it possible ranks as a lasting statement itself to the commu-

■ *The fortress-like Alley Theatre building is home to the nation's oldest resident professional Equity group—the well-respected Alley Theatre Company. Photo by C. Bryan Jones*

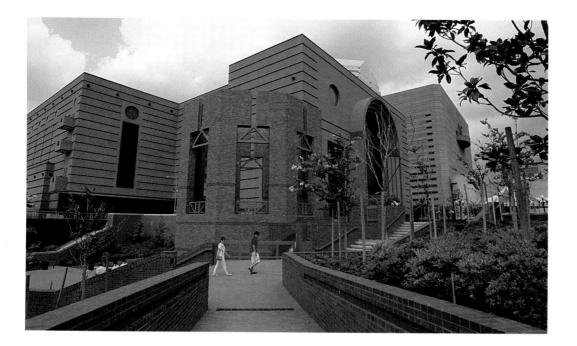

nity's desire to be included among the big leagues of fine arts endeavors.

Constructed on land beside the Alley Theatre and across from the Jesse H. Jones Hall for the
Performing Arts, the Wortham Center ranks as the most expensive privately funded performing
arts center in the United States. Considered with the Alley and Jones Hall, both built 20 years
before, the Wortham now stands as the linchpin for a true downtown theater district of international proportions.

Home to the Houston Grand Opera and Houston Ballet, the Wortham stands as another outstanding piece of downtown architecture. Its entranceway is a Romanesque arch 87.5 feet tall and
50 feet wide. "Spanned with lightly tinted clear glass and supported by a thin structural system
painted deep burgandy, it heralds in scale, form, color, tone and refinement the design and architectural details discovered inside," writes the Houston Chapter of the American Institute of Architects. Its lower nine feet of exterior facing is done in carmen red Finnish granite, cut and
dressed in Italy. Rose brick sheathing above came from Henderson, Texas. Windows, balconies,
and darker-hued protruding horizontal rows of custom fabricated bricks accent the structure.
Inside it holds the 2,178-seat Brown Theater for the opera and the 1,100-seat Cullen Theater for
the ballet.

Neighboring Jones Hall was completed in 1966 as a home for all of Houston's performing
arts. Its opening coincided with the founding of the Houston Society for the Performing Arts.
Jones Hall was built to supersede the city's once premier entertainment complex in the Sam
Houston Coliseum and Music Hall, constructed a few blocks away as a mid-1930s U.S. Public
Works Administration project. With seating for 3,001, Jones Hall was funded entirely by the
Houston Endowment Inc., a foundation established by Jesse H. Jones and his wife.

Just across the street stands the Alley Theatre. Built in 1968, it is home to the Alley Theatre
Company, a nationally known professional dramatic group. The theatre building, with its nine
towers and rounded sentinel walks, resembles a fortress, "a stronghold of the dramatic arts," according to Houston's AIA chapter. It houses two stages: the 798-seat Large Theatre and the co-
zier 296-seat Arena stage. A grand staircase sweeps up the multilevel lobby, and the ceiling peaks
high above in a triangular clerestory window.

As a privately funded building, the Wortham commands a large share of civic pride. And the

■ Above: Sculptures are set amid the grounds of the Museum of Fine Arts. Photo by Bob Rowan/ Progressive Image Photography

■ Right: The Glassel School of Art features the work of its students. Photo by Bob Rowan/ Progressive Image Photography

■ *Left: The pursuit of art and culture permeates every square mile of the Houston area. Photo by Bill Ross*

story of its construction illustrates the importance of that northeastern influence on Houston's growing cultural stature, for it was a transplanted corporate executive named Robert Cizik who has attracted much of the credit for making the project work. In naming Cizik one of its Houstonians of the Year in 1987, *Houston City Magazine* noted, "Without him, Houston's largest private civic project may have become one of its most embarrassing fiascos."

As chairman and president of Cooper Industries, he moved the company to Houston in 1967 and built the conglomerate from one with $100 million in sales to one with more than $3 billion in sales by the end of the 1980s. A longtime supporter and past president of Houston Grand Opera, he seized the initiative on the Wortham when the project stalled in 1983 with $45 million in financial commitments and a tentative design that could have boosted costs to $115 million. Cizik organized three major financing campaigns to complete the work that had started in 1977 when the foundation was first launched.

By the time the Wortham opened, the Houston economy had endured the longest period of suffering it had ever known, but Cizik managed to raise the funds from allies in the corporate network. Commenting on the timing of the Wortham opening, Cizik said, "Some might say, 'Who needs it? We're cutting back our budgets.' But the fact of the matter is that it is important. Houston will recover. It will resume its growth. And I'm convinced that 10 years from now this facility will be viewed as 'How could we have gotten here without it?'"

With world-class structures in place and the economy on the rebound, Houston entered the 1990s with a new outlook from business development leaders where the city's state of the arts was concerned. City leaders no longer saw the arts as a frill but as a quality-of-life factor required, according to the Houston Economic Development Council, as a base to attract those who will build the city's industries of the future. Commenting on the business connection with the arts, John Seidl, president and chief operating officer of Enron Corp., told *Houston Magazine* in

1988: "The arts make it easier to attract first class employees to Houston. We've recently relocated a number of employees here and they were very nervous about the move. But they are finding the city a great place to live because of the arts. I just ran into two relocated executives at the opera and they were delighted to be here."

In contrasting the two cultural Houstons—wild west and highbrow—it's important to consider other elements of the fine arts equation. One significant factor has been the contribution of Dominique de Menil, a French native who emigrated to Houston with her late husband during World War II. She was 19 when her father and uncle founded the international Schlumberger Inc. to sell an invention for locating oil deposits. It progressed to become the world's largest oil field services company. And de Menil—one of Houston's most important patrons of the arts—has regularly appeared on the *Forbes* 400 list of the nation's wealthiest citizens.

When she and husband John moved to the company's U.S. headquarters in Houston after the Nazi invasion of France, they found their adopted city had only one official museum—the Mu-

seum of Fine Arts—and virtually no modern arts collection. Having developed an interest in art before the war, the de Menils continued their collecting as they established roots in Houston. During the decades after World War II they traveled the world in search of gallery treasures, and their home became a gathering place for celebrated artists. John became a charter member of the new Contemporary Arts Association and the couple organized a showing of 24 Van Gogh paintings at the small museum that drew large crowds. They influenced arts consciousness at the Museum of Fine Arts, the University of St. Thomas, and Rice University. Indeed, it was the de Menils who first brought architect Philip Johnson to town, hiring him to challenge residential construction convention in Houston's posh River Oaks neighborhood and design a modern, one story home for them there.

But the most lasting de Menil contribution will undoubtedly be the Menil Collection (the "de" is dropped for simplicity), a stunning museum built in 1987 in the Montrose area as the permanent home for her $150 million, 10,000 work collection of surrealist, Oceanic, and African art. Several years after her husband's death in 1973 she began planning for the museum, designed by Renzo Piano, who collaborated with Richard Rogers on the high-tech Centre Pompidou in Paris. Piano adopted a dramatic new approach to the architecture of the building, which occupies an entire city block yet blends with the residential structures around it. While most objects are stored on the second floor, a relatively small number remain on display downstairs where diffused natural lighting intensifies the focus.

The Menil Collection has become a cornerstone for an exciting museum district in the vicinity of the Texas Medical Center, Rice University, and the Montrose neighborhood. Within a mile lie the Museum of Fine Arts, the Contemporary Arts Museum, several commercial galleries, Rice

■ *Children, of course, enjoy*
any opportunity to visit the
Contemporary Arts Museum
Photo by Jay W. Sharp

University, and the University of St. Thomas, all within sight of the Postmodern skyscrapers that electrify the downtown skyline.

All this has converged to attract an intriguing cadre of young artists to the city. With playwright Edward Albee in residence in the 1980s as a professor at the University of Houston, where an influential creative writing program had begun to blossom, the city was fast becoming a kind of blank slate where creative minds could work unfettered. Photographer Wendy Watriss, who has exhibited her work in the Soviet Union, offered her view of Houston's attractions in a 1989 article for *Discovery Magazine:* "There's a lot of energy here and it's a place where you can dream. There isn't a strong art power structure here that would make it difficult to try new projects. There's freedom to experiment and develop." The result has been impressive enough for former *Houston Post* columnist Keith Watson to make a simple declaration in that same *Discovery* story: "In keeping with the Texans' affinity for things big, Houston has become the arts capital of the South."

JUDGE HOFHEINZ BUILDS THE EIGHTH WONDER OF THE WORLD

Cowboy chic and fine art collide in Houston to create a cultural atmosphere unique in America. That atmosphere becomes even more unusual in light of another entertainment option, one familiar to people all over the world as another symbol of Houston's grip on the future. Other cities have built domed stadia as homes for their own sports franchises, concert productions, and convention business. But Houston's Astrodome will always be remembered as the first of this breed.

It became fashionable a few years ago to heckle the Astrodome as a building past its prime, one that compares unfavorably with sleeker models constructed elsewhere. Nothing could be further from the truth. Thanks to its rich legacy, the Astrodome as a pioneering effort will always be the best. Refurbishing has made it just as modern as imitators in other locations. A visit there kindles a connection to the past and a time when plenty of supposedly knowledgeable folks said that something like this just couldn't be done. As a monument to Houstonian ingenuity, it ranks with the Houston Ship Channel. Thus, it is more than a building where grownups go to play. And, as a Houston institution, the story of the Astrodome is more the story of a forceful, visionary individual than it is the story of a construction project. It is the story of the late Judge Roy Hofheinz, one of the most remarkable people in a city famous for eccentrics.

Houstonians remember Hofheinz in a special way. Others gained fame in the oilpatch, medicine, or space, but Hofheinz was a product of the political arena. His style, however, made him the P.T. Barnum of his day. First and foremost he was a showman, and the title of his biography by Edgar W. Ray says its all: *The Grand Huckster—Houston's Judge Roy Hofheinz, genius of the Astrodome.* To call him a huckster may have seemed unfair, but the judge probably loved it. And the legacy of the Astrodome bears witness to the title.

They called Hofheinz "the judge" because the Beaumont native had been at age 24 the youngest county judge in Texas. County judge is an administrative rather than a judicial position, equal to being mayor of a city or supervisor of county government. Born in 1912, Hofheinz was the son of a hardworking shipyard laborer who moved to Houston in 1924 and launched his own cleaning and pressing business, which failed after a year.

While his father went on to earn a living as a truckdriver, young Roy was proving his talents as a scholar and promoter. He made top grades and demonstrated his potential for controversy as the yell leader for San Jacinto High School, often becoming the target for anger from opposing teams because of his enthusiasm.

He demonstrated his entrepreneurial instincts by selling programs at sports events and developed a knack for performance that would one day find its peak of recognition in development of the entertainment empire that's known in Houston as Astrodomain.

He refused a scholarship to the University of Texas, attending Rice Institute instead because it charged no tuition. He supplemented the family's income by promoting dances at Rice. He transferred to Houston Junior College and in 1930 accepted one of the first free scholarships awarded for Houston Law School, a private school based in the Harris County Courthouse. Hofheinz learned quickly and by 1931, at age 19, had passed the bar and opened an office. Ambitious and charismatic, he won a term in the legislature, then won election in 1936 as Harris

■ Left: The enormity of the Astrodome is apparent in this aerial view showing the stadium and AstroWorld amusement park. Photo by James Blank

■ Facing page left: Old and new co-exist in urban harmony in Sam Houston Park downtown. Photo by Al Stephenson

■ Left: Home to baseball's Houston Astros, the Astrodome, with its artificial turf, presents some unique problems for ballplayers. Photo by Bob Rowan/ Progressive Image Photography

■ These football players are a blur of motion as they take to the field. Photo by Jim Baron

County judge, earning a title that would stick for the rest of his life, although he only held the post for two terms.

Hofheinz always had something cooking. Controversial and flamboyant, he amassed a fortune in land speculation and returned to politics, winning election as Houston's mayor in 1952. Impatient with those who seemed to be holding his city back, Hofheinz endured two controversial and stormy terms as mayor highlighted by impeachment proceedings and battles with a stodgy city council.

Voted out of office in 1956, Hofheinz left politics behind with a grander scheme—some would call it insanity—burning in his brain. The year before, he had vacationed in Rome and toured the ruins of the Colosseum. Legend said that the Colosseum originally had a velarium, or awning, that was pulled across the top by slaves when the weather turned sour. Intrigued and maybe a little obsessed, the judge contacted Buckminster Fuller, inventor of the geodesic dome, and devoured the literature on dome architecture. Fuller convinced him it was possible to cover any space with a dome—if you had enough money. He first thought he'd try the concept with a shopping center. Then one of the city's wealthiest oil and real estate entrepreneurs, R.E. "Bob" Smith, approached Hofheinz with a better idea. They decided to bring major league baseball to Houston and do it in style. He drew a picture of a dome on a piece of yellow legal paper and knew it would be the perfect hook to win a franchise from the National League.

Without the judge's political acumen, charisma, and drive, the Astrodome would certainly never have been built. Transferring that yellow sketch into the reality that stands today along the South Loop required more than construction workers and materials. First he formed the Houston Sports Association (HSA), the business that today officially owns the Houston Astros and a number of other sports-related entities, including the lease for the county-owned Astrodome. He convinced the National League that Houston deserved a team and promised a dome as the Eighth Wonder of the World to promote it.

By 1960 Houston had its team—called the Colt .45s—but its dome remained a plan for the future. City government laughed when approached to serve an administrative role over what Hofheinz envisioned as a public facility. But 34-year-old Harris County Judge Bill Elliott liked the idea and convinced the Commissioners Court to accept that role. First, however, they had to convince voters to spend $9 million building the thing. HSA had agreed to lease the county's stadium—if it ever got built—for $750,000 per year, covering principal and interest and giving the county a landmark facility practically for free. Hofheinz, Elliott, and other supporters worked around the clock to promote their bond issue. It passed by a meager 51 percent. Then when construction costs exceeded expectations, they had to promote a second bond election. By then Houstonians figured they were along for another wild Hofheinz roller coaster ride and couldn't get off if they'd wanted.

With his penchant for detail and flair, the judge personally took command of every aspect of construction. Although specialists assured him that grass would grow in the dome, Hofheinz fortunately pursued investigation of artificial turf, which eventually had to be used and became known as Astroturf—the Ninth Wonder of the World? He recruited baseball's greatest fungo hitter, Ed Roebuck, to determine how far a baseball could be hit before it would touch the roof. He asked Elliott, a former pipefitter, to climb 218 feet to the top of the dome and fasten the final rivet. The day before the Astrodome opened on April 9, 1965, Hofheinz even inspected every restroom himself to make sure that toilet paper had been installed everywhere. Despite construction delays, political warfare, engineering dilemmas, and a Pandora's Box of other problems, the Astrodome took shape on Houston's south side and became a roaring success. Its real name is the Harris County Domed Stadium.

Dare we call the Astrodome a facility of cultural enterprise in Houston? It's hard to call it anything else. With the judge at the helm, Houston's Astrodome quickly overshadowed the baseball team renamed the Astros and to great extent, the city itself. The Hofheinz imagination ran wild as the Astrodome became the host for all manner of grandiose events, much like its inspiration, the Colosseum in Rome. In June 1965, Ringling Brothers and Barnum & Bailey Circus stopped there, drawing the largest crowds in its 96-year history. September 11, 1965, marked the world's first indoor football game as the University of Houston Cougars lost 14-0 to Tulsa University. The Reverend Billy Graham brought his crusade, setting a single-event attendance record that would withstand all challengers until 1981 when the Rolling Stones showed up.

In February 1966 the judge presented one of his dream events, bloodless bullfights, which attracted 107,250 fans and prompted an encore in 1969. Cassius Clay reclaimed his heavyweight title there in 1966, and the collegiate basketball game of the decade saw UH defeat UCLA in 1968. Hubert Humphrey held a political rally there in November 1968, with Frank Sinatra providing entertainment. Evel Knievel set a world record for an indoor motorcycle jump there in 1971 and in 1973 the Great Wallenda walked a high wire above an auto thrill show in the Astrodome. Later that year Billie Jean King beat tennis bigmouth Bobby Riggs there in the heralded "Tennis Battle of the Sexes." What's happened at the Astrodome over the years? Better to ask what hasn't.

Just as interesting were some of the events behind the scenes. Besides building a sports arena, the judge also constructed a wonderland of special suites and offices in his dome. Some of the original rooms have since been removed, but they bear noting because of what they reveal about the Hofheinz flare and its impact on Houston. He wanted a scoreboard like no other before it, one that would entertain as well as inform. The result was a new era in scoreboard design, with a $2-million extravaganza that required a crew of six technicians to operate its 50,000 bulbs across 474 feet of surface. The board immediately became controversial, as the technicians used it in ways some ball teams found offensive. They could, for example, simulate the sound of a toilet flushing from center field as a way to ridicule an opposing pitcher removed from the game. The league even ordered a $400 fine against the team one season after it flashed an insulting message at an umpire. The scoreboard was removed in the late 1980s to make room for more seats, and today sports fans take extravagant scoreboard mechanics for granted. But the Astrodome scoreboard must be remembered as the first of a special breed.

In addition, Hofheinz designed an elegant Presidential Suite in the walls around the Astrodome, hoping that his old pal Lyndon Johnson might want to bunk there sometime. He decorated club boxes at the top of the dome in different motifs. Behind the scoreboard was a beauty parlor, a puppet theater, and a children's playroom complete with circus pedestals and a big top for VIP guests who brought their children for a visit. There was also a medieval chapel with simulated stone arches and six concrete benches, built in anticipation of the bloodless bullfights, so the bullfighters would have a place for prayer before entering the arena.

The judge even lived in an apartment in the Astrodome for a couple of years after his first wife died in 1966. Imagine looking out your window one morning about 2 a.m. to see Elvis Presley in rehearsal for the next day's concert at the Houston Livestock Show & Rodeo. That's one memory held by the judge's second wife who lived there, too, before they retired to a mansion in River Oaks: "It's most beautiful in the morning with the eastern sun reflecting off the seats," she has recalled. "When you live in the Astrodome you are completely isolated from the outside world."

Fortune didn't smile so fondly on the judge in the 1970s. He added to the Astrodome empire with construction of a Disneyesque amusement park called AstroWorld, a hotel complex now known as Astro Village Hotel, the Astrohall, and Astroarena—projects that demanded massive outlays of cash and energy. He suffered a stroke in 1970, and in 1971 had to borrow $48 million

■ *The Six Flags Corporation's AstroWorld, a major Houston tourist attraction, features the Texas Cyclone roller coaster. Courtesy, Cathy Ferris*

to continue with his plans. By the mid-1970s those creditors, Ford Motor Credit Company and General Electric Credit Corporation, had taken control and had begun looking for a successor.

AstroWorld was sold to the Six Flags Corporation in 1975 and has since rebounded to become one of Houston's prime tourist attractions. When Dr. John McMullen, a New York entrepreneur, bought controlling interest in HSA in 1979, he ushered in a new era, one more refined and businesslike than that distinguished by the judge. But he appreciated the tradition he inherited, noting immediately: "The dome is the most spectacular stadium in the country. It's magnificent. It has the potential of being the most magnificent thing in Houston and we intend to make it that."

When Roy Hofheinz died from a heart attack at the age of 70 in 1982, city flags were flown at half staff. The Grand Huckster had left a permanent impact on his city. He planted seeds that have become integral parts of the quality of life Houstonians will enjoy for the rest of their days. Beyond construction of the Astrodome, Hofheinz proved to be a pivotal force in bringing big league sports to the city. With the contributions of oilman K.S. "Bud" Adams—owner of the Houston Oilers—the city can claim a colorful sporting tradition. And in HSA Hofheinz created a powerful entertainment entity that has gone forward under McMullen to become a prosperous enterprise.

An HSA study in the mid-1980s concluded that the Astrodome complex generated some $574 million for the local economy in 1985—about 1 percent of the city's entire economy, or 4 percent of its nonenergy- sector value. The Astrodome itself represents about one-fourth the economic impact of the Texas Medical Center, and about half that of the Johnson Space Center. It generated about 11,000 jobs, provided $147 million worth of income, and paid $61 million in local taxes. Those statistics were compiled as the county wrestled with plans to continue improving and upgrading the historic facility.

By the end of the 1980s, HSA and Harris County enjoyed a business relationship that had HSA holding a lease on the Astrodome complex, with sublets to the Houston Oilers, the University of Houston Cougars football team, the Houston Livestock Show & Rodeo, and several other important regular event promoters. Besides owning the Astros, HSA received revenue from the complex concessions and parking, plus revenue from radio and television contracts. It owned a telecommunications company, a small interest in the Home Sports Entertainment (HSE) cable-TV network, an interest in Florida's Kissimmee Bay Resort country club/residential complex where the Astros hold spring training, and a management contract with Miami Arena, where the National Basketball Association expansion franchise Miami Heat ranked as primary tenant.

HSA had grown into a business worth an estimated $200 million by the end of the decade. Although they had yet to win the National League pennant, the Astros had proven themselves a competitive and entertaining team, twice ranking as Western Division champions (1980 and 1986) and actually posting one of the best win-loss records in the majors. The Astros are usually in the race for the World Series until the very end and that keeps fans coming to the park.

In addition to big league baseball, Houston has made its mark in football and basketball. In the Oilers and their founder Adams, Houston boasts a significant slice of pro football history. Adams was one of the movers responsible for creation of the American Football League, which now is the American Conference of the National Football League. It was from his office in the basement of the Adams Petroleum Center that formation of the AFL was announced in August 1959. Adams mounted the first challenge to the established National Football League in 1959 by signing Heisman Trophy winner Billy Cannon, already under contract to the NFL, and engineering a courtroom victory to confirm the new league's viability.

His upstart Oilers won the AFL's first two championships but it's been a rocky road for Houston football fans ever since. Between the beginning and the glory years of the late 1970s when

Coach Bum Phillips and running back Earl Campbell sparked the frenzy of the "Luv ya Blue" era and the playoff days of the late 1980s have been sandwiched years of nearly total embarrassment. Always the maverick, Adams did not start playing in the Astrodome until 1968, and his relationship with HSA has had its ups and downs. One thing rings clear, however, from any review of the Oilers relationship with Houston: When that team is competitive, the city literally vibrates with excitement, demonstrating beyond all doubt its sentiments as a football town. Although the Astrodome was built initially as a home for baseball, anyone attending a big game for the Oilers can feel the difference. Oilers of the late 1980s have dubbed the structure with a nickname to reflect their reputation. They call it "The House of Pain," and they've become as much a symbol of the Astrodome tradition as the Astros themselves.

Despite longer traditions in baseball and football, Houston has probably experienced its most prominent successes in professional basketball, with the Rockets reaching the world championship series on two occasions (1981 and 1986), losing both times to the Boston Celtics. The Rockets moved to Houston from San Diego for the 1971 NBA season but it wasn't until 1976-77 that the team began to capture the city's imagination. That's when they extended the powerful Philadelphia 76ers to six games in the Eastern Conference finals.

The Rockets also stimulated construction of another important Houston entertainment facility, The Summit, in Greenway Plaza between downtown and the Galleria. Besides hosting Rockets games, the 17,000-seat Summit offers concert promoters a large arena for world-class productions. With his $11-million purchase of the Rockets in 1982, Houston auto retail magnate Charlie Thomas ensured local ownership of the franchise and pledged to operate the team like a business. Thomas has easily been the most consistently popular owner among the three professional sports franchises of Houston. By drafting local hero Akeem Olajuwon out of the University of Houston, the Rockets staked a claim to the sport's dominant center of the next decade. But the challenge of building a team around the superstar remained the key to future prominence as the Rockets entered the 1990s.

From the land of the urban cowboy, through the realm of true cultural arts, to professional sports, the Houston area represents its own blend of culture. Recreational sports enthusiasts can find plenty to keep them busy, too, among the parks and playgrounds in a city where winter stalls outdoor activities but a few weeks every year. With Galveston's beaches just 60 minutes away, it's easy to see why Houstonians always have plenty to keep them on the go.

EPILOGUE

In the 1980s, Houston took its reputation for boom and bust cycles to new heights. Perched atop the price of oil, its economy endured a roller coaster ride of dramatic proportions that will influence the city's development for decades to come. Centered on a theme of survival, the story of Houston in the 1980s is one with universal appeal. It marked a time when the city came to grips with its own identity and saw modern leaders respond to adversity in a way the city's founders would certainly have admired.

"Houston was built on resourcefulness, and the ingenuity of Houstonians has always been one of our greatest assets," observed Stanford J. Alexander, president of Houston-based Weingarten Realty, Inc., in 1986 during what might have been the city's darkest hours. "Houston has successfully sought its own destiny. Houstonians have a positive attitude and that translates into making great things happen."

Responding to adversity, the city has managed a remarkable rebound aboard an economic recovery officially recognized by state government economists in 1989.

"Hit hard by the 1986-87 statewide oil price recession, the Houston economy has since bounced back and is now enjoying a broadbased recovery," reported the Economic Analysis Center of the Texas Comptroller's office in December 1989. "New growth was initially stimulated by a rebound in manufacturing. Now other industries, especially services, government and trade are posing the largest gains . . . Because of economic diversification, Houston is now less dependent on the energy industry than ever before."

Looking back on the trauma of the 1980s, University of Houston economist Barton Smith explained in 1987: "Houston is a new city that has undergone dynamic changes. Deciding who we are has always been a problem. That's changing now. Boom towns are places where you come to make a quick buck without plans for the future. Now we've got people saying, 'Let's make this a place to live.' There's a newfound commitment to the future, an incredible change in attitude. The downturn has solidified the community and made us think about the future. We were all doing our own things in the 1970s. But when you're forced to think about the future, you start thinking about your dependence on others. Our economic health is tied to one another. Planning is itself a statement about cooperative effort."

The downturn actually gave the city time to revitalize an infrastructure overtaxed during the boom. It launched its first professional economic development entity in the Houston Economic Development Council (HEDC) and revitalized community spirit with the creation of Houston Proud. Initially launched as an energizing booster arm for HEDC, Houston Proud organized volunteer efforts for neighborhood revitalizations and other important work projects.

Besides rebuilding civic spirit, Houston also added to its physical prowess. By 1989, the city was spending more money on road improvements than any state, with the exception of California. And it joined the big leagues of convention towns with the 1987 completion of the $136 million George R. Brown Convention Center.

As he closed out the 1980s, Lee Hogan, a former president of the Greater Houston Partnership, summarized the city's past as a prelude to its future:

"Forty years ago, few would have included among Houston's assets a major medical infrastructure. Twenty-five years ago, no one would have indentified Houston as a leader in space exploration. And just five years ago, few would have predicted our emergence as a principal center for personal computer development and manufacturing . . . I am confident that a citizenry cured, over the past decade, in the furnaces of recession, foreclosure and unemployment has gained through that experience the necessary strength to face any challenge—expected or otherwise—that the 90s may bring."

■ *Facing page: Photo by Dave Jacobs*

HOUSTON'S ENTERPRISES

Photo by Jay W. Sharp

9

NETWORKS

The aerospace industry and energy and communications firms play an important role in Houston's economy, providing employment as well as power and information to the area's residents.

■ *Photo by Bob Rowan/
Progressive Image*

McDONNELL DOUGLAS

Space has long played an important role in the city, and boosters are quick to point out that Houston was the first word said on the moon. The Johnson Space Center and its employees, including astronauts, call the community home. Moreover, as recent economic cycles have dictated diversification, the potential in space-related industries appears to be tremendous. McDonnell Douglas has long recognized this, and its Space Systems Company is playing a vital role as one of the prime contractors in the design and construction of the Space Station Freedom.

That role comes as no surprise to those familiar with McDonnell Douglas. Formed as the result of a merger in 1967, both the McDonnell and Douglas companies had independently earned their reputations as leaders in pioneering aviation, best known

for their military, particularly fighter, aircraft. The resulting company is one of the largest in the nation, comprised of a variety of subsidiary companies.

The McDonnell Douglas Space Systems Company is now at work with NASA on the next phase of the space program, the development and deployment of the Space Station Freedom. On December 1, 1987, the Space Systems Company was designated one of four prime contractors on the project. In 1988 the company signed a $2.6-billion contract to perform the work over the next decade. The Space Systems Company, as a prime contractor, will provide program management, systems engineering and integration, design and development, and manufacturing and testing.

Scheduled to begin operations by the

end of the 1990s, NASA envisions the Space Station Freedom as a basic framework called a truss structure, with laboratory facilities, crew quarters for up to eight people, utilities for science and technology work, satellite repair stations, co-orbiting and polar-orbiting platforms, and rocket-powered orbital maneuvering vehicles, or "tugboats."

The Freedom Station will be an international facility and will be used as a manufacturing site for advanced computer circuitry, the production of new metal alloys, and a "garage in space" for the servicing of satellites. New satellite production now incorporates designs for repair and refueling in orbit.

The McDonnell Douglas Space Systems Company is responsible for the design, development, assembly, and checkout of the

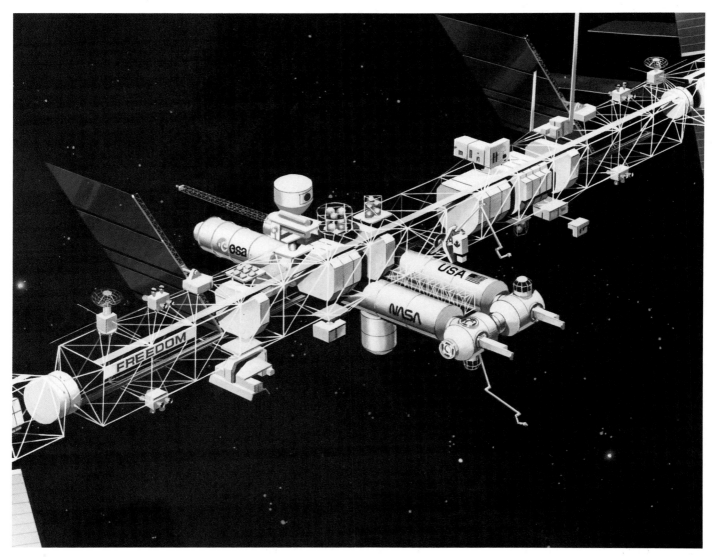

■ *ABOVE AND FACING PAGE: McDonnell Douglas Space Systems Company is now at work with NASA on the next phase of the space program, the development and deployment of the Space Station Freedom.*

integrated truss, airlocks, propulsion, mobile transporter base, attachment systems, inter-element hardware and software, and the outfitting of the resource nodes. Other activities include operations planning, avionics integration, software development, and support to the Johnson Space Center project office.

No one organization could undertake such a massive project by itself. All four prime contractors work in coordination with NASA, and McDonnell Douglas Space Systems has subcontracted a significant portion of its work to primary subcontractors: Honeywell, IBM, and RCA. These entities will join together in produc-

ing the work package. Included in this effort will be the construction of an integration facility at Ellington Field.

Many of the truss structure pieces will be built elsewhere, and eventually the entire package will be assembled in phases prior to the actual launch. The project calls for the launching of useful pieces that can begin operating once in orbit, without depending on subsequent launches to begin work. Built into the project is the ability to upgrade systems as technology allows and demands; one example would be the upgrading of the project's computers.

Needless to say, this will demand a tremendous number of highly qualified individuals. McDonnell Douglas estimates that it will add significantly to its work force in the coming years. Initial plans call for an estimated 500 to 800 new employees, some of whom may transfer from other regions. McDonnell Douglas has always been keenly interested in its community and has made significant contributions in the area's devel-

opment. The company has made long-term investments in the community and sees a synergistic relationship with good universities in the area, developing programs and exploring the horizons of knowledge together.

That role is not new to McDonnell Douglas, which has more than a quarter-century of experience in manned space programs, serving as one of the prime contractors on the Mercury, Gemini, Skylab, and Spacelab programs. Also responsible for the third stage of the powerful Saturn rocket of the moonflight, the company is currently providing cargo processing, on-orbit maneuvering, and booster parts for the space shuttle.

The Space Systems Company relishes the work of the coming decade and the success of the Space Station Freedom. And beyond, there is the possibility of a lunar base and a mission to Mars. McDonnell Douglas looks forward to continuing its role as a leader in the space industry.

UNIVERSAL WEATHER AND AVIATION, INC.

Beginning with the ideas of founder Tom Evans during the late 1950s, Universal Weather and Aviation, Inc., has become an expert in the fields of weather and aviation. The firm has enjoyed decades of continual growth, attributable to an aggressive and progressive attitude in its fields of endeavor.

With the advent of corporate aviation, there was a growing demand for personalized yet professional weather information. When the first Universal Weather Station was established in 1959 at Love Field in Dallas, the company started with contracts from 35 corporate operators. Within one year another office was opened in Houston to serve aviation and industry. Today that Houston office occupies a modern complex of more than 62,000 square feet and has become headquarters for a global organization that employs more than 300 people.

■ *Universal Weather & Aviation's world headquarters is located adjacent to Houston's Hobby Airport. The company has 24 offices throughout the world.*

Detailed weather information is critical in many industries, often affecting the bottom line. Universal provides its clients with a complete weather service 24 hours a day, 365 days a year, for any location in the world. Today that client base includes not only the aviation and marine industries, but also government agencies, construction, media, sporting events, and many others.

One year after opening the Houston office, the proximity to the Gulf of Mexico led to a natural expansion as Universal developed its Marine Forecast Division. From tugs to barges to offshore operations, Universal provides real-time weather support for the marine industry. Site-specific and area forecasts are monitored for weather and sea conditions. Moreover, for clients affected by a specific type, intensity, or duration of weather, severe weather advisories are automatically issued when conditions are expected to exceed the client's designated parameters. Advisories are continuously updated as conditions dictate.

Beginning with a staff of trained meteo-

■ *Universal chairman Marjorie Evans with vice president of operations Greg Evans.*

rologists, Universal has continued to hone its skills and apply new technologies to improving its product. An original teletype link was expanded with Universal's global HF (high-frequency) station. Today a satellite link has access to four geostationary and one polar-orbiting satellites. The

net result is an accurate picture of the world's weather that is never more than 30 minutes old.

Coupled with this, Universal has another division, named UView. UView is a computer-generated weather communications system that transmits color graphics. More than 400 graphics are available and represent past, present, and forecast products. They also include radar sites, satellite images, and other graphics originally designed for users. In addition to this is the EDRS, or Electronic Data Retrieval System, that delivers complete domestic and international weather information in text form. Additional data can be stored and transmitted using the the system's mailbox.

In the interim years the aviation aspect of the company has grown by leaps and bounds to become the primary focus of the organization. As Universal's corporate clients began more international travel, their needs grew more complicated. Those complications included overfly and landing permits, fuel, parking and ground transportation, customs, catering, hotels, and credit. Universal has added services each year and now has more than 20 offices around the world, from Italy to India, Ecuador to Singapore, along with a vast network of agents supporting them.

In 1974 Universal began laying the

groundwork for what has turned into a global network to provide its clients with fuel discounts through its UVair program. By 1987 the UVair fueling card was accepted at more than 650 airports worldwide. In the mid-1980s Universal once again broadened its service base with the development of Universal Aircraft Support, Inc., which provides parts, engines, and

■ *ABOVE: Fifty staff members provide more than 1,000 written and verbal weather briefings to marine, sports, media, construction, and aviation clients each month.*

■ *BELOW LEFT: This year the flight planning department will file more than 5,000 computerized flight plans, obtain take off and landing slots, diplomatic and customs clearances, provide crew transportation, make discount hotel room reservations, uplift discount fuel, and reserve onboard catering for passengers, aircraft, and crew.*

avionics requirements.

More recently, the company has developed its Windstar program, which enables a flight crew to easily receive a computer printout with complete, point-to-point information on a given route. Never content to rest on its laurels, the organization has also started its own travel agency that not only handles all arrangements and reservations, but has developed an extensive network of more than 3,000 hotels and other travel services that will provide discounts to Universal clients.

As evidenced through its development over the years, Universal Weather and Aviation, Inc., has a proven track record of meeting its clients' requirements. One of the most innovative in its industry, Universal has built its reputation by giving its clients personalized service they will not find elsewhere.

HOUSTON LIGHTING & POWER COMPANY

Houston Lighting & Power Company has powered the growth of Houston for more than a century. HL&P serves 3 million people in a 5,000-square-mile service area along the upper Texas Gulf Coast. Its 11 power plants are capable of generating more than 13,000 megawatts of electricity—enough to supply the area's anticipated needs through the mid-1990s.

Houston is one of the most energy-intensive areas in the world. It is the most air-conditioned city in America. As a result, HL&P's residential customers use about 60 percent more electricity than the national average. Industrial use of electricity is also high, due to the fact that one of the heaviest concentrations of petrochemical plants in the world is in the Houston/Gulf Coast area. This demand for electricity has made HL&P the eighth-largest investor-owned utility in the country, in terms of electricity sales.

Houston Lighting & Power Company has been serving Houston for more than 108 years. In 1882, less than four months after Thomas Edison's first generating plant was put into operation in New York City, Houston's first electric arc lights pierced the darkness of a December night.

Houston's first generating plant was later destroyed by a boiler explosion in 1898. It was replaced by a plant on the banks of Buffalo Bayou that could generate up to four megawatts of electricity. Today four megawatts is what it takes to operate the rides at the AstroWorld amusement park.

With the rapid growth of the upper Texas Gulf Coast, Houston Lighting & Power Company bought more than 20 small power companies in the 1920s and provided the first electric service to 125 villages and towns. This expansion established the size of the company's present service area.

Following World War II the economy of the greater Houston area kicked into high gear. Peak demand for electricity doubled from 1,000 megawatts to 2,000 megawatts in the 1950s. And today peak demand is more than 11,800 megawatts.

The 1973 OPEC oil embargo triggered a major change in HL&P's operations. Up until that time all of its generating plants burned natural gas for boiler fuel. But to reduce its dependence on gas, the company

■ *The control room of HL&P's state-of-the-art energy management and control system. It controls the flow of energy throughout the company's electrical network and automatically selects the most cost-efficient mix of generators.*

began a massive program to diversify its fuel mix with fuels other than natural gas. In 1978 HL&P completed its first coal-fired generating unit. It has since built three other western coal-fired units. In 1985 and 1986 it completed two units fired by Texas lignite.

The most recent addition to its fuel mix has been uranium. HL&P is the project manager and the largest of four participants of the jointly owned South Texas Project (STP), the state's first nuclear power plant. STP is the most advanced nuclear plant in the nation, with more safety systems than any other nuclear generating station in the United States.

Located 80 miles southwest of Houston, STP has two 1,250-megawatt units, that generate enough electricity to serve 500,000 homes. The first unit went into

commercial operation in August 1988, followed by the second in June 1989. HL&P receives nearly 31 percent of STP's electrical output. At its formal dedication Department of Energy Secretary James Watkins proclaimed that STP "represents the strategic commitment to energy security essential to a prosperous America."

Nuclear fuel costs about one-fourth as much as conventional power plant fuels. As a result the South Texas Project is expected to save customers more than $40 billion in fuel costs during its 40-year life, compared to electricty generated by natural gas.

STP's operation replaces the equivalent of 25 million barrels of imported oil, or 8.4 million tons of coal annually. It also supports 2,000 permanent jobs and pumps $200 million annually into the southern Texas economy.

In 1988 the Nuclear Regulatory Commission chose the South Texas Project to represent the United States in an exchange of nuclear power safety information with the Soviet Union. The NRC selected STP because it was the state of the art in nuclear construction.

As a result of its fuel diversification efforts, Houston Lighting & Power Company has a boiler fuel mix of 9 percent natural gas, 41 percent coal and lignite, 15 percent cogeneration and purchased power, and 5 percent nuclear power. This mix ensures the reliability of Houston's electric supply will not be threatened by events, foreign or domestic, that might disrupt the supply of any single fuel source.

Controlling the flow of energy throughout the area's network of transmission and distribution lines is HL&P's Energy Management and Control System. This advanced computer system automatically selects the most cost-efficient combination

■ *RIGHT: Don D. Jordan, chairman and chief executive officer of Houston Lighting & Power Company.*

■ *BELOW: An aerial view of the South Texas Project, Texas' first nuclear power plant. HL&P is project manager and receives nearly 31 percent of the plant's electrical output.*

of generators to meet the area's energy needs. This saves consumers millions of dollars each year in lower fuel costs.

Service is the driving force for HL&P and its 11,000 employees. The words "Service First" have been a part of the company's logo for more than a half-century. A staff of 300 telephone service representatives handles customer inquiries 24 hours a day in English and Spanish.

HL&P's dedication to service during emergencies has long been recognized by its customers and the electric utility industry. In 1984 HL&P received the Edison Award for its outstanding performance in restoring service to 750,000 homes when Hurricane Alicia struck Houston a year earlier.

The company's service ethic also extends to its concern for the community. Through its corporate volunteer program, Project People, more than 1,800 employees donate their talents to a variety of community outreach programs annually. During a typical year HL&P volunteers log more than 25,000 hours walking for the March of Dimes, donating clothes and canned goods for the needy, restoring the homes of low-income and elderly residents, and performing numerous other volunteer activities.

HL&P also has a major stake in education—by virtue of the fact that it pays taxes to 78 school distrcts and 13 college districts in the service area. Employees spend about 4,000 hours every year tutoring Houston area students identified by the schools as potential dropouts.

The company also is an active supporter of the business community. HL&P's economic development division, in cooperation with local economic development agencies, encourages businesses to relocate to or expand in Houston. Houston Lighting & Power Company is proud of the role it has played in the city's development and is dedicated to providing the energy Houston will need to power its growth into the next century.

KZFX
Z-107 FM

It was the summer of 1986 when Bill Clark, president of Shamrock Broadcasting, was driving in from the airport to look at a small, religious FM station that was for sale. He was caught in a monstrous traffic jam that made Los Angeles traffic look like life in the fast lane. It happened to be the day of the "Rendezvous Houston" light show.

"Wouldn't it be great," Clark mused that day, "to have a radio station capable of making that kind of a positive impact on a

great city like Houston."

Less than three years later, Clark's wish was realized as the station he eventually purchased hosted the nation's largest outdoor Fourth of July celebration, the Houston Freedom Festival.

KZFX, better known as Z-107 FM, astounded much of the radio industry with it's spectacular growth during Houston's tough economic times. But it didn't happen by accident. Shamrock Broadcasting is owned by Roy Disney, and it shares the famous Walt Disney philosophy of focusing on customer service and quality people.

Extensive marketing research was conducted. It confirmed that there was a void and need for classic rock and roll—the album hits of the 1960s, 1970s, and 1980s. The large and very influential listener group that had been in college in the 1960s and

■ *The Houston Fourth of July Freedom Festival, which includes a major evening concert event by classic rock and roll bands such as Chicago as part of its festivities (ABOVE), draws record-breaking crowds each year (TOP).*

1970s had grown up with the music and still valued it.

John Dew, who had managed KRBE for nine successful years, was hired as the general manager. In turn he brought some of the Houston radio industry's top professionals such as operations manager Ted Carson, general sales manager Mark Krueger, and national sales manager John Poche.

Top professionals were brought into the programming, sales, and business offices. New, state-of-the-art studios were constructed in the Lakes on Post Oak office

in uptown Houston, and a strong commitment to community service and involvement was made.

One of the main assets of the station has been its morning show. Rick Walker has a unique style of humor to start the listener's day with a smile. Supplementing the jovial side of the morning is the serious information people need throughout the day, with the latest news reports and traffic bulletins from Z-107's traffic team, which includes a helicopter and roving mobile units.

Beyond morning antics and a winning format, KZFX attributes its rapid success to its commitment to community involvement. Throughout the calendar year, Z-107 provides a wide array of events that not only its audience but the entire city can participate in and enjoy.

Perhaps no event illustrates this better than the Houston Freedom Festival. Despite the city's size, it had never really developed a Fourth of July event. Beginning in early 1987 KZFX, in conjunction with three other major corporate sponsors, launched plans for the Houston Freedom Festival. With the cooperation of the city's parks department, a site downtown was selected. Attendance at the first festival was estimated at almost 300,000 people. It has more than doubled

In the ensuing years the Houston Freedom Festival has become the city's official Fourth of July celebration, a day-long event filled with local and regional bands, along with performing stages in Sam Houston and Buffalo Bayou Parks. Following a major evening concert, the day culminates in a spectacular fireworks display: a 35-minute choreographed program with music simulcast on Z-107 FM. Each year the Houston Freedom Festival committee bestows The Freedom Five Award on five prominent Houstonians.

■ *KZFX welcomes in the new year with the rest of downtown Houston.*

While the Freedom Festival is one of the biggest events in the Z-107 year, it is just one of the many that take place in myriad forms of service to the community. One particularly successful item has been the Party on the Plaza. This evening concert takes place on Jones Plaza downtown, every Thursday night from March through November. These concerts have grown tremendously popular and bring together a varied population on the downtown square. Featuring a different live band each week, musical groups are now calling KZFX to request a performing date. Furthermore, 40 percent of the contributions generated by Party on the Plaza are given to the Central Houston and the Theatre District as well as the Houston Parks and Recreation Department.

KZFX is a participant in the city's marathon, a growing event of world-class status. As the region has developed a Mardi Gras, so too has Z-107 participated in promoting the fun in February as the official radio sponsor. With March comes the celebration of St. Patrick's Day. Rounding out the year is the station's sponsorship of the Uptown Grand Lighting Ceremony in the Galleria area, the promotion of the Dickens on the Strand activities in Galveston, and welcoming in another year with New Year's Eve in downtown Houston.

In addition, KZFX holds many other events benefiting the Leukemia Society, the March of Dimes, food banks, the Houston Hospice, the Houston Zoological Society, and Amnesty International. Z-107 also participates in sports and cycling events, regatta, golf tournaments, beach volleyball, pep rallies, and the Italian Festival parade.

With a great organization with all of the tools, facilities, top-notch professionals, and the deep community involvement, it is no surprise to find KZFX Z-107 FM at or near the top in the Houston's key 25 to 50-year-old audience rankings.

KHOU CHANNEL 11

KHOU Channel 11 has been located on the banks of Buffalo Bayou, on the edge of downtown Houston, for more than 30 years. During that time it has grown with its industry from the tentative efforts of a new medium to the powerful force that television now enjoys. Through the ensuing years Channel 11 has become an integral part of its community.

KHOU, a CBS affiliate, began its broadcast life as station KGUL in Galveston. It originally signed on the air March 22, 1953. Within a year and a half the station had opened a studio in Houston. Within five years the station received its license to open its main studio in Houston. In 1959 Walter Cronkite and the mayor were on hand for ceremonies marking the ground breaking for construction of its current site. In June of that year the station changed its call letters and officially became KHOU.

KHOU established its commitment to the community early on, especially with its strong dedication to news during the days when such efforts were pioneering. With the burgeoning space program located in its own backyard, KHOU's news division has played a critical role from the station's inception. Today news accounts for 50 percent of the station's production. Channel 11 has a team of professionals dedicated to doing what it takes to bring home the news to its viewers, from not only the city's immediate environs but beyond

■ *Air 11.*

to the state, nation, and world. Never has that been more important than today, when television is the sole information source for an estimated 65 to 70 percent of the people living in the United States.

Technology has revolutionized the television industry and television news. ENG, or electronic news gathering, has evolved, and the newest trend sweeping the industry is SNG, satellite news gathering. From computerizing its newsroom to

satellite technology, KHOU has continued making the capital improvements in technology required to remain competitive.

One trend has been the development of satellite news trucks and the extended range they can provide in news coverage and production. To that end KHOU has added an SNG truck, unique to the market in that it is a dual pathway truck—it can both send and receive information concurrently. Channel 11 has also recently added a new 2,000-foot tower, designed to enhance the station's reception in certain portions of its viewing area.

Perhaps nowhere are the technological changes more readily evident than in the gathering and presentation of weather news. In the early 1960s Dan Rather, longtime CBS newsman and evening network anchor, worked at KHOU. During coverage of Hurricane Carla he thought that if viewers could sense the magnitude of the storm as seen on radar, they might have a healthier appreciation for its disastrous potential. In a primitive fashion (by today's standards), the station broadcast a picture of a radar screen.

In contrast, today's weather forecasts routinely use satellite pictures and data. Looming on the horizon is the use of three-dimensional satellite photographs and the addition of the fourth dimension of motion to weather presentation. KHOU

■ *The KHOU-TV newsroom.*

■ *KHOU-TV's Sky Scan satellite truck.*

has coupled sophisticated technology with the expertise of someone who can easily translate the wealth of data to viewers, namely Dr. Neil Frank, former director of the National Hurricane Center. A good illustration is the example he uses to describe a 75 miles-per-hour wind—standing on the roof of a car traveling on a freeway at the same speed.

KHOU's commitment to news is easy to understand when looking at its parent company, the A.H. Belo Corporation. Belo, which purchased KHOU Channel 11 in the mid-1980s, also owns network affiliated television stations in Dallas, Texas; Sacramento, California; Tulsa, Oklahoma; and Hampton/Norfolk, Virginia. Beyond television the Belo Corporation publishes the *Dallas Morning News* and seven community newspapers in the Dallas/Fort

Worth area. In operation since 1834, it is the state's oldest continuing company.

Management's philosophy, from the parent company down, has always been that a strong commitment and concern for the community pays the best dividends. Perhaps the best demonstration of what that commitment can accomplish is the case of a recent food drive. KHOU was approached by area food pantries for help in replenishing rapidly emptying shelves. A food drive was launched in conjunction with Texas Commerce Bank, and announcements were made throughout all the station's programming. Within two days the drive had garnered more than

300,000 pounds of food. This drive has become an annual event conducted in the memory of the late congressman Mickey Leland, who died helping the hungry of Ethopia.

No isolated incident, the same success story was repeated with a clothing drive in conjunction with Pilgrim Cleaners. Viewers were invited to drop off servicable used clothing at any of the cleaner's locations, where it would be cleaned and passed on. Within two days the cleaner was at capacity with donated clothing.

"The Spirit of Texas" has been the station slogan at Channel 11 for several years. Never has that spirit been more evident than in the recent past. KHOU Channel 11 celebrated and participated in Houston's renaissance and stands eagerly poised for its future.

K-NUZ AM/K-QUE FM

K-NUZ AM signed on the air on February 18, 1948. Since then the radio station has seen its hometown grow tenfold to become one of the nation's great cities.

K-NUZ has seen the proliferation within its own industry as well, watching as the number of stations grew from a handful to roughly 50 today.

In 1960 K-QUE FM signed on the air as a sister station. In an age where formats can literally change at the switch of a button with some stations, K-QUE has maintained the same format from day one, described as middle-of-the-road nostalgia. K-NUZ was for many years the dominant Top 40 station in the market, and now it plays oldies—hits from the 1950s and 1960s.

The station has always had a progressive attitude and, as a result, can lay claim to many firsts in its market. In 1948 the station had the first black disc jockey and the first female account executive in the city, showing a prescience beyond its years. The year 1950 saw the first remote broadcast studio, and 1951 ushered in the first helicopter reporting, the first use of wireless microphones, and the first station with a computer traffic system. The latter being yet another example where K-NUZ has been a pioneer in what is commonplace today.

The 1970s saw the first female sales manager and the additions of a full-dimensional FM antenna and a solid-state AM transmitter. As the 1980s introduced the burgeoning of computers in every facet of life, K-NUZ/K-QUE once again recognized the future and, in 1985, became the first station in town with a completely computerized news-gathering system.

The computerization of the newsroom provided instant access to local, regional, and national news feeds. Those stories are sorted into the computer and create a working archive system. The system automatically catalogues tapes, giving instant answers to the numbers of stories, their length, and even the speed of a reporter's voice. Reporters can access this warehouse of information anywhere and anytime they need it. All of this provides listeners with the latest news they need, from a

■ *ABOVE LEFT: Pictured here (from left) are Paul Berlin, K-QUE personality; Dave Morris, president of K-NUZ/K-QUE; Biff Collie, original DJ on K-NUZ; and Dave Ward, anchor for ABC Channel 13 Houston. Dave Ward was interviewing Biff Collie on the occasion of proclamation by the mayor of Houston that February 18, 1988, be named K-NUZ Day.*

■ *LEFT: The K-NUZ/K-QUE headquarters.*

■ *LEFT AND BELOW LEFT: The Astroworld
Hotel Grand Ballroom was the scene of the roast and
dance for Paul Berlin's 40th year on the air. The Tommy
Dorsey Orchestra was directed by Buddy Morrow.*

QUE are owned by Texas Coast Broadcasters, Inc., a privately held company.

As the Houston market has grown, it has changed in ways that could not have been predicted three decades ago. One of those changes has been the transfer of music almost exclusively to FM carriers and the specialization of AM carriers as a result.

The management has been the same since the station's inception and has always remained committed to serving the community in which it lives and works. One simple example is the station's firm commitment to news. As its name implies, K-NUZ has always been news oriented and remains so, even in a time when changing regulations require less news coverage by stations.

Beyond the news there is the station's commitment to relay community events and assist it where and when it can. President David Morris has long been involved in the 100 Club, a local organization that aids the spouses and children of slain law officers. The group also funds equipment and education for law-enforcement agencies.

Other activities include work with the Society for the Prevention of Blindness and a charity golf tournament that raises an estimated $75,000 per year. K-NUZ/K-QUE takes pride in belonging to this community and is having the opportunity to give back some of the good fortune the community has bestowed on it. Morris has been president of the Texas Association of Broadcasters and is a board member of the National Radio Advertising Bureau.

The experience of more than 40 years in the market is a definite asset, according to Morris, who once paid a young unknown named Elvis Presley and his three-piece band $125 for a performance. Few can match that history or the station's adherence to integrity. K-NUZ AM/K-QUE FM takes pride in its reputation as being a full-service station and looks forward to the future of the city and its industry.

source they can trust. The station employs a staff of about 50 people.

Many listeners started their allegiance to K-NUZ/K-QUE as teenagers and have grown up with the station. That solid reputation has earned the stations a dominant place in their market—the 35-plus age range. The stations have always remained committed to this good, solid audience.

Overall the stations have about a four to five share in the market. That increased to an estimated eight share in the 35-plus market. They are generally within the top three in their time periods for their designated markets.

Houston has become a very large radio market. Many of the major broadcast chains now have operations in the city and predictions call for the city to continue to grow and eventually become one of the nation's top markets. The K-NUZ/K-QUE station is one of only four that remain locally owned. K-NUZ/K-

■ *Mickey Rooney visits Dave Morris at
K-NUZ/K-QUE.*

HOUSTON CHRONICLE

With the approach of the twenty-first century, the *Houston Chronicle* rapidly approaches its own century mark of service to the city. When the first edition of the *Houston Chronicle* hit the streets in 1901, the city was really a town of less than 50,000 residents. Today Houston is one of the nation's largest cities, and the newspaper has grown along with it, playing an important role in that development. The *Houston Chronicle* is now the largest newspaper in the Southwest.

The dawn of the twentieth century was a period of tremendous worldwide change. In 1901 Marconi sent the first wireless telegraph. Also in 1901 an event that was to have far-reaching effects in Texas took place: the Spindletop oil gusher came in, forever altering the Texas and Houston landscapes.

It was Spindletop that gave birth to the *Houston Chronicle*. A young reporter named Marcellus Foster was on hand to report the Spindletop phenomenon, and he became a part of the ensuing whirlwind. Taking a week's pay of $30, he invested in an option on the oil well. One week later

■ *The offices of the* Houston Chronicle *have remained at the same downtown location, at the corner of Texas and Travis, since 1910. The* Chronicle *building built by Jesse Jones (ABOVE), seen here circa 1910-1920, underwent a massive renovation in 1968 that resulted in today's modern structure (BELOW).*

he sold it for $5,000. With this principal he raised another $20,000 from investors and set himself up as a publisher in a three-story building on Texas Avenue.

The first edition hit the streets on October 14, 1901. By the end of the first month, circulation totaled 4,378. The following year the *Chronicle* bought another afternoon paper, the *Daily Herald*. For decades thereafter the newspaper's masthead read the *Houston Chronicle and Herald*.

Within three years the *Chronicle* launched its first Sunday edition, which was 44 pages strong, including four pages of color comics. The solid growth and development of the newspaper's early years has been repeated throughout its history.

By 1908 the paper's expansion was forcing it out of its original home. In another portentous move, Jesse Jones, a leading builder in the city, was hired to build a new 10-story home for the *Chronicle* at the corner of Texas and Travis. In exchange he was given an interest in the paper. In 1910 the paper, with bigger and better equipment, moved to the location it has occupied since. Foster, the reporter who started it all, sold his interest to Jesse Jones in June 1926, making Jones sole owner and publisher. Despite the Depression, the *Chronicle* maintained its steady growth. In 1937 the paper added a four-story building next door to handle the growing production department.

One dozen years later, yet another expansion occurred. The Palace Theatre was rebuilt and became a part of the main building. The same year, 1949, Jesse Jones retired as president of the paper. Jones, however, remained publisher of the *Chronicle,* a position he would hold for 30 years, until his death in 1956.

The continuing history of growth at the *Chronicle* forced a major decision in the process. In the early 1960s, as the building space grew cramped, consideration was given to moving out of the city and into spacious suburban accommodations. However, the newspaper management believed that all great cities require a strong business district and opted to remain where it began, in the heart of downtown and its history.

Thus, in 1967, plans were announced for a new production facility to be located next to the old Chronicle building. One year later major renovations were made to the existing 10-story building and another adjacent to it. The two were literally combined into a single building and then given facelifts in glass, marble, and stainless steel. The entrance lobby was situated where the two structures joined. The result was almost 300,000 square feet of office space in the main building, and some interesting interior split levels as the only remaining clue to the massive undertaking.

As the production plant began nearing completion in 1970, the paper was faced with the daunting task of moving and setting up anew the massive equipment required to print a major daily newspaper, with a minimum amount of disruption. Following months of planning, the move was completed in a marathon 33 hours in August of that year. Not a single edition was missed as a result. The building now encompassed the entire city block on which it had begun.

One of the keys to the newspaper's steady growth has been its adaptability to the marketplace. A good example is the introduction of the "Saturday Sunrise," a morning edition, in the fall of 1974. Designed to meet Houstonians' changing needs, the change required months of planning. Having always been an afternoon and evening newspaper, the *Chronicle* had to change some editorial policies and deadlines, rework production schedules, and

■ *After the newspapers come off the press folded, a high-speed conveyor belt moves them to the stacker in the mail room.*

organize new delivery times. Much as it had four years earlier with the production plant move, the advance planning made for a smooth and successful transition. The "Saturday Sunrise" was a success from its inception. Within four years the *Chronicle*'s Saturday circulation led its competitor's circulation, traditionally a morning newspaper, for the first time.

That success was a harbinger of dramatic changes to come. In September 1979 the *Chronicle* became both a morning and evening daily when its first daily morning edition hit the streets. The edition was initially available only in outlying counties or at racks and newsstands in Harris County. Since then it has expanded and developed into an integral part of the newspaper's continued success. Those efforts are reflected in the total circulation numbers at publication deadline: more than 442,000

daily and more than 620,000 on Sundays.

Beyond sheer physical growth the *Chronicle* has faced and at times led the challenges of a changing industry and world. The advent of computers has enhanced the publishing of newspapers and altered the workplace immeasurably.

The best example is pagination, the electronic positioning of all the elements of a newspaper page. MAGIChron, a system the *Chronicle* has pioneered, is providing the foundation for the total integration of advertising, editorial, and graphics, or full pagination.

Technology has improved the engraving and color processes. With the advent of microwave and satellite technology, the possibilities for news gathering, production, and delivery seem limitless.

Automation includes the finished product. The *Chronicle* was one of the first newspapers in the world to adopt palletizing. (The process wherein bundles of newspapers flow at the rate of one bundle per second into the machine known as a palletizer.) Then they are stacked and placed on a conveyor platform. When the platform is full, the entire pallet, hence the name, is loaded onto a waiting truck. With the publication of several daily editions, speed is of the essence.

The *Chronicle* is also an industry leader when it comes to insertion technology. Readers are accustomed to the colorful special sections and advertisements that are inserted into the paper. The purchase of Promotional Printing Company (PPC), an offset printing facility, has enhanced the paper's production abilities for such special inserts. In addition, several weekly *Chronicle* sections, including fashion and travel, are printed at PPC using the heatset offset

process, producing extremely high-quality color printing.

As society's awareness of the environment and its sensitivity has increased, so has the *Chronicle*'s. The paper developed an ink reclamation system. Small amounts of reclaimed ink are added before printing ink heads for the presses. The impurities filtered from the scrap ink not only saves money but considers the environment in the process. The newspaper is also actively involved in the recycling process of newsprint.

The *Chronicle*'s theme is "Houston's leading information source." It is dedicated to bringing its readers the latest in news, sports, business, the arts and entertainment, and new ideas in the community and the world. To that end, the *Chronicle* has extended its coverage over the years. It has bureaus in Austin, Dallas, Mexico City, and Washington, D.C. Along with the regular daily sections, the paper also produces weekly sections such as food, fashion, religion, and many more. The creation of the state and national desks, and more than 300 people on the editorial staff, has enhanced the paper's reporting abilities. Those talents have reaped numerous awards in local, state, regional, and national competitions across the spectrum of

reporting.

A new era in the *Chronicle*'s history began on May 1, 1987, when the Hearst Corporation purchased the newspaper from Houston Endowment, the entity to which Jesse Jones had transferred ownership of the paper prior to his death. Houston

Endowment is a charitable foundation founded by Jones and his wife, Mary Gibbs Jones. It eventually had to sell the paper to comply with federal tax laws requiring charitable institutions to dispose of profit-making subsidiaries.

After many months of careful research and negotiations, the Hearst Corporation purchased the *Houston Chronicle* for $415 million. The newspaper is now a division of the Hearst Corporation, and Richard J.V. Johnson, who was first named executive vice president in 1972, and later president, remained as president and was named publisher of the *Chronicle*.

The Hearst Corporation has long been synonymous with the newspaper business and has become one of the nation's largest communications companies. Hearst not only publishes newspapers, some 15 in all, but also magazines and books. The corporation also has broadcast and cable television interests.

The Houston READ Commission
Leading the Way to Literacy

■ *Richard J.V. Johnson, president and publisher of the* Houston Chronicle, *accepted the Outstanding Literacy Leader Award in September 1989 from Raymond Kerr, president of the Houston READ Commission.*

The change of ownership did not alter the Chronicle's status as the city's major daily and one of its major supporters. The tradition of community involvement started early in the paper's history with the establishment of the Goodfellows Club. The story behind the club begins in 1911, when an editor on his way home for Christmas festivities saw a waif outside the paper. Determined that no child should be without toys during Christmas, to this day the Goodfellows Club collects donations of money with which toys are purchased for

■ *Staff members of the Newspaper in Education department direct students in the use of the paper as a "living textbook."*

distribution each Christmas, with the paper shouldering the cost of administration. More than 75,000 children receive toys from Goodfellows each holiday season.

In recent years the *Chronicle* has concentrated a great deal of staff and financial resources toward making the community fully literate. The process was initiated with a Forum on Literacy, which brought the public and private sectors together to focus on the literacy needs in the community. From that beginning, the Houston READ Commission was formed by the mayor and city council to promote adult literacy in Houston. The *Chronicle* is a strong supporter of the efforts of the READ Commission. The *Chronicle* also has an active Newspaper in Education department,

which not only sponsors well-known programs such as the regional spelling bee and citizen bee, but also works actively in the schools year-round to encourage the use of the newspaper as a "living textbook."

The publication of a major daily newspaper encompasses a broad range of people and skills. Although newspaper reporters are the first to come to mind, the editorial staff is like the visible tip of the iceberg, supported by a vast array of people and equipment: from the salespeople who provide the advertising that fuels the fire, to the ink and paper handlers, composers and pressmen, to the person who may toss it to your doorstep each day.

Perhaps the best summation of the *Chronicle*'s purpose can be found in the words of its longtime publisher, Jesse Jones, which are etched in the marble of the newspaper's entrance.

"The publication of a newspaper is a distinct public trust, and one not to be treated lightly or abused for selfish purposes or to gratify selfish whims. A great daily newspaper can remain a power for good only so long as it is uninfluenced by unworthy motives, and unbought by the desire for gain. A newspaper which can be neither bought nor bullied is the greatest asset of a city or state. Naturally a newspaper makes mistakes in judgement, as it does in type; but, so long as errors are honestly made, they are not serious when general results are considered. The success or failure of a particular issue is of little consequence compared with the all-important principle of a fearless and honest newspaper."

ENTEX

The Entex of the 1990s is far removed from the gas company that began serving Houston in 1866, only one year after the end of the Civil War. That predecessor of Entex, the Houston Gas Light Company, was given a 25-year franchise and a contract to provide gas for the 75 gaslights scattered throughout the small community. In contrast, Entex today provides natural-gas service to almost 600,000 Houston customers and a total of more than one million customers throughout its three-state service area.

When Houston Gas Light Company was organized, the company was forced to use manufactured gas, produced by burning coal. Houston customers used this "coal gas" until 1925, when a pipeline was constructed from the East Texas gas fields and natural gas was brought to Houston for the first time.

A key turning point in Entex's history came in 1930, when more than 40 independent gas companies, including the one in Houston, were joined together to form one large entity—United Gas Corporation. In 1965 United Gas was acquired by Pennzoil, and many of United's original properties were either sold or merged with other companies.

Today Entex operates most of the gas properties that comprised United Gas Corporation's distribution division. These properties were expanded in 1974, when Entex acquired the distribution business of Houston Natural Gas, adding 360,000 new customers to the approximately 700,000 the company was already serving.

The most recent change in Entex's operations came in February 1988, when the company became a division of Arkla, Inc., a diversified energy concern based in Little Rock, Arkansas. Arkla and Entex together serve roughly 2 million customers in more than 1,000 communities throughout a six-state area.

Entex's tremendous growth over the years can be attributed to the company's commitment to provide its customers with quality, dependable, courteous gas service. Entex places a high priority on individual

■ *Looking to the future, an Entex serviceman pauses on the fringe of downtown Houston before answering his next call.*

community involvement and overall corporate citizenship through involvement in both civic organizations and a series of customer service programs.

Entex believes good service requires good people, but those people must have the right tools to do their best. New technology is constantly being used by Entex as a means of enhancing the quality of customer service and increasing operator efficiency. By capitalizing on new technology, Entex has earned a reputation as a pacesetter in its field and has gained nationwide recognition for implementing an impressive array of high-technology applications such as computer-aided dispatching of trucks, hand-held electronic meter reading devices, automated mapping systems, radio telemetry, and other similar innovations.

The future of Entex and the natural-gas industry has never looked brighter. As environmental concerns become increasingly important, natural gas appears to be the fuel of the future. Its clean-burning capabilities, as well as its versatility as an energy source, make natural gas a favorable choice for legislators, environmentalists, and the public in general.

As Houston and Entex stride boldly into the decade of the 1990s, the company eagerly looks forward to expanding its gas distribution system to meet the growing requirements of a dynamic city.

■ *Entex customer service employees, using sophisticated computer equipment, handle thousands of telephone calls each month.*

10

BUILDING GREATER HOUSTON

Houston's developers, property management firms, contractors, and real estate professionals, as well as suppliers and manufacturers of construction materials, work to revitalize and create the urban landscapes of today and tomorrow.

■ *Photo by Larry Lee/Stills, Inc.*

FLUOR DANIEL INC.

Fluor Daniel Inc. is one of the world's leading engineering and construction firms. It is also a company that has emerged from Houston's stormy economic decade stronger and better than before.

Fluor Daniel came into being in 1985, when the Fluor Corporation merged the operations of Daniel International and Fluor Engineers and Constructors. The resulting firm is wholly owned by the Fluor Corporation. It is the largest publicly owned engineering, construction, maintenance, and technical services company in the United States.

The organization offers its clients a wide range of diverse services. These include site selection, procurement, architectural, design engineering, and project management services. The company handles construction and construction management, as well as turnaround and maintenance services.

Moreover, as one of the industry leaders globally, Fluor Daniel can provide its clients with a vast network of resources, both domestically and internationally. In the United States alone the firm has 25 offices, six of which are major engineering centers. Houston is home to one such center with others in California, South Carolina, Illinois, and Pennsylvania.

At the international level Fluor Daniel maintains large engineering centers in London, Dusseldorf, Haarlem, Dhahran, Tokyo, Melbourne, and Calgary. In sum, Fluor Daniel's network is an organization more than 20,000 employees strong, located in 56 cities and spanning 20 nations. Few firms can offer their clients such global capability.

That capability encompasses a wide range of areas. In the 1980s Fluor Daniel had a heavy investment in the petrochemical industries, from which it drew the majority of its clientele and business. The company was affected, like most Houston businesses, with the industry's downturn. Fluor Daniel began an aggressive diversification program to ensure continued growth and prosperity. That diversification was undertaken in a very formalized manner, with structured changes occurring over three to four years.

Today that diversification program is strongly in evidence as the company has successfully pursued five areas of business.

■ *Process—the Amgen microbial facility in Thousand Oaks, California.*

Those sectors are government, industrial, process, hydrocarbon, and power.

In the government sector, inherently a more complex regulatory process than strictly commercial ventures, Fluor Daniel provides services for projects ranging from local to national in scope and size. The industrial sector runs the gamut of industries from food, beverage and consumer products, to automotive and electronics, metals, pulp and paper, and commercial facilities.

The process sector handles such industries as chemicals and fine chemicals, in addition to plastics, pharmaceuticals, and biotechnology. The hydrocarbon sector serves the energy industry in petroleum

and petrochemicals, mining and metallurgy, onshore and offshore production, and pipelines.

The power sector handles services for nuclear as well as fossil-fueled power plants, cogeneration operations, and municipal waste to energy facilities. Fluor Daniel is keyed into the power industry and anticipates a strong growth market in this area. The combination of these sectors provides the array of expertise needed in today's marketplace.

In short, Fluor Daniel is an organization that has the expertise and resources to develop whatever a client may need— from

■ *FACING PAGE: Industrial—Lincoln Properties' C&S Plaza in Columbia, South Carolina.*

■ *BELOW: Power—CAPCO's facility in Madera, California.*

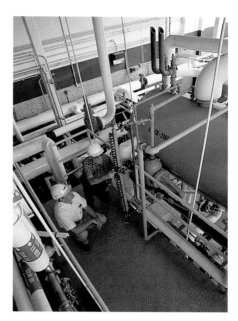

■ *ABOVE: Hydrocarbon—the Lagoven facility in Amuay, Venezuela.*

■ *LEFT: Government—the City of Houston's wastewater treatment facility in Houston, Texas.*

a small facility to a complex chemical manufacturing plant, from a refinery modernization to the George Observatory for the Ft. Bend County Museum of Natural Science. Some of its Texas clients include

Chevron, Alcoa, IBM, Tenneco, NASA, the City of Houston, and St. Joseph's Hospital.

The company has consistently been ranked at the top of its field by ENR, the industry's leading journal. That success has been achieved, in no small measure, by the firm's emphasis on the words quality, value, and safety. These simple words that make common and business sense. Fluor Daniel is a company that cares about its people, its clients, and its community.

Fluor Daniel Inc. has built its reputation on a combined history of 175 years. During that time the firm has witnessed four wars and four times that many presidencies. Today it is a major local and world organization whose mission is to help clients attain a competitive advantage by delivering quality services of unmatched value.

≡ BRAE BURN CONSTRUCTION COMPANY

Brae Burn Construction Company was the logical choice for Trammell Crow's Houston retail division when the company decided to undertake the construction of the city's first shopping center anchored by six large national retailers in a strict time frame. Brae Burn Construction Company's use of fast-track techniques and performing all their own job-site concrete work was essential to meeting the demands of the task. The decision to use Brae Burn Construction was a sound one for Trammell Crow; the project was completed on time and added a landmark retail center to the area.

Brae Burn Construction Company is a privately owned and independent general-contracting firm serving Houston and Texas. The majority of Brae Burn's work is in commercial construction, with particular emphasis on concrete and structural steel facilities, including office buildings, hospitals, schools, grocery stores, tilt-up and structural steel shopping centers with both high finish and/or plain decor exteriors, high-tech service centers, dock high warehouses, distribution warehouses, and industrial facilities.

Brae Burn's area of expertise has always been serving its clients. Throughout their more than 20 years of experience, the principals and employees of Brae Burn have employed the methods of value engineering, design-build coordination, budget and preliminary planning, and turnkey bidding and construction. Brae Burn satisfies its clients by producing the best value for the construction dollar.

In the design-build process, Brae Burn provides a comparison of various construction methods through value engineering to

determine the method best suited for the particular project. To increase economy the individuals initially assigned to the project follow it through estimating to actual completion.

More than half of Brae Burn's work is competitively bid. This allows Brae Burn Construction to know the market and the value of the construction materials required and also the value of all the subcontractor's work. Maintaining professional relationships with suppliers and subcontractors and providing well-organized, tightly scheduled projects has earned the most competitive pricing available in the marketplace.

■ *Brae Burn has 20 years of experience in the construction of all types of buildings, from commerical offices (BELOW) to high rises (ABOVE RIGHT).*

Some of Brae Burn's contracts are "guaranteed maximum" with cost savings split between the owner and contractor. Savings are realized in two distinct ways. When the contractor is included as part of the design team, savings can be realized prior to determining the guaranteed maximum. Secondly, Brae Burn has returned considerable savings as a result of superior construction performance.

Brae Burn maintains a staff of highly skilled superintendents to direct field work. Brae Burn consequently performs a large percentage of work that is traditionally subcontracted, including concrete formwork, placing and finishing of concrete, reinforcing steel, and rough and finish carpentry.

Brae Burn Construction has accomplished a long list of repeat and referral clients. In every project Brae Burn undertakes, it strives to provide the very best attention and discipline to produce the best job-site product in the most strict time frame.

Notable past and present projects include the million-square-foot Brazos Mall in Lake Jackson, Texas; the Drama and Fine Arts Building at Concordia Lutheran College in Austin, Texas; such Houston projects as the Flying Tiger Air Cargo facility at Houston Intercontinental Airport; Quentin Mease Community Hospital Addition and Renovation; Bering Drive Office Tower at 2000 Bering Drive; and Centre One Building at 9800 Centre Parkway; as well as the Commons at Greenspoint Power Center.

PIONEER CONCRETE OF TEXAS

While a person may not often stop to consider concrete as an integral part of everyday life in Houston, it is in fact the foundation for homes, office buildings, and roads. As such, Pioneer Concrete of Texas has played a major role in the city's development.

Pioneer Concrete of Texas and its sister companies throughout the United States are wholly owned subsidiaries of Pioneer Concrete of America, Inc. The Texas

concrete product specified for each project. Projects can range from a slab for a new home to a major building mat pour involving thousands of cubic yards.

Pioneer's strength is remarkable given the city's recent economic history. In the early 1980s, when the building boom was

Throughout the economic downturn, commitment and stability has enabled Pioneer to stay in the market. It has become a leaner operation and has been innovative and adapted to a changing market. One such adjustment was the move into highway work and specialized materials when residential and commercial projects were becoming scarce. The company keeps abreast of the latest changes in technology, such as new aggregate materials,

company was established and headquartered in Houston in 1978. Pioneer is the second-largest concrete supplier in the state and the largest in the city.

Pioneer Concrete of Texas operates concrete, aggregate, asphalt hot mix, and transport trucks statewide. In Houston there are 14 concrete plants, seven sand and gravel operations, and one asphalt hot mix plant. In the Dallas/Ft. Worth area Pioneer operates more than 20 facilities. Operations are also in place in San Antonio, Austin, and throughout central Texas. Statewide the company employs nearly 1,500 people.

Pioneer's concrete business is relatively easy to understand. Cement, sand, aggregate, and admixtures are formulated at the plant, weighed and loaded into ready-mix concrete trucks and delivered to the job site. Pioneer formulates different types of

admixtures, among others, all used to formulate better, higher strength concrete. Pioneer's management approach demonstrates a participatory philosophy. A good example is the plant manager system, where each manager is responsible for the total operation of the unit plant including operations, staffing, and, ultimately, profit or loss. Ready-mix truck drivers can participate in an owner-driver plan, an entrepreneurial program wherein drivers work toward purchase of their truck, giving drivers the opportunity to build equity as they work. Both programs emphasize delivery of a quality product in a timely manner at a competitive price.

■ *Pioneer Concrete's diversification is evident throughout Houston. Pioneer has been a major supplier to: (clockwise from top) downtown office development, the George R. Brown Convention Center, highway expansion and development, residential markets, municipal water and waste-treatment plants, and the petrochemical industry.*

on, the Houston concrete market averaged 8 to 9 million cubic yards annually. The city's demand plunged dramatically to less than 4 million cubic yards per year in the late 1980s. The number of concrete companies, plants, and truck fleets dropped proportionately as well.

In an industry where the product is a perishable commodity, Pioneer Concrete of Texas prides itself on the quality and service it delivers as it participates in Houston and Texas' development.

WHOLESALE ELECTRIC SUPPLY CO.

Beginning with a metal building, Clyde G. Rutland has built Wholesale Electric Supply Co. into one of the largest electrical suppliers in the Texas Gulf Coast region. He has seen his hometown grow from a city of 200,000 people to one of the top five largest in the nation. He has watched his company play a vital role in that development.

Founded (ironically) on April Fool's Day, 1949, Wholesale Electric Supply started life in a small metal building at 3800 McKinney Avenue. A separate office measuring 800 square feet served as headquarters for the personnel; in addition to Rutland, the staff included a salesman, counterman, warehouseman, driver, and two office people. The warehouse space totaled 5,000 square feet.

Rutland, a U.S. Air Force veteran, had spent four years in the electrical distributing business. He determined he would go after the industrial and large commercial market. Long hours of hard work paid off, and the company moved to a new office and ware-

house, totaling 30,000 square feet, built for the company along the Gulf Freeway. The number of employees gradually grew to more than 80 people, and more industrial

■ *ABOVE: Clyde G. Rutland, company founder, president, and chief executive officer.*

■ *LEFT: Wholesale Electric Supply Co. furnished electrical materials when Dome Stadium was originally built and again when the facility was recently enlarged and refurbished.*

lines became available.

Through the next 17 years at this location, Wholesale Electric Supply Co. continued to expand and earned a respected reputation in the industry. The company then relocated to its present site, on four acres of land just off the Gulf Freeway near downtown. Company headquarters are located in the offices that total 50,000 square feet. Two warehouses, totaling more than 100,000 square feet each, house an extensive inventory.

As Houston and the Texas Gulf Coast experienced dramatic growth, Wholesale Electric Supply Co. built a branch operation in Brazosport in 1980. The two-story facility totals more than 30,000 square feet

and enables the company to better serve its industrial customers in the area. In 1986 the company started another branch operation in Deer Park, which serves customers along the Ship Channel, Texas City, and the Gulf Coast.

In keeping with the changes affecting the marketplace, Wholesale Electric Supply Co. is in its third generation of computers, and it has fully integrated computers within its daily operations. The entire inventory, literally thousands of items, has been computerized. This enables speedy, constant monitoring and the ability to respond quickly to a customer's need. The computer network allows continuous communications between all the branch operations.

Wholesale Electrical Supply Co. has three basic markets: commercial, industrial, and export. Combined they represent 90 percent of the company's business. The remainder is derived through original equipment manufacturing. In the commercial market the company has provided supplies for many of the downtown skyscrapers, literally, in some cases, from the ground up. The same applies for the Galleria area and the Texas Medical Center, where the integrity of supplies is even more critical.

While the commercial market fueled tremendous growth for the company, that has tapered off and now the industrial mar-

ket is waxing. The Texas Gulf Coast region is home to one of the largest petrochemical complexes in the world. The work involved gets very technical and often requires that equipment be vapor proof or hazard proof. By carrying the best in industrial lines, the company has the inventory demanded for such critical work.

Another large segment of the company is its export business. Wholesale Electric Supply Co. has shipped to practically every country in the world. Over the years the company has met the higher standards demanded by the largest and best manufacturers of equipment. Consequently it now has the best products available.

One recent development at Wholesale Electric Supply Co. and business in general, has been the adoption of quality management theories. The company was one of the first in its industry to develop quality control and improved management systems that allow participation by all employees, with active problem resolution by management.

The net result has been partnerships developed with some of its biggest customers, particularly in the industrial area. In these partnership arrangements the

company has what is, essentially, a blanket order form to fill the partner's requests for a given time period. While Wholesale Electric Supply Co. is often one of the first approached, it must still bid and produce, from beginning to end. In a partnership, price is not always the most important factor; decisions hinge on the overall quality.

Personnel is the biggest resource of an organization and the company has always recognized that. During the downturn in the region, the company trimmed expenses but did not lay off any employees. Rutland has lost only one of his outside salespeole during the past 25 years. Employees have a history of years of service, a continuity not often found in today's businesses.

At Wholesale Electric Supply Co. the motto is, "Do it right the first time." A simple concept, perhaps, but one that has a tremendous impact—proof of which lies in the numerous awards for best and largest distributor.

EMILY INVESTMENTS INC.

Starting from scratch was nothing new to Emily Guillen. In 1968 her family arrived from Cuba as refugees. Resettling in New Jersey, she went to school, learned English, and became a chemical engineer. She went to work in 1976 for Analyst Incorporated as an oil analyst. She spent three years with that company in New Jersey.

After moving to Houston she started anew in real estate, where her expertise has grown for the past decade. Guillen began as a salesperson and within six years opened her own firm: Emily Investments Inc. She attributes much of her success to having started her business in a market with growing opportunities for those with foresight, such as herself.

Initially there were five agents on staff, a number that has tripled. Many of those in staff today honed their skills by attending seminars offered by professional consultants and members of the National Association of Realtors.

The agents of Emily Investments Inc. sell business, commercial, and residential properties. The business brokers specialize in selling beauty shops, restaurants, daycare centers, and liquor stores. In the commercial area the firm handles apartment complexes and office buildings. The

■ *ABOVE: Emily Guillen, founder of Emily Investments Inc.*

■ *BELOW: The agents of Emily Investments Inc. sell business, commercial, and residential properties.*

firm's residential areas include: Bellaire, Kelliwood, Memorial, River Oaks, Sweet Water, and West University. Individual agents of the firm specialize in each area.

Her success is primarily the result of serving a broad base of clientele. The ability of her agents to speak Spanish has increased her international appeal, as was proven when *Hispanic Business Magazine* recognized Emily Investments Inc. among the top 500 Hispanic businesses in the United States in 1988 and again in 1989.

Emily Investments Inc. is committed to serve the public with high professional standards. Ultimately, Emily Guillen would like to add to her accomplishments a listing of her firm, Emily Investments Inc., in the New York Stock Exchange. If past performance is any indication, there is little doubt that the goal will be realized.

SUNBELT HOTELS, INC.

Marked by innovative thinking and guided by standards of the highest quality since its inception in 1978, Sunbelt Hotels has quickly become one of the leading hotel management companies in the country. This success has been achieved by operating lodging facilities that provide guests with quality service and owners with increased value in their assets.

Offering an array of services that range from actual site selection for the development of a new property to managing the day-to-day operations of an existing hotel, Sunbelt is equipped with staff of highly qualified professionals who are experts in every phase of the lodging industry.

More specifically, Sunbelt's services include property development and construction management that entails market-study analysis, budget and schedule control, and site selection. For existing properties Sunbelt offers support in sales and marketing, purchasing, food and beverage operations, personnel training, internal control, and customized financial reporting.

In the highly competitive hotel business it is a lodging facility's efforts in

the area of sales and marketing that can separate it from the competition. Sunbelt's understanding of the critical role of sales and marketing is reflected in its unique approach to each hotel. Individual marketing plans are developed that contain specific goals. These plans include everything from the tracking of individual sales efforts to overall campaigns for the hotel's food and beverage outlets.

Purchasing is an area that requires key financial controls. Sunbelt has developed a computerized group purchasing system through which managed properties can realize immediate savings on a full range of items, thus eliminating the need for a purchasing manager in each hotel. This knowledge allows Sunbelt to track trends, pricing, and usage to effect savings at each hotel. Each Sunbelt-managed hotel acquires maximum purchasing power through close monitoring of cost trends and the established relationship Sunbelt has with national vendors.

Sunbelt has developed a level of expertise on food and beverages due to the understanding that these hotel components are vital to successful property. The company uses experienced judgment and detailed research to develop restaurants and lounges that are not only attractive and appealing to hotel guests but to the local market as well. This enhances the amenities for the guest as well as pro-

viding a valuable marketing tool.

At the base of Sunbelt's approach to hotel management is the realization that the hotel business is a people business. This understanding has led the company to develop a concise and strong personnel training program. Because Sunbelt places a high priority on employee development and training, Sunbelt employees know that their job is important in the operation of their hotel and that attitude is reflected in their treatment of the guests.

In addition to these services, Sunbelt has an ongoing maintenance and energy conservation system at each managed hotel that assures that this important area is also operated in an efficient and cost-effective manner. Sunbelt's data processing and systems management provides information quickly and accurately while also providing the important service of financial management.

In a competitive industry such as hotel operations, the measure of success can sometimes be a fine line. Sunbelt Hotels, Inc., has a proven track record to establish itself as a leader in the business of successful hotel management through a proven innovative marketing system, a people-oriented management style, and strict control systems that result in significant value increases for ownership.

■ *The Hobby Airport Hilton in Houston is just one example of Sunbelt Hotel's successful approach to hotel management.*

HOUSTON SHELL AND CONCRETE COMPANY

Houston Shell and Concrete, a private company established in 1946, has grown with the city and developed into one of the largest ready-mix concrete producers in the area. Over the years the company has expanded its operations throughout the greater Houston metropolitan area and beyond. Today Houston Shell and Concrete's client base encompasses the entire region, serving Brazoria, Galveston, Ft. Bend, Montgomery, Waller, and Harris counties.

which includes some 28 plants and more than 200 trucks, gives the company the strength, scope, and flexibility to compete for any type of contract. This is supplemented by another key factor—personnel.

The company considers its employees the best-kept secret of its success. In what is becoming increasingly rare today, most Houston Shell and Concrete employees stay with the firm through their retirement. The president has been on board for almost

als include sack goods and expansion joints. Houston Shell and Concrete has ensured its current and future success by keeping abreast of the latest trends and technologies, such as new uses for plastics. While each new product and technological development requires a slightly different process, the company's philosophy is to grow with the demands required to care for their clients.

Houston Shell and Concrete anticipates a future strong in governmental work and

Adaptability has been the key to Houston Shell and Concrete maintaining its position as an industry leader. Throughout the economic cycles since its inception, the company has been successful in diversifying its operations to garner the available business. The strength of its operations allows Houston Shell and Concrete to compete for all types of work, from home building to apartment complexes, commercial building to industrial work, and private paving to state road contracts.

Houston Shell and Concrete's size,

■ *As one of the oldest companies in Houston, Houston Shell and Concrete Company is an industry leader providing quality work in many segments of the Houston economy.*

40 years. That stability, competence, and professionalism are reflected in the dedication of the 400 employees and the quality of the work they produce.

In addition to the concrete its name implies, the company also provides sand, gravel, and limestone base. Building materi-

industrial construction, as many companies undertake new projects and maintenance work. The company's size has been a tremendous value through diversification of its work load.

Having weathered the city's economic cycles, the company brings a historical perspective to its business operations that benefits its clients. A long and successful history as one of the oldest companies in the region has earned Houston Shell and Concrete Company an edge when it comes to respect and quality.

SHIPPING

From the maintenance and repair of oceangoing vessels to oil spill cleanup to transporting cargo, Houston's shipping industry plays a vital role in the area's economy.

■ *Photo by C.B. Jones*

BARWIL AGENCIES (TEXAS) INC.

As cargo moves around the world and through the Port of Houston, it is reliant on agents to provide the services needed for its safe and prompt delivery. Barwil Agencies (Texas) Inc. are shipping agents with the expertise and experience required.

Shipping agents sell service to their customers. Barwil solicits cargo for vessels, and its representatives handle the receipt of cargo deliveries for their customers, including customs clearance. They also provide attendance for tramp and tank vessels, crew changes and repatriation, clearance and forwarding of spares, and repairs and dry-docking. Competing in a field of roughly 70 firms, Barwil ranks among the top five in Houston and third in the number of vessels attended.

With the third-largest port in the nation and a skilled labor pool, Houston is a natural site for Barwil's headquarters. With much of the port's activity related to the oil industry, Barwil was not exempt from the

economic decline that affected most of the city. It honed new skills to adapt to the changes in the shipping market.

One such innovation was the development of turnkey projects for large manufacturers. In these instances Barwil agents literally handle the cargo from A to Z. They offer services that include packing at the manufacturing site, loading, transporting, customs clearance, and delivery to the final destination—all at a fixed cost. Barwil had not done that in the past but has the expertise required to successfully do the work.

■ *Barwil agents can provide all facets of cargo handling. Shown here is the loading of turnkey project cargoes, which is being handled by Barwil.*

Also new to Barwil is marine surveying. Marine surveyors are employed by the vessel owner, charterer, or shipper. Their duties include examination of the packing of cargo to determine if the loading by stevedores is appropriate and if the storage is suitable for the cargo. Service may also require the measuring of cargo, whose rates are determined by weight or volume. Another new development for Barwil is the chartering of vessels for commodity transfers.

Barwil Agencies (Texas) Inc., so renamed in late 1986 during corporate restructuring, is a wholly owned subsidiary of Barwil Agencies North America, Inc. Headquartered in Houston, Barwil North America has offices in New Orleans, Los Angeles, San Francisco, Seattle, and Portland. Barwil is a subsidiary of Wilh. Wilhelmson, Norway. Barwil has more than 60 offices worldwide—a tremendous advantage to Barwil Texas and its customers.

■ *Barwil Agencies (Texas) Inc.'s corporate headquarters in Houston.*

KERR STEAMSHIP COMPANY, INC.

Since its establishment in 1916, Kerr Steamship Company, Inc., has built a solid reputation for service and expertise. As its name implies, the organization began this century as a steamship company, but beginning in the mid-1950s it has made the successful transition to a modern, full-service agency house, representing a number of major lines and numerous tramp vessel operators.

■ *Well diversified and situated nationwide, Kerr Steamship Company, Inc., is one of the largest agencies in the world and can provide its clients with the full range of services they require.*

from hundreds of interior points.

Kerr has kept pace with these developments. In spite of the trend towards the creation of in-house agencies by major container carriers and prompted by their heavy capital investments, Kerr has, as an agency house, progressed in meeting the new challenges. Building upon its long-term relationships with several worldwide liner operators, this agency has developed the degree of sophistication and flexibility required to effectively compete in today's demanding and ever changing market.

Apart from its involvement in liner agency business, Kerr has created a separate marine division. Staffed with experienced technical and operational personnel throughout

As proof of that success, today Kerr Steamship is one of the largest agencies in the world. In the United States alone, Kerr operates more than 30 offices nationwide, staffed by more than 500 employees. Kerr has established operational bases on the East, West, and Gulf coasts, along with the Great Lakes area. With the development of a stevedoring and terminal network throughout the nation, Kerr can provide its clients with the full range of services they require, nationwide.

The subsidiaries provide the network that clients demand and include Stevens Shipping and Terminal Company, Kerr Steamships (Canada) Limited, Kerr

Steamship Company Limited (Vancouver), California United Terminals, Gulf and Southern Terminal Corporation, Southern Dock Company, Inc., and Kerr Terminals, Inc. Kerr also are partners in various additional terminal, stevedoring, and other maritime related companies.

Perhaps the greatest change in the shipping industry over the past two decades has been the move toward containerization. While the use of containers has simplified the movement of freight for shippers, it has drastically expanded the operational scope of ocean carriers from providing the traditional port-to-port service to include inland transportation via rail and truck to and

North American port offices, this division is dedicated to the handling of liquid and dry full cargo and special cargo operations which are so prominent, particularly in Houston and other U.S. Gulf ports.

Kerr Steamship Company, Inc., is unique in that it can provide, in house, all the services a line may require. Being well diversified and well situated nationwide means that Kerr can offer attractive and complete packages to its principal customers. Coupled with this is the ability to tailor its services to a client's needs. Kerr's future success seems assured as it remains sensitive to trends and changes within the industry.

PORT OF HOUSTON AUTHORITY

People are often surprised to discover that Houston, located 50 miles from the Gulf of Mexico, is a major port city, ranking third largest in the nation and among the top 10 ports worldwide. The Port of Houston recently celebrated its 75th anniversary as a deep-water port, but its history goes back to the meandering bayou on which the city was founded.

In 1828 the Clopper family plied their wares on the bayou in their schooner *Little Zoe*. But it took the city's founders, real esate developers and brothers John and Augustus Allen, to ascertain the real potential of the wandering Buffalo Bayou. In 1837 they persuaded Captain Thomas Wigg Grayson to navigate his steamship, *Laura,* up the bayou from Galveston. Thus, in a sense, was the port begun. Within four short years the city council had established the Port of Houston, and more than 4,000 bales of cotton were shipped out from the port in 1842. Within a dozen years that number had multiplied to 40,000 bales of cotton.

By the turn of the century it became apparent that Houston needed a deep-

water port, and community leaders redoubled their efforts to achieve it. In 1914 President Woodrow Wilson, while seated at his desk in the White House, pressed a button that was wired to a cannon in Houston. The cannon fired, and the city had opened its deep-water port.

Over the ensuing years the Port of Houston has evolved into a 25-mile long complex of private and public facilities. The private sector includes terminals, shipyards, and towboat docks, and manufacturing and processing plants. The public part of this entity is managed by the Port of Houston

Authority. The Port of Houston Authority is an authorized state agency. The Port Authority also serves as the sponsor of the Houston Ship Channel. It operates autonomously on a self-generated budget and is governed by the port commission. The seven commission members are appointed by Harris County Commissioners, Houston City Council, as well as representatives from surrounding communities actively involved with the port. The Port of Houston Authority is a public agency that deftly blends with the private sector.

Since its inception the port has benefited from the service and vision of the authority's commissioners, coupled with the public support it receives. That support comes naturally since the port is a big revenue maker locally and has played a role in attracting new industries to the area. NASA cited the port as one of the reasons it established the Manned Space Center in Houston, and one of the nation's largest industrial and petrochemical complexes has evolved along the banks of the Houston

■ *The Port of Houston Authority's Turning Basin Terminal lies at the navigational head of the country's third-largest port. In 1988 more than 4,700 ships and barges called at the terminal, which is capable of handling palletized, break-bulk, and containerized goods. The terminal can also handle automobiles and cargo that are directly discharged from vessels to trucks and railcars. Photos by Ray Soto*

Ship Channel. The Port of Houston's facilities are essential in attracting business and the Port Authority has always been enthusiastic in developing the facilities required to keep abreast of a changing marketplace.

Located just six miles from the city's downtown business district, the Turning Basin Terminal serves as the navigational head of the ship channel. This is a modern complex of wharves, transit sheds, and other facilities that stretches almost three miles along the ship channel. The turning basin can accommodate almost any kind of cargo, from heavy lift, to containers, to cars. It is home to the Houston Public Elevator, which has a grain storage capacity of more than six million bushels. The Houston Public Elevator, together with four private elevators located on the ship channel, provide Houston with more grain storage capacity than any other U.S. port.

Wharf No. 32 on the ship channel was specifically designed for project and heavy-lift cargo. With 806 marshaling feet of quay and 20 acres of marshaling area paved for heavy-duty traffic, this wharf can handle almost any large shipment. The Port of Houston Authority owns 39 general cargo and two liquid cargo wharves available for public hire.

The Fentress Bracewell Barbours Cut Container Terminal is located at the head of Galveston Bay and is considered the most modern intermodal facility on the

■ *Wharf No. 32, located at the Turning Basin Terminal, was built for heavy-lift and long-term cargo projects. The $11-million wharf has 806 feet of quay and 20 acres of paved marshaling area. Photo by Ray Soto*

■ *The Turning Basin Terminal is ideally designed for the direct discharge and direct load of cargo. Using this method, cargo is transferred directly from ship to truck or railcar (or vice versa), saving the shipper costly freight handling charges. Photo by Ray Soto*

Gulf of Mexico. The terminal has four berths, each 1,000 feet long, with two more under construction, and a marshaling area for 100 barges. On land, there is access to 44 acres of paved marshaling area and 23

acres available for temporary staging of vehicles, with auto processing facilities nearby. All this makes for quick turnaround, popular with shippers. For example, a driver with the proper documentation can deliver a

■ *The Port of Houston Authority's Fentress Bracewell Barbours Cut Terminal is the most modern intermodal facility on the Gulf Coast. The $150-million terminal has four container berths, state-of-the-art cranes, and a computerized inventory control system. Approximately $80 million has been earmarked for improvements and expansion at Barbours Cut, including more berths and additional paved storage area. Photo by Ray Soto*

container, load a new one, and be back on the road in under an hour.

Located mid-channel between these facilities is the Bulk Materials Handling Plant. As its name implies, the plant is equipped to handle all kinds of bulk commodities. In addition, a ship loading system valued at almost $5 million has been installed. The shiploader travels the length of the wharf with a loading chute mounted on its boom, keeping dust to a minimum. This enables the plant to handle dusty commodities, such as petroleum coke and potash.

The port's newest facility is the Jacintoport Terminal, a 125-acre site located on the north side of the ship channel near the town of Channelview. Houston Transmodal Owning Co., a private consortium, has leased 31 acres from the Port Authority for an automated facility for the handling of boxed and bagged commodities. The facility, called Omniport, opened in 1989 and is the first operation of its kind in the United States. The remaining acreage at Jacintoport will be used for the

storage and handling of other types of cargo.

The Bayport Turning Basin was developed by the Port of Houston Authority in cooperation with Friendswood Development Company, a subsidiary of Exxon Corporation. This deep-water, bulk liquid and chemical complex has two privately owned terminals available for public use. The Port Authority also has land available for lease to be used in the development of

■ *RIGHT: The Port of Houston handles more export cotton than all other U.S. Gulf ports combined, according to figures released in 1988. Houston ranked fifth in the country in export cotton tonnage, moving more than 93,100 tons during the first six months of 1987. Other Gulf ports handled approximately 53,400 tons of export cotton during the same period.*

■ *BELOW: Steel is a major cargo at Port Authority wharves. It comes in many forms, including beams, wire, and nails. Photo by Ray Soto*

private bulk or general cargo terminals. Located two hours from open sea, Bayport is one of the largest chemical complexes in the United States, with an estimated value of $2.2 billion. The Bayport development is home to more than 50 national and foreign companies, including some of the largest chemical manufacturing firms in the world.

Supplementing these facilities is the Malcolm Baldrige Foreign Trade Zone. This multisite zone is managed and sponsored by the Port of Houston Authority and offers its users several advantages. At various FTZ sites along the ship channel and surrounding areas, customs duties on imported goods can be delayed until the

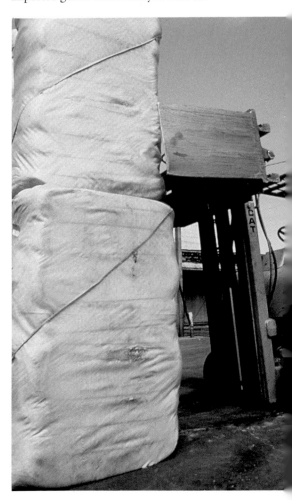

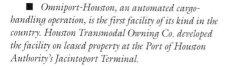

■ *Omniport-Houston, an automated cargo-handling operation, is the first facility of its kind in the country. Houston Transmodal Owning Co. developed the facility on leased property at the Port of Houston Authority's Jacintoport Terminal.*

cargo is distributed domestically. Or duties can be waived on commodities that are marked for export to another foreign port and are just traveling through Houston. Houston's FTZ sites include warehouses, a refrigerated storage area for foods, bulk liquid storage, and a steel pipe finishing facility.

Strategic location makes the Port of Houston a natural gateway to inland points. The port is served by four major railroads and every wharf at the turning basin is served by rail. Almost 150 common carrier lines provide trucking service for cargo. Port Authority officials work with shippers to find the best way to move their

cargos. Using a procedure called "mini-land bridge," a shipper can shave almost a week of transportation time on cargo headed from South America to the West Coast by sending it to Houston by rail instead of going through the Panama Canal.

The Port of Houston authority aggressively seeks new business, targeting major shipping lines in much the same way that cities target airlines for hubs. A shipping line generally chooses only one Gulf port

for its trade, and the Port of Houston wants to be that choice. The key is efficient service at competitive rates.

Tonnage figures tell this port's success story at a glance. In 1989 the port handled an estimated 126 million tons. Container tonnage totaled the equivalent of 3.9 million tons, and 4,656 vessels called at the port in 1989. Goods moved in foreign trade that year totaled 62.6 million tons valued at $22 billion dollars, ranking Houston second among U.S. ports in foreign tonnage.

The Port of Houston is well positioned in the matrix of international trade. Top import countries in tonnage include Algeria, Saudi Arabia, Mexico, and the United Kingdom. Top exporting countries in tonnage were the Soviet Union, Japan, China, Venezuela, and Taiwan. That international trading has carried over to Houston at large. More than 250 import/export companies operate in the area and more than 50 foreign governments are represented there. Nearly 30 nations have investment and tourism offices in the metropolitan area, and 29 chambers of commerce and trade associations are also represented.

Closer to home, a study done in 1987 found that more than 110,000 Texas jobs are related to the port's activity, and 28,000 of those jobs are the direct result of the Port of Houston. Port activity generates about $3 billion annually in benefits to the regional economy. Those numbers continue to grow.

The Port Authority works closely with shippers and private companies to make the improvements necessary for the port to survive and grow in a competitive industry. Moreover, the Port of Houston enhances the city's business base immeasurably. Ongoing capital improvements, coupled with a commitment to dependable service and competitive rates, ensures the Port of Houston a comfortable stride into the twenty-first century.

■ *A 6-million-bushel public grain elevator is located in the turning basin area. In 1988 more than one million tons of grain moved through the Houston Public Elevator. This facility and the four privately operated elevators located elsewhere on the channel give Houston more grain storage capacity than any other U.S. port. Photo by Ray Soto*

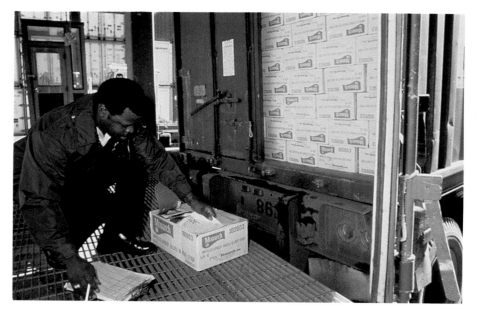

HOUSTON SHIP REPAIR INC.

In a port where 5,000 vessels call annually, Houston Ship Repair Inc. has become an international leader in the maintenance and repair of oceangoing vessels. HSR is one of the largest topside ship-repair companies in North America.

Houston Ship Repair has the facilities and the expertise required to do almost any kind of work and has a worldwide reputation in marine industrial repair, tank and hold cleaning, and oil-spill cleanup. Houston Ship Repair is the factory-authorized service facility for MAN-B&W and Sulzer, the major manufacturers of marine diesel engines, and is on the list of repair companies qualified to submit bids to the U.S. Government for repair work on the vessels of the U.S. Department of the Navy Military Sealift Command (MSC), the U.S. Department of Transportation Maritime Administration (MARAD), and the Coast Guard.

In addition to bid work (often government contracts), the company performs emergency repairs, regular maintenance, and warranty work. This work may be ordered by local agents or by the ship owners directly. Phones are answered round the clock, 365 days a year, and work can begin at any time. Jobs can vary from costing a mere $300 to more than $10 million.

With corporate offices in Houston, Houston Ship Repair has facilities in Hous-

■ *Proof of a job well done: the SS Hattiesburg Victory on sea trials.*

ton, Galveston, and the Orange/Port Arthur area. In Houston HSR has more than 120,000 square feet of space, including offices, a fully equipped machine shop, motor shop, and fabrication shop, on 21 acres near the ship channel and in Chan-

nelview. The company's repair berth at Brady Island on the Houston Ship Channel can handle vessels up to 800 feet in length and provide full utilities.

Houston Ship Repair operates two berths in the Port of Galveston for vessels up to 850 feet with full utilities.

In the Orange/ Port Arthur area, Houston Ship Repair has two repair berths that can handle vessels to 750 feet with full utilities available.

The company does a considerable amount of work in the MARAD Ready Reserve Fleet and has 65,000 square feet of space, including a machine shop and a fabrication shop, located on more than 10 acres on the Port of Orange Ship Channel.

Supplementing these physical plants is a marine fleet that includes crane barges and workboats and a complete fleet of trucks and mobile equipment.

Beyond its physical facilities Houston Ship Repair sends skilled crews wherever required. Riding crews work on vessels en route from one port to another and perform sea trials after major repairs are completed. Crews work on vessels at all docks in the Houston area and may be sent to ports elsewhere in the United States or abroad.

The skilled work force, that at times numbers almost 500 people, consists of experts in mechanical, structural, and electrical repairs. The technical management staff is made up of marine, mechanical, and electrical engineers as well as structural designers and naval architects. Houston Ship Repair's skilled work force and superior management have enabled the company to grow steadily, even during the city's lean years. Houston Ship Repair Inc. has proved to be a Houston success story.

■ *The SS Chesapeake under conversion at HSR's Brady Island ship repair facility.*

Photo by Jay W. Sharp

12

NATURAL RESOURCES

Houston's reserves of natural gas and oil have provided the backdrop for oil exploration and the area's booming petrochemical industry.

■ *Photo by C.B. Jonesa*

GLOBAL MARINE INC.

Thirty years ago four oil companies got together and began a tentative move into the waters off the coast of California in search of oil. Global Marine Inc. is the end result, and offshore drilling is an integral part of the energy industry today.

Global Marine Inc., which moved to Houston in 1982, has three operating subsidiaries and 2,000 employees backing up their expertise worldwide. Foremost is Global Marine Drilling Company. After 30 years in the business it is one of the leaders in international offshore drilling. The company ranks third in the number of rigs, 27, and second in terms of revenues.

Challenger Minerals Inc., an oil and gas exploration company, was developed in recognition of the cyclical nature of the offshore-drilling industry. As part of its cap-

■ *Shown is the crew of the Glomar Pacific tripping pipe utilizing the Global Marine-patented lay down system.*

■ *The Glomar High Island I at work in the Gulf of Mexico. This rig was the first jack-up purchased by Glomar Marine. The rig is a Marathon LeTourneau 82 SD-C 250-foot, water-depth-capability, cantilevered jack-up.*

ital expansion the corporation decided to develop oil and gas reserves. Though not unscathed by the problems encountered throughout the industry, Challenger's proven oil and gas reserves in the mid-1980s totaled more than 9 million barrels of oil equivalent.

Rounding out the corporation is Applied Drilling Technology Inc., a turnkey drilling operation. Turnkey drilling essentially means that the drilling contractor will drill a specific well to a specific depth at a specific cost. In 1980 ADTI became the first contractor to offer the service offshore. Ultimately turnkey drilling opened the door for smaller, independent companies for whom offshore-drilling expertise had been prohibitively expensive.

The heart of the company is Global Marine Drilling Co. The company

currently has 20 jack-up rigs. These are mobile, bottom-supported drilling rigs that stand on legs in water at depths of up to 300 feet. The company also has four semisubmersible rigs where the support columns sit on submerged pontoons. There are also two drill ships, which are exactly what their names imply. They are positioned over the well and anchored. One is outfitted with a dynamic positioning assist, which means a shipboard computer monitors and aligns the ship's position continually in relation to the well bore on the ocean floor.

Finally there is the CIDS, or concrete island drilling system. This was designed, built, and operated by Global Marine in Alaska's Beaufort Sea. The CIDS can work year-round in water depths of 35 to 55 feet and in moving ice flows up to 12 feet thick.

Each of the various rig types has its advantages and disadvantages, and many are designed with specific drilling environments in mind. Global Marine operates rigs all over the world: western Africa, India, Australia, the North Sea, Alaska's Beaufort Sea, the Mediterranean, and the Gulf of Mexico. Beginning with the first floating drilling vessel, Global Marine has pioneered drilling in many of the world's severe environments, as well as advances in drilling technology.

At a cost of $20 million to $100 million

company emerged whole in 1989, having done two things to strengthen itself. The first was to dramatically lower its debt, and the second was a scheduled repayment of that new debt on very flexible terms.

Global Marine, which has the most modern rig fleets in the world, is now poised to benefit from oil prices. Most experts predict that OPEC will regain control in the decade ahead; the only question is when. Yet no one expects a return to the whirlwind of the late 1970s and early 1980s. Global Marine believes that it is a different market with a different set of rules now. While the industry has always been competitive, the company today has to compete in ways it has not before. Competition notwithstanding, Global Marine stands ready for the future, having weathered the stormy past and emerged stronger for it.

■ LEFT: *The Glomar Beaufort Sea I shown working on the Alaskan North Slope for Exxon. The rig is shown at work spraying water during building of a defensive ice barrier for use against moving pack ice.*

■ BELOW: *The Glomar Atlantic, a Global Marine drillship. The Glomar Atlantic has dynamic positioning as well as conventional mooring capabilities. The rig is capable of drilling in water to a depth of 2,000 feet.*

each to build, these rigs represent a tremendous capital investment. Given that investment, the biggest problem in offshore drilling is the cyclical nature of the industry. Rigs are generally in undersupply or oversupply, and the change from drilling in one state to the other can occur dramatically. The problem, given that initial investment cost, is keeping the rigs operating at a profitable rate. It is somewhat analogous to building an office tower—the owner is dependent on rent to pay the bills. Rigs do not earn large profits until the utilization rate gets into the 90 percent range. Then prices can jump, literally in weeks, from a rate of $20 thousand per day to $90 thousand per day. Conversely, prices can plummet just as fast.

In the late 1970s Global Marine undertook a tremendous capital investment program, renovating its fleet with $1.6 billion in new equipment. Completed in 1984, the fleet was the most advanced in the industry. Unfortunately oil prices had begun their tumble from the range of more than $30 a barrel to less than $10 a barrel. Global Marine, along with everyone else in the industry, experienced tremendous difficulties. It was saddled with a crippling debt structure. Following a Chapter 11 reorganization the

STERLING CHEMICALS, INC.

Sterling Chemicals, Inc., was created in 1986 to acquire and operate petro-chemical facilities previously owned by Monsanto Company. Organized by one of the giants of the chemicals industry, Gordon Cain, and another veteran, Virgil Waggoner, Sterling's founders accurately forecast a window of opportunity to purchase major petrochemical assets at attractive prices. The company was structured to be an efficient, low cost producer of commodity petrochemicals. Employees were given an opportunity to share in the company's future.

Sterling Chemicals, which is publicly traded on the New York Stock Exchange, is headquartered in Houston. The company's petrochemical facilities in Texas City are located on a 250-acre site on Galveston Bay. This convenient location makes possible shipments of commodities by container, truck, rail, barge, and ocean tanker, to both domestic and foreign markets. Sterling is a major producer of seven petrochemical products. These are acrylonitrile, styrene monomer, lactic acid,

■ ABOVE: An expansion for acrylonitrile increased capacity by more than 50 percent in 1989. Photo by Chris Salvo

■ LEFT: The largest U.S. producer of styrene monomer, Sterling has 17 percent of domestic capacity.

acetic acid, tertiary butylamine, plasticizers, and sodium cyanide.

The intermediate petrochemicals produced by Sterling serve as building blocks for innumerable products. Not well known by their chemical names, these products are found in countless everyday items. Acrylonitrile is used in the production of furnishings and upholstery, apparel and household appliances, carpet, and automotive components. Sterling's acrylonitrile production unit was expanded in 1989 to increase its capacity by 50 percent, to more than 700 million pounds annually. The world-class facility uses state-of-the-art technology and has the potential for additional expansion.

Styrene monomer is used in the production of disposable cups, packaging and containers, synthetic rubber and housewares, video cassettes, insulation, luggage, toys, boat and vehicle components, paper coating, and appliance parts. Capable of producing 1,500 million pounds per year, Sterling has almost 20 percent of U.S. capacity for styrene and is the largest domestic producer.

The uses for lactic acids are found in

packaging, and construction materials such as wall and floor coverings. Sterling's plasticizer production capability is more than 280 million pounds per year.

Sterling has begun production of sodium cyanide in a joint project with Du Pont. The unit, owned by Du Pont and operated by Sterling, is designed to produce up to 100 million pounds annually. The sodium cyanide, used in precious metals recovery and electroplating, will be marketed through Du Pont's international network.

Sterling's management felt that shareholders benefit if employees own stock in the business. Nearly 12 percent of the company's common stock is held by employees who have taken a stake in Sterling's future through the company's employee stock-ownership plan. Combined with directors and officers, the nearly 1,000 employees of Sterling own almost 50 percent of the company's common stock.

Sterling Chemicals made a strong commitment to four specific groups when it was formed: to its employees; to its shareholders; to its customers; and finally to the community. Those commitments and a farsighted management philosophy have made Sterling Chemicals, Inc., the success it is today, having reached number 403 on the *Fortune* 500 list the second year it was in business.

■ *ABOVE: Sterling is the only U.S. producer of synthetic lactic acid. Photo by Fred Carr*

■ *RIGHT: A cryogenic gas separation unit provides raw material for production of acetic acid and oxo-alcohols. Photo by Fred Carr*

food additives and preservatives, in pharmaceuticals and as surface coatings. Sterling's lactic acid unit has a production capacity of 20 million pounds annually. The company is the only domestic producer of synthetic lactic acid and one of only two in the world.

Acetic acid is used in the production of paint and surface coatings, adhesives, glues, solvents, windshield safety liners, and cigarette filters. With almost 15 percent of domestic capacity, Sterling produces almost 600 million pounds of acetic acid annually and is studying the feasibility of a major increase in capacity.

Tertiary butylamine, known as TBA, is used in pesticides, lube oil additives,

solvents, pharmaceuticals, and synthetic rubber. Sterling has an annual production capacity of 12 million pounds and is the only domestic producer and one of only two worldwide.

Plasticizers are used in footwear and outerwear, luggage, shower curtains, floor coverings, cable insulation, calendared film, swimming pool liners, commercial

THE DOW CHEMICAL COMPANY

In 1891 Herbert H. Dow went into business to extract chlorine, caustic soda, and other elements from the brine fields underlying Midland, Michigan. This entrepreneurial effort eventually gave birth to The Dow Chemical Company in 1897, the world's sixth-largest chemical company.

Today Dow is a diversified, worldwide manufacturer and supplier of more than 2,000 products, including chemicals and performance products, plastics, hydrocarbons, energy, and consumer specialties, which include agricultural products, consumer products, and pharmaceuticals. It operates 179 manufacturing sites in 31 countries, and it employs 62,000 men and women around the world. In 1989 the company had sales of $17.6 billion and earnings of $2.49 billion.

As Houston and its Gulf Coast environs developed into a world-class petrochemical complex during the twentieth century, Dow USA was a major contributor to that growth and development. Dow brought to the Houston Gulf Coast technological innovation, talented and enterprising people, and the vitality of a global organization.

Dow purchased its first tract land in 1940, some 800 acres located along the Gulf of Mexico and the Brazos River. The abundance of natural resources in the area made the selection a perfect site for the start of Dow's Texas Operations. Seawater, natural gas, oyster beds, fresh water, and salt domes were readily available and plentiful. In addition, there was good rail and water transportation, particularly the proximity of deep-water port.

Dow's Texas Gulf Coast operations have since expanded to encompass more than 5,000 acres today. At the original site alone, Dow has more than 7,000 employees, of whom more than 1,000 are involved in research and development and technology. These chemists, engineers, and technicians are at work on a variety of innovative projects, ranging from new processes to new products.

HYDROCARBONS AND ENERGY

One of Dow USA's major businesses, Hydrocarbons and Energy, is headquartered in Houston. Its major objective is to provide low cost and reliable supplies of olefins and aromatics for Dow's production of chemicals and plastics, and to supply process

■ *Bill Waycaster, vice president and general manager, Dow Hydrocarbons and Energy, Houston.*

fuels, steam, and electricity to Dow's major manufacturing facilities.

Its position in the industry is significant. Dow is the largest producer of ethylene in the United States and the world, and among the three largest propylene producers in the world. Dow USA converts more than 10 million metric tons of olefin feedstocks to ehtylene and propylene annually, ranking it as the number one global consumer of olefin feedstocks.

Dow's production of steam and electricity make it the world's largest producer of cogenerated power. Cogenerated power is the production of electricity and thermal energy (steam) from a single fuel source, usually natural gas. Cogenerated plants add value to Dow because they are approximately 20 percent more efficient than conventional fossil fuel plants.

Hydrocarbons and Energy manages and operates roughly one-third of Dow USA's capital assets and accounts for about two thirds of Dow USA's purchases. The total material flow of hydrocarbon fuels, feedstocks, and products currently amounts to some 16 billion pounds and represents about 40 percent of the total Dow USA movements.

The total Dow USA Hydrocarbons and Energy material flow effort employs extensive assets, including more than 60 barges, 600 rail cars, and equipment of 4 ships. In addition, Dow USA Hydrocarbons and Energy uses 1,200 miles of fuel gas pipelines and 3,000 miles of olefin feedstock pipelines. In a published listing of U.S. pipeline companies, Dow is the only company in the top 50 for both gas and liquid pipelines.

Based on growth projections for Dow's

derivative products in plastics and chemicals, the Hydrocarbons and Energy business is proceeding with several projects to replace old capacity and expiring purchase contracts, and to meet expanding internal hydrocarbon demands. A new 1.5-billion-pound olefins facility with added feedstock flexibility and state-of-the-art technology is being added at its Freeport site.

CARING FOR THE ENVIRONMENT
As a responsible corporate citizen, Dow has long been committed to protecting and caring for the environment. Throughout the organization, Dow is reducing and eliminating waste, encouraging customers to use its products properly, promoting recycling, and sharing knowledge and expertise.

Dow's goal is to cut waste at the source—the manufacturing site. To spur improvements, Dow gives plant managers a direct incentive to reduce waste by charging each plant for all waste management. Reducing waste at the source results in lower operating costs and improved productivity when waste can be recycled into valuable products.

The company supports a national waste reduction data base to measure and communicate the chemical industry's progress

■ *Dow's Texas Gulf Coast operations encompass more than 5,000 acres today.*

in reducing waste and emissions. This accountability can foster industry-wide waste reduction efforts and encourage voluntary waste-reduction programs.

Dow has made consistent progress in reducing levels of airborne and water emissions. Total air emissions from its plants in the United States are down by more than 50 percent since 1985 and 85 percent since 1974. Organic discharges to the water, meanwhile, have been reduced by 95 percent in the past 15 years.

Dow also is actively involved in solid-waste management. When it is necessary to use landfills, Dow takes precautions to ensure that they are secure. Its hazardous-waste landfills meet strict permit limits and are engineered to assure long-term stability of contents. They are also closely monitored by Dow.

In recognition for these efforts, the World Environment Center awarded Dow the 1989 Gold Medal for International Corporate Environmental Achievement.

The Electric Power Institute awarded Dow the Innovative Technology Award and the Council on Alternate Fuels

presented Dow with its Walter Flowers Achievement Award for developing a proprietary process to produce synthetic natural gas from coal. Considered one of the cleanest of coal-based technologies, the process produces significantly lower emissions than related fossil-fuel technologies.

LOOKING TO THE FUTURE
Dow's continued commitment to the environment is a long-term investment. In 1989 Dow spent more than $260 million on environmental, health, and safety controls, and that capital investment will steadily increase in the 1990s as new technology is developed. The company also is undertaking several environmental initiatives in 1990, including: a commitment to further emission reduction, a major conservation program, plastic recycling programs, and a search for greater external involvement in Dow's environmental activities.

Except for the space industry, The Dow Chemical Company is the region's largest single capital investor and anticipates the future with confidence. By embracing an active and progressive management applied with clear and common sense, Dow has become, and will remain, a leader in the petrochemical industry and in the U.S. Gulf Coast region.

CHEVRON COMPANIES

The bright new signs going up at service stations all over the city and statewide are a symbol of the greater presence of Chevron in this area. Established in its original form more than 110 years ago, Chevron has been in Houston for more than 20 years. But it was the merger with Gulf in 1984 that propelled Chevron into an even greater role within the city.

The flagship of this expansion is the Chevron Tower, so designated and dedicated in June 1989. The gleaming 51-story building has been honored as one of the top two buildings in the city. With more than 20 different tenants, it was designed, engineered, and built beyond the norm to make it a super-class building. It was named the 1989 Houston Building Owners and Managers Association Building of the Year.

More readily recognized by consumers are the new Chevron service stations. In the merger with Gulf, Chevron acquired all of its former retail outlets. A campaign was launched to assure motorists that their neighborhood service station was changing for the better. Chevron reassured its new customers that the friendly and familiar service would remain, and the gasoline would get better.

Facing the conversion of its acquired outlets, Chevron took this project a step further, redesigning its paint scheme, adding new signage, and sprucing up all of its locations. Texas, with more than 2,000 Chevron outlets, is leading the nation in this conversion. It is also fair to say that Chevron is now one of the top retail marketers in Houston.

Chevron Chemical Company's Cedar Bayou plant is yet another impressive asset in this area. Located 30 miles east of the city, the plant sits on 1,000 acres and produces almost 4 billion pounds of chemicals annually, many of which are used by people on a daily basis. Principal products include ethylene, polyethelene, propylene, and a category of olefins later marketed to other chemical companies. Cedar Bayou produces two finished products: acetylene black, used in making dry-cell batteries and Synfluid R, a synthetic lubricating oil.

Beyond its primary function as a manufacturing facility, Cedar Bayou is a tremendous contributor to the community where it operates. The plant employs 570 people and has an additional 300 or more em-

ployed by a local contractor to maintain and service the facilities. Cedar Bayou pays more than $7.5 million in taxes each year and triple that amount to employees. More than another $40 million each year is provided for purchasing area goods and

■ *ABOVE: One of Chevron's new Houston stations at Beltway 8 and Woodforest.*

■ *FACING PAGE: Honored as 1989 Building of the Year by the Houston Building Owners and Managers Association, the gleaming, 51-story Chevron Tower visibly establishes Chevron's presence in Houston.*

services, and a similar amount is paid to area utilities. As such a prominent member of the business community, Cedar Bayou also plays a role in the community through a variety of programs it sponsors.

Cedar Bayou is just one of a number of Chevron operations in the greater Houston area. Chevron began the route to its present form when the Pacific Coast Oil Company

was started in 1878 and purchased by Standard Oil in 1900. Through other changes the company became Standard Oil California, later Socal, and continued its expansion. In 1934 the Chevron name was first introduced to the public. Fifty years later the metamorphosis was complete, when Socal bid more than $13 billion and merged with Gulf in 1984. In July of that year the organization became the Chevron Corporation.

The merger was synergistic, with the assets of both corporations giving the new Chevron a strong and diversified portfolio. In Houston alone there are 31 operations working independently of each other, reporting to headquarters in California. Houston is the headquarters for Chevron

Exploration and Production Services Company, the petrochemical divisions of Chevron Chemical Company, and the natural-gas sales and supply unit. These logical choices given the industry concentration there. Houston is the center of the refining and petrochemical industries in the United States, with roughly 50 percent of the nation's refineries and 60 percent of the petrochemical plants located along the Golden Crescent, the 700-mile strip on the southeast Texas coast.

The size of Chevron is easily demonstrated with a look at its operations in Texas. It has more than 7,000 employees, roughly 2,300 in Houston alone, and pays them more than $400 million. Chevron also has retirees in the Houston area and in Texas as a whole. Beyond the organizations in Houston, some of the operations statewide include exploration and natural-gas and oil production, pipelines, refining, and supply and distribution.

In addition to its commitment to the business at hand, Chevron Companies is equally committed to the city as a whole and the quality of life for its residents. Many Chevron employees are involved in volunteering their time to service groups, education, and the arts. At the corporate level, Chevron is committed to the quality of education, from kindergarten through the 12th grade, particularly in math and science. Support is also given to environmental and conservation programs.

■ *Located 30 miles east of Houston near Baytown, Chevron Chemical Company's Cedar Bayou plant is a major contributor to the local economy.*

BUSINESS AND PROFESSIONS

Houston's business and professional community provides the necessary professional services and insight and ability for financial growth for both individuals and businesses in the community.

■ *Photo by Bob Rowan/Progressive Image*

COMPUTEL BUSINESS COMMUNICATIONS

The communications business has changed dramatically in recent years, and the business world is ever more dependent on excellent communications to survive. In this crowded and competitive field, Computel Business Communications is a proven contender.

Started in 1984 by President Julie Williams, the company is now one of the top five in the city, with more than 4,000 customer accounts. Established when the city's economy was faltering, Computel has thrived because of knowledge, dedication, and financial stability.

In a nutshell the firm is an interconnect company that sells, installs, and maintains business communications systems. These run the gamut from phones and intercoms to paging systems and the recent addition of facsimile technology. Clients range from small office accounts to one with more

■ *ABOVE: The team of technicians fulfills Computel's commitment to quality and service.*

■ *RIGHT: Julie Williams, president.*

■ *BELOW: Williams meets with her skilled staff. Her expertise has led the company to its position of strength.*

than 68 branches.

On the horizon the company is expanding into voice mail. The latest wrinkle in this everchanging industry, voice mail is a type of electronic PBX that works along with telephone operators. These systems have been used for years in the hotel and airline industries but were cost prohibitive to smaller firms until recently.

Computel draws on the experience of Williams, who began in the communications field in 1966. She and a partner were contractors for ITT, one of 71 such operations scattered nationwide. At that time the only business available to independents were the intercom and paging systems.

In 1984 that operation ceased and Williams started Computel, relying on almost 20 years worth of experience to succeed. The technicians who had been with her original operation remained on staff, providing a wealth of expertise in the technical support for systems that is essential to clients.

"This is an easy business to get into and a difficult one to stay in," says Williams. She attributes a large part of her success to the stabilty and experience her firm offers to its clients, some of whom call for specific technicians by name, having worked with them for years.

The bulk of the company's sales comes from its ITT equipment. Computel Business Communications sells primarily U.S.-made systems, per Williams' decision. When Computel purchased the Houston client base from ITT in 1987, it also purchased their inventory, valued at more than $500,000. A warehouse of more than 3,000 square feet gives them the space to stock the inventory they need to provide speedy reliable service to their customers.

AIM MANAGEMENT GROUP INC.

AIM Management Group Inc. is an investment management firm established in 1976 with definite ideas on management—principally that talented investment people are its primary product. Those ideas have borne success. AIM, through a number of subsidiaries, manages assets valued at $15 billion, making it among the top such firms nationally.

The AIM Group's primary business is the management of its clients' investments. AIM invests in a wide range of securities for both mutual funds and private accounts. AIM, through its two investment advisory subsidiaries, AIM Advisors and AIM Capital Management, advises some $15 billion for mutual funds and private accounts. Account size varies from $8,000 to $10,000 for retail mutual fund customers to more than $100 million for large institutional accounts.

Among the different types of mutual funds underwritten by AIM Distributors, Inc., are retail funds which are sold by brokers. These retail funds are known collectively as the AIM Family of Funds due to the ease with which shareholders may

switch from one fund to another. There is also AIM Summit Fund, a fund purchased only by making regularly scheduled monthly investments through a contractual plan.

The biggest part of AIM's assets lies in its institutional funds. These are the mutual funds that invest primarily in short-term money market securities on behalf of large financial institutions, such as banks or broker/dealers. The money-market trading room averages three-quarters of a billion dollars in transactions daily. Rounding out

■ *AIM manages assets valued at $15 billion, making it among the top 20 investment management firms in the nation.*

the picture are the private-label funds, mutual funds sold primarily to customers of a particular organization, such as a bank that is associated with the fund.

In little more than a dozen years, AIM Management Group Inc. has grown from a small organization with 15 employees to a significant and respected money manager with approximately to 180 employees. Houston is home to AIM, which also maintains smaller offices in New York and Dallas.

AIM Management Group Inc. has succeeded in a highly complicated and competitive business, one in which the report card comes in every day. Clients seek outstanding performance, innovative products, and excellent service. AIM's success can be attributed to the attention of its people to these competitive challenges.

■ *Robert H. Graham, Charles T. Bauer, and Gary T. Crum (left to right) work hard to guarantee success in a complicated and competitive business.*

STEWART & STEVENSON SERVICES, INC.

Stewart & Stevenson Services, Inc., may not be a household name, but as one of the largest providers of engineered power in the world, millions of people are affected by its products and services everyday. Some quick examples include airline ground support equipment, buses, military vehicles, forklifts, cargo tractors, marine propulsion, diesel-driven generator sets, and gas turbine powered cogeneration units. In short, it designs, manufactures, and maintains virtually anything that has a turbine or diesel engine

This corporation is a diverse organization with offices worldwide and more than 2,500 employees. In Houston it ranks as the 25th largest among the publicly traded companies and in the top 25 in number of employees. Beyond these numbers, however, Stewart & Stevenson shares in the heritage of this community. It began, grew, and prospered there.

In 1903 C. Jim Stewart went into a partnership with J.R. Stevenson. Each partner invested $300 toward the establishment

of a horseshoeing parlor, for blacksmithing and carriage making, handled by Stewart and Stevenson, respectively. Within the original "pardnership" agreement, as it was written at the time, is the philosophy that

■ *ABOVE: The partnership was established in 1903 between Jim Stewart and Joe R. Stevenson.*

■ *BELOW: The business was started with an indoor horseshoeing parlor and blacksmith shop.*

has fueled the company's phenomenal success. Each partner was committed to doing whatever was necessary, beyond his own duties, to satisfy the customer and ensure success.

Within two short years the partners' fate was determined with the arrival of a badly burned Dixie Flyer—their first repair of a "horseless" carriage. The damage was so great that a new handcrafted wooden body had to be built. That task was the first step from the world of horseshoes to worldwide horsepower.

Through the ensuing years Stewart & Stevenson continued to modify and service many types of the new vehicles of the early century. In 1938 they decided to take a much bigger step into the power business with the development of a new, untried diesel engine by General Motors. GM was looking for dependable firms to market and service their new diesel engines, while S&S was interested in becoming a distributor for these new engines. That original partnership has grown to the point where Stewart & Stevenson is now the world's largest distributor of Detroit Diesel engines.

The Engine Division was soon selling to rice farmers, lumber mills, and other small power-plant users until the advent of World War II. The company converted from

■ *Stewart & Stevenson was granted a franchise in 1938 for the distributorship of Detroit Diesel engines.*

commercial to wartime production and remanufactured thousands of engines for use in tanks and jeeps, as well as a large number of generator sets.

A telling illustration of the patriotism of this company can be found during the press of World War II production. Detroit Diesel asked S&S to join them, as a subcontractor, in a project to rebuild 4,000 Sherman tanks, providing the rebuilt diesel engines. Although S&S intially declined, saying it was already beyond its limits with wartime manufacturing, the firm eventually agreed.

A facility was put together within 90 days, and soon S&S was turning out the engines at a rate of 40 a day, an astonishing

number at that time. The cost was $1,900 per pair for the 6-71 engines, a price Detroit Diesel said was too low, but S&S stood by it. Moreover, when the contract was met, S&S felt it had overpriced its product and returned one million dollars to the government.

As it developed, Houston was the perfect site for S&S as the city became the center of the burgeoning petrochemical industry. S&S expanded with a growing industry by providing the power required in the oil field. By 1981 roughly one-third of the company's business was petroleum related. When the petroleum industry took a plunge, S&S saw its own assets declining as well. But this is not a firm that waits around for things to occur—it makes them happen.

In maintaining its own oil field equipment, S&S realized there was tremendous need for maintenance of idle drilling rigs throughout the area. Investors, many of whom were new to the business having acquired oil field equipment as a result of repossession, were looking for a way to protect their assets worth millions of dollars. S&S found a way to make money in a declining industry by contracting to service and maintain those idle drilling rigs.

Nothing better illustrates the "can-do" spirit of this company than the case of the

■ *A typical LM2500 gas turbine powered cogeneration unit that supplies 20 megawatts of electrical energy and uses the recovered waste heat to produce steam.*

■ *ABOVE: One of the many diverse product lines included in S&S airline ground support products.*

■ *LEFT: Since World War II S&S has been manufacturing products for the defense industry such as this 1000-kilowatt ship service generator set.*

vertical engine. Approached with the need for a certain amount of power in a limited space, S&S set out to turn the engine on end to accommodate this application. The manufacturer, along with other skeptics, said it could not be done. S&S engineers and management tackled the problem, reconfigured the engine, and obtained a patent on its modifications. Today there are many of these vertical engines in use worldwide.

Another good example was the development of a safe and economical diesel engine for customized application in marine pleasure craft. Once again, faced by skeptics, S&S led the way and is now a major provider of marine propulsion engines.

A spirit of willingness to try new things and professional ability has led S&S to diversify into a wide variety of areas. S&S has been a major figure in the material handling industry since 1959. This division carries the full line of Hyster lift trucks, from narrow-aisle to diesel-powered heavy-lift trucks. The division also offers the Unisource program, which provides customers with parts for Hyster as well as competitive equipment. Beginning in January 1989, the material handling division added the complete John Deere construction equipment products line to its distributorships in the Houston metropolitan area.

Commercial airline passengers may not see the S&S logo on their trips, but S&S is an integral part of their journeys. With the onset of turbine powered aircraft, S&S entered the aviation industry and began providing ground-power equipment. It now offers a range of ground-power and air-start units, along with tow and cargo tractors.

S&S is also a manufacturer of the Elephant Beta aircraft deicer, under license from its European inventor. The Beta is considered one of the finest in speed, efficiency, effectiveness, reliability, and economy. A proven design provides an enclosure for the operator, allowing the operator to remain protected from the elements.

While almost never needed in balmy Houston, the firm has signed a manufacturing and distribution agreement with Rolba A.G., Switzerland, through Stewart & Stevenson Power in Denver, for its full product line of snow-removal equipment.

The largest contributor to growth in the past five years has been the gas turbine products division. Focusing on cogeneration plants and electrical utilities, S&S has, through knowledge and experience, become a leader in the industry. Today it provides a world-class cogenerating package.

The way it reached that position of strength can be told with the story of a country that needed several cogenerating plants on line in four months, a process that normally takes 12 to 14 months. Most people said it could not be done. S&S tackled the job and with the fortuitous request for a delay on delivery of another order was able to supply the requested equipment within the allotted time.

The prime mover is always the focus for S&S, and in diversifying it looks for new applications of that power, followed by pro-viding for the parts and service required after the sale. Its entry into the transit industry is a good example of a new application. S&S now offers three new bus models: coach, transit, and shuttle in a range of sizes and is building on its existing network of dealers, branches, and subsidiaries.

Stewart & Stevenson is one of only three firms funded to do research in the uses of compressed natural gas as an alternative fuel. In conjunction with the Gas Research Institute, S&S is working toward a government mandated deadline of this decade for the delivery of an alternate fuel in transit systems.

A reputation for excellence in engineering, construction, and support has long made S&S a steady supplier for U.S. defense forces. S&S is now working on a prototype of a new U.S. Army truck for the Depart-ment of Defense. The 15 prototype vehicles will be subjected to a rigorous testing process and then may become the future trucks for the army. Defense work includes backup power supplies throughout the world and ship service generator sets for the Aegis and Spruance class U.S. Navy vessels.

Since its inception Stewart & Stevenson has been committed to a quality product at a fair price and customer satisfaction. Some S&S customers include NASA and the Texas Medical Center, areas where the tolerance for a power loss is minimal and backup generators must function. It is also critical that service is available 24 hours a day, 365 days a year. S&S will go anywhere anytime, to service its products.

The company has grown because of the dedication of its employees, many of whom have more than 30 years with S&S. Combined with management's open-minded approach and willingness to change and adapt as needed, the future seems limitless. S&S believes the key to continued strength and success is the desire and will to set the pace, not simply follow the crowd.

WILLIAM M. MERCER, INCORPORATED

William M. Mercer, Incorporated, is the largest employee benefits and compensation consulting firm in the United States and in the world. Founded in 1945, the company now has more than 4,000 employees serving more than 9,000 employers from offices in 46 cities in the United States and more than 7,000 employees serving clients from offices in 101 principal cities in 20 countries worldwide.

Although the company is large and diverse, Mercer maintains a strong commitment to provide local service with professionals who understand local problems and issues in each market served. The Houston office, located at 1221 Lamar in downtown Houston, has a staff of almost 100 people, including experts in almost every aspect of employee benefits and compensation concerns, from retirement to health care to salary and incentive compensation issues.

Mercer consultants can assist employers in designing and administering employee benefits, including group benefit programs, flexible benefits, and pension and savings plans that are carefully tailored to suit the needs of the individual client.

An important portion of the Mercer practice in Houston is devoted to assisting companies in managing health care costs, both by plan design and by evaluating and negotiating alternative delivery systems, establishing utilization management and

■ *The professionals at William M. Mercer, Incorporated, are uniquely qualified to provide the finest counsel.*

peer review consulting, structuring and managing health care services, auditing claims, and helping clients set up wellness and preventive programs.

Mercer's compensation consultants will help employers with wage and salary administration, executive compensation and incentives, and compensation surveys and research. The objectives of all Mercer-de-

signed compensation programs are to assist clients in meeting their objectives of rewarding employees for performance and maintaining a strategic competitive position in the marketplace.

One of the most important aspects of human resources consulting is communications. Mercer communications and human resources professionals can assist employers in communicating benefits and compensation programs, in researching and documenting employee attitudes in order to design the best benefits and compensation program for the company, and in human resources planning and development.

Mercer also provides guidance to employers in the funding and financing of benefits and compensation programs through actuarial services, analysis and forecasting of benefit costs, evaluation of funding and investment alternatives, selection and evaluation of investment managers and trustees, and monitoring and evaluation of investment performance.

As more Houston companies expand and establish international operations, Mercer's international consultants can also help in the planning and implementation of compensation and benefits programs for managers and employees working in other countries.

In today's business climate employers are coping with rising health care costs, increasing government regulation, pressure to step up productivity, changing economic and demographic patterns, and changing individual attitudes toward the workplace. Houston employers faced with all of these challenges can benefit immeasurably from the wide range of services and counseling William M. Mercer, Incorporated, professionals provide.

■ *Mercer's Houston office staff of nearly 100 people includes experts in almost every aspect of employee benefits and compensation concerns, and the company can call upon the expertise of its more than 4,000 employees in 46 cities across the United States.*

BROOKS/COLLIER

Since 1977 the architectural, planning, and interior design firm of Brooks/Collier has excelled in the realization of complex projects. The company's founding partners combined years of experience with innovative approaches in targeting the areas of health and education projects.

In the ensuing years Brooks/Collier's substantial expertise and fresh ideas have

■ *ABOVE AND BELOW: The design of medical facilities like the San Jacinto Hospital in Baytown, Texas, makes up an estimated 75 percent of Brooks/Collier's business. Photos by Richard Payne*

proven to be a successful formula. An estimated 75 precent of the firm's business is related to the medical field—a market in which projects are inherently complicated. Attention to detail is essential in these projects, which can range from the addition of a magnetic resonance imaging (MRI) unit to a complete mental health care campus. Brooks/Collier has designed award-winning full-service hospitals, professional buildings, and ambulatory care centers.

Beyond the requisite attention to the technical requirements, the firm approaches the health care environment with the goal of making it less intimidating. After the dramatic advances in technology achieved in recent years, there is a renewed realization of the patient's intangible needs and a commitment to a more humane and less confusing environment.

Brooks/Collier has the expertise required to handle any aspect of a project, sometimes defining and crystallizing the

basic need for a given facility. Clients must look at the initial cost and the long-term operating cost to determine the level of durability they can afford. Brooks/Collier is active in this budget formulation process and in some cases, prepares the financial package for lenders' review.

Once a project has been defined, the firm uses a participative design process, or

user friendly approach, with the people who will be using the space. While the initial work on a project is very client and people oriented, the end phase involves building technology, which is highly regulated in the medical field, and administration of the actual construction.

Educational, commercial, and general institutional work accounts for roughly one-quarter of the firm's business. Brooks/Collier, through a merit selection process, won the distinction of designing the Texas Supreme Court and Attorney General Buildings in the Texas Capitol Complex, including two new office buildings and extensive remodeling of the existing Supreme Court Building, a combined total of 700,000 square feet.

Brooks/Collier has extended its professional portfolio with its ability to work out of a suitcase. Projects have been completed throughout the Southwest, as well as in the states of Virginia and Indiana, as clients relocate and refer their new organizations to the firm. These referrals represent roughly half of Brooks/Collier's volume, a percentage certain to grow in the future.

BUTLER & BINION

Houston, as one of the nation's largest cities, is a hub of private and public enterprise. As that realm has grown more demanding and complex, so have the abilities of the law firm of Butler & Binion. Established in 1941, Butler & Binion has grown to one of the largest firms in the city and one that is respected nationally.

Butler & Binion's practice covers the broad spectrum of civil law. The firm's clients include multinational corporations and leading financial institutions, new com-

panies and sole proprietorships, and public entities and private individuals. With more than 165 lawyers on board, and a total staff approaching 500 people, the firm has the depth of expertise required to competently and efficiently advise its clients. As testament to the abilities of its staff, many attor-

neys have left the firm for the bench, including three federal judgeships.

Since its establishment in Houston, the firm has added offices in Dallas, San Antonio, and Washington, D.C. The Dallas office handles principally corporate and finance work, the San Antonio office handles trial work and general practice, and the Washington office was established to handle energy law and other regulatory matters.

Litigation has always played an important role since the firm's organization; today roughly one-third of the firm's attorneys are involved in litigation. The founding partners were trial specialists, and as the firm's caseload has changed in size and complexity, so have its trial capabilities. Those litigative abilities do not stand alone; they are woven into the fabric that is the whole cloth of the firm's practice.

As its clients' interests and endeavors have changed, so have the skills and specialties of Butler & Binion. A quick tour of law practiced includes admiralty, antitrust, banking, bankruptcy, condemnation, constitutional law, contracts, corporate takeovers, creditors' rights, deceptive trade practices, defamation, environmental, franchising and licensing, fraud, labor, oil and gas, patent, price discrimination, probate, real estate, and trademark issues.

Beyond this broad range Butler & Binion has developed a substantial caseload of insurance defense, including medical and professional malpractice and product liability. Health care clients include hospitals, physicians groups, and medical equipment manufacturers.

Admiralty law is a natural in a city that is home to

■ *Partners in the firm today include (from left) Dan M. Cain, Dallas; Louis Paine, managing partner in Houston; and John K. McDonald, Washington, D.C.*

one of the nation's leading ports. Butler & Binion attorneys specialize in the representation of domestic and international companies that own or charter traditional vessels, along with offshore rigs and drill ships. Attorneys also negogiate maritime transactions and advise clients on a wide range of matters, from cargo transportation and construction to charter of new vessels. Litigation covers everything from personal injuries cases to cargo, collision, and salvage operations.

Throughout a turbulent economic decade in the region, Butler & Binion has developed a tremendous expertise in the areas of bankruptcy and creditors' rights. Not only does this area involve specialized litigation but also the development of effective strategies for the resolution of troubled finances.

The firm's finance and banking attorneys handle a wide range of client interests, including commercial banks and bank holding companies, insurance companies, and other providers of credit. Naturally incorporated within that representation are matters of credit and project financing, regulatory compliance, and mezzanine,

■ *Early senior partners in the firm included (from left) George W. Rice, Frank J. Knapp, William C. Perry, B. Hunter Loftin, and George A. Butler.*

subordinated debt, and leveraged buyout financing. Counsel includes formation, acquisition, reorganization, and sale of various financial institutions.

With any financial matter there are taxes involved, and the firm's tax attorneys often touch upon many of its areas of specialization. While available for a variety of issues, the tax team primarily handles corporate acquisitions and mergers, and reorganizations and dissolutions. Other areas include securities offerings, natural resource and real estate transactions, joint ventures, and licensing and royalty agreements.

These groups work hand in hand with the corporate section, where specialists handle domestic and international ventures, from sole proprietorships to complex organizational structures. Services range from the planning, structuring, and negogiation of major transactions to the full range of financial services a corporate client may require.

Other areas of special expertise include the real estate section, which covers everything from property acquisition and finance, through project development and construction and leasing and sales. Yet another special section (a natural one in the Southwest), the firm's resource specialists provide clients with the counsel they require in the areas of mineral rights—acquisition, development, and sales of those products.

Rounding out the the areas of specialty are the administrative and public law sections, and the intellectual property, or patent, division. Many of the attorneys in the latter are engineers, giving them the expertise required to operate in the field of high technology. Yet another section that has experienced tremndous growth in recent years has been the practice of environmental law.

All these specialties are woven together to provide a blanket of expertise required by clients in today's marketplace. Whatever a client's given need, Butler & Binion has the ability to perform the task at hand with competence and efficiency.

ARTHUR ANDERSEN & CO., S.C.

The name of Arthur Andersen & Co., S.C., is synonymous with strength and professionalism in accounting and consulting services. The Houston office is no exception, standing as the preeminent practice in the market.

The Houston office was first established in 1937, a demonstration of Arthur Andersen's commitment to a "young" city with potential. Arthur Andersen has been part of Houston's phenomenal growth for more than 50 years now and has an historical perspective that is unmatched among its competitors.

When the first office opened its doors, the staff totaled 11 people. That number has grown to more than 1,200 today, making it the largest organization of its kind in Houston—larger than the next two firms combined. The Houston office ranks first in a number of Arthur Andersen categories measured internally and has provided the firm with a number of its leaders.

Arthur Andersen & Co., S.C., is divided into two basic groups: accounting, tax, and financial consulting services, offered

■ *(From left to right) Southwest regional managing partner Von Graham; partner-in-charge of Houston accounting and audit practice Terry Hatchett; and partner-in-charge of Houston tax practice Richard Spivak.*

through Arthur Andersen; and management information and strategic consulting, business integration services, and software sales, offered through Andersen Consulting. Clients are the beneficiaries of the synergy provided by these services, combined with the scope and strength of the entire corporation.

Arthur Andersen is proud of its leadership as auditors and accountants. In this capacity the firm's primary responsibility is understanding the client's business and internal systems. Using its experience, staff identifies risk areas and then evaluates and quantifies those risks. In perhaps the most important aspect of their work, Arthur

helping businesses absorb technology advances and then integrate those advances with the multitude of systems already in place.

But the spectrum of services supplied by Andersen Consulting goes far beyond systems integration. Information and technology planning, systems design and installation, strategic planning, facilities management, and software sales are all part of this consulting practice's scope of services.

Such new areas as Andersen's change management practice are vital services for today's constantly changing corporate environments. Change management professionals assist clients in managing and training their personnel who are dealing with organizational changes, and ensuring that change remains a positive catalyst for growth.

Andersen Consulting has the breadth of skills required to integrate business and technology. The firm can provide the solution—be it strategic planning and systems design and development, facilities management, or hardware and software.

One of the greatest strengths of the Houston office is the foundation provided by Arthur Andersen & Co., S.C., in its entirety—a global organization employing more than 56,000 people in 299 offices located in 66 countries. With a client portfolio numbering almost 100,000, the firm generated more than $4 billion in 1990. Those clients represent an entire range of products and services, needs, and goals. All benefit from the unparalleled scope of Arthur Andersen & Co., S.C.

Andersen people maintain constant communication with clients, reviewing progress, sharing ideas, and anticipating problems.

A critical element to the success of any business venture is a thorough understanding of and compliance with its tax responsibilities. This area of enterprise is marked by constantly changing and increasingly complicated tax codes. Arthur Andersen provides its clients with a team of professionals who are experienced in the full range of tax specialties, from state and local taxes, to ad valorem tax services, to personal financial planning.

Furthermore, the firm provides many special financial services that an organization may require. In merger and acquisition assistance, the firm can construct the financial models and review and research the economics of the deal. For the established business there are productivity enhancement and cost-reduction services for an

■ *Houston Andersen Consulting leaders: (from left to right) consulting managing partner Randell Thomas; partner-in-charge of Houston energy practice Wayne Miers; partner-in-charge of Houston advanced systems Tom Pincus; and partner-in-charge of Houston financial services Jacque Passino.*

improved bottom line. Appraisal and valuation services provide important information in business planning. Compensation planning helps employers offer attractive benefits programs while remaining cost effective in today's changing marketplace. This range of skills provides the tools necessary to help clients achieve their financial goals.

From the beginning of the computer age, the world has seen an information explosion. Since installing the first business computer in 1954, Andersen Consulting has become a global leader in information technology services. Andersen Consulting is

BECHTEL CORPORATION

Bechtel broke ground for its first project almost a century ago. Since then Bechtel has become a giant in the engineering and construction industry. Its massive projects around the globe have earned the company a reputation for excellence and innovation.

In Texas Bechtel has been a presence since 1948. That was the year it began its first project in the state: a 200-mile natural gas pipeline from El Campo to Natchitoches, Louisiana. In a sense, that project was a harbinger of the important role the petroleum and chemical industry would play in Bechtel's growth in this region.

In the ensuing years Bechtel participated in hundreds of projects across the state and region. The corporation opened its first Houston office in 1956 and has provided full and uninterrupted service since that time. In 1989 Bechtel restructured its operations and made Houston one of four regional offices in the country.

The Houston regional office has grown to more than 2,000 employees on site with roughly another 1,000 in the United States who report to Houston. The office also works with international projects and is world headquarters for the corporation's petroleum, chemical, pipeline, pulp and paper, and industrial lines.

Bechtel concentrates all its business lines and all its resources—development, engineering, procurement, construction, and management—into one-stop centers for its clients. While continuing service in the petroleum, chemical, pipeline, nuclear and fossil power, and environmental business, the Houston office has broadened its range of abilities. Those include serving industry, space and defense, mining and metals, air and ground transportation, waste-to-energy, buildings and infrastructure, and water resouces.

Further success lies in Bechtel's ability to remain flexible and look to new markets and technology. Glimpses of that future can

■ *Bechtel is a leading engineering, construction, and management company, serving clients worldwide from its Houston headquarters in the Lake on Post Oak complex. Photo by Jay Coberley*

be found in the dramatic increase in usage and the increasingly sophisticated design found in the telecommunications industry. In Houston the space program and its spinoffs are other areas of tremendous potential growth.

Bechtel project teams in Houston work with leading edge technology, such as Bechtel's own 3 DM and WALKTHRU, to design facilities in three dimensions and review the animated model with project owners. For a chemical plant expansion all piping, civil, and electrical control systems were modeled electronically using the 3 DM system.

One trend that is changing the manner of business for Bechtel is the development of partnerships with some of its major clients. One such association is with Union

Carbide. As with any large operation, Union Carbide's capital expansion has varied dramatically from year to year. Facing a big, annual variable cost and expansion beyond its in-house capability, Union Carbide was looking for someone with whom it could form a long-term relationship. Bechtel signed on with a seven-year, renewable contract. Now the two work toward each other's benefit, with a combined strength not present in either one singly. This association enables Bechtel to better serve the client as well as plan its own future needs.

■ *Chevron Chemical Company's petrochemical expansion included building a normal alpha olefin unit at its Cedar Bayou chemical complex in Baytown, Texas. Chevron Corporation and Bechtel have a long-term alliance in which Bechtel provides engineering, procurement, construction management, and other related services to support a portion of Chevron's capital programs. Photo by Glenn Robichau*

Bechtel has undertaken several such partnerships, usually within the framework of long-term associations. These are more than just the by-product of lengthy association. They are the realization of the need for quality work. Partnerships also help ensure Bechtel employees an unprecedented stability.

The Bechtel organization has transformed to incorporate quality management programs worldwide, with the Houston Regional Office at the forefront. Based on the principles of management consultant W. Edwards Deming, this Commitment to Continuous Improvement program includes all employees in advancing the company's work processes. The quality management approach fosters a participative environment that enables those involved to share their ideas and concerns, resulting in a better product for the customer.

That search for quality led Bechtel to take on a responsibility in the community. Bechtel, along with many in corporate America, has recognized that the key to success lies in reaching, educating, and mo-

■ *Bechtel is proud of its accomplishments as the architect-engineer and construction manager of the South Texas Nuclear plant in Bay City, Texas. The plant is called a model of safety.*

tivating the young. To that end the Houston office "adopted" a high school and

middle and elementary schools. More than 150 employees volunteer their time as tutors, role models, and friends to children who need them most.

Bechtel looks forward to a steady growth as it builds and serves its community, both regionally and globally, throughout the 1990s and beyond.

■ *Patti Carhart tutors a student as part of Bechtel's Business/School Partnership Program with L.T. Cunningham Elementary School.*

McFALL & SARTWELLE

McFall & Sartwelle was established in Houston, Texas, by eight veteran trial lawyers in March 1985. Since that time the firm has maintained its commitment to the representation of its clients in the field of litigation. The firm has grown to more than 35 lawyers who handle virtually every area of civil and white-collar criminal law from the beginning of the case through the appellate process. The firm now includes experienced trial lawyers who joined the firm from the city's largest and most established law firms. The firm intends to grow with the needs of its clients so that it can provide competent and creative representation in the context of the adversary proceeding. The firm fully recognizes that its success depends on the quality and value of the professional services that it gives to its clients. The firm has quickly become a leader in the legal community.

Each client is represented by the entire firm. Yet the firm attempts to provide each client with a smaller team adapted to the particular needs at hand. This approach allows the firm to commit the necessary resources to protect the interests of the client but still maintain a direct line of accountability for the conduct of the case. Because the legal practice is limited to litigation, the firm provides the necessary knowledge, skill, and experiences at a reasonable cost consistent with the nature of the case. The firm respects its clients' time and resources, adapting each team to fit the clients' special needs and business goals.

The firm recognizes that its primary and compelling duty is to present and advocate the position of the client before the court and jury or administrative body in a manner consistent with the bounds of the adversary process and professional ethics. Efforts are directed toward the courtroom in a manner that will achieve results in terms of favorable judgments or reasonable settlements. McFall & Sartwelle also recognizes its duty to the community at large to develop legal precedent consistent with the highest standards and principles.

THE ATTORNEYS
The firm has attracted some of the most effective attorneys in Texas due to its excellent reputation and breadth of practice. These attorneys have attended and succeeded in the country's leading law

■ *Donald B. McFall (left) and Thomas P. Sartwelle.*

schools. One of the firm's founding partners, Eugene A. Cook, was elected to the Texas Supreme Court and serves with distinction as an associate justice of the highest court in the state. Attorneys at the firm lecture frequently at legal and other professional seminars and have written articles for legal periodicals and law reviews. All attorneys are active in bar associations and are members of numerous and various bar committees. Most importantly, the firm's experienced attorneys have tried numerous cases to jury verdicts.

In addition to its legal presence, the firm is heavily involved in community, bar, and political activities. The firm believes that its attorneys must contribute time and effort to improve conditions in Houston and across Texas in terms of education and business opportunities. The firm contributes significantly to charitable and political campaigns and has served as a sponsor at numerous fund-raising events. This commitment to the local community not only has a direct effect on the quality of life in the Houston area but also enhances the firm's effectiveness in its efforts for its clients.

FIRM CLIENTS
Since it began in March 1985, McFall & Sartwelle has been fortunate to represent

numerous clients among the *Fortune* 100 and *Fortune* 500 list of multinational corporations. The firm represents many such companies on both a local and regional basis. The client base covers a wide range of manufacturers, oil-field related firms, financial institutions, health care providers, insurance carriers, and professional service providers. The firm also represents individuals on a regular basis. The firm has the experience and skill necessary to represent the interests of a wide variety of clients in both simple and complex litigation in virtually every field of trial law. The success of the firm to date is reflected in the confidence of the country's leading corporations and business leaders.

Among the regular clients of the firm are ARA Services Inc.; Baylor College of Medicine; Channel Two Television Company; Dresser Industries, Inc.; First Interstate Bank of Texas; General Electric Company; Hospital Corporation of America; Humana Inc.; Lyondell Petrochemical Company; Marmon Group; Memorial Healthcare System; National Medical Enterprises, Inc.; St. Paul Fire & Marine

Insurance Co.; Texas Lawyers' Insurance Exchange; Texas Medical Liability Trust; The Procter & Gamble Company; Travelers Insurance Company; TRW Inc.; and Westinghouse Electric Corporation.

The firm handles nearly every aspect of civil and white-collar criminal trial law. McFall & Sartwelle is well known for its expertise in a wide range of cases. The firm has represented clients in cases involving allegations of professional malpractice, general negligence, environmental and

■ *ABOVE: Pictured here (from left) are Mathew C. Guilfoyle, Donald B. McFall, Thomas P. Sartwelle, and Joseph R. Alexander.*

toxic torts, products liability, civil rights, media law, and all aspects of commercial litigation whether based on theories of contract, tort, or violations of statute. The firm has the background and experience to represent a wide range of clients with their varied and unique litigation problems. This background and experience applies not only at the trial level but throughout the entire appellate process.

McFall & Sartwelle is committed to excellence in the representation of its clients in the judicial and administrative system. This commitment requires hiring and training the most qualified young attorneys available in the legal community. The firm recognizes its duty to provide quality legal representation at a reasonable cost to each and every one of its clients. The firm intends to commit the resources necessary in the years ahead to represent its clients consistent with the highest professional and ethical standards.

HIRSCH, GLOVER, ROBINSON & SHEINESS, P.C.

Hirsch, Glover, Robinson & Sheiness, established more than 20 years ago, has earned a reputation as a civil litigation firm providing top-flight legal representation for the many corporations and entrepreneurs who make up its clientele. From a core group of some of Houston's leading trial lawyers, the law firm has expanded over the past two decades to serve clients with a broad range of commercial needs, including energy, banking, real estate, corporate, and securities law. Those practice areas, and virtually all types of civil litigation, now command the attention of 60 attorneys. The firm is committed to provide its clients with the expertise they expect, and its growth will always be determined by their needs.

Hirsch, Glover, Robinson & Sheiness initially built its reputation on skillful litigation. The firm's subsequent growth in business representation has not blunted the vigor of its trial lawyers, whose frequent trials in Texas courthouses are essential to maintaining the litigation skills needed to achieve the best results for their clients. Areas of particular trial expertise within the firm include product liability and profes-

sional liability lawsuits. The firm represents professionals in the medical, legal, accounting, architectural, engineering, and insurance fields, and it defends several self-insured manufacturers throughout the state of Texas.

General litigation describes many non-notorious but still threatening lawsuits, such as those asserting premises liability, which now often equal product liability claims in their potential for risk to businesses and property owners. Hirsch, Glover, Robinson & Sheiness defends self-insured and insured corporations in lawsuits arising out of accidents, assaults, business torts, defamation, and other torts alleged by physically or financially injured people seeking damages. The firm also defends trucking companies and other common users of vehicles in cases alleging motor vehicle negligence. Less well-known defense work includes the representation of municipalities, counties, and even businesses in civil rights lawsuits.

Houston is home to one of the nation's largest ports, which has resulted in the firm defending the interests of ship owners and marine contractors in many of the circumstances leading to maritime litigation, and in disputes over marine contracts and insurance policies. Gulf coast refining and manufacturing activities have also led Houston courts to regularly address environmental law issues. The firm's environmental section has expertise grounded in the representation of major participants in hazardous waste and toxic tort litigation.

So many liabilities can be insured against, in language so arcane, that the expert interpretation of insurance policies is invaluable to any business. Several of the firm's attorneys concentrate their practices in the interpretation of and litigation over every type of insurance policy, representing both insurers and insureds. The firm's ap-

■ RIGHT: Name partners (left to right) Marc A. Sheiness, Arthur M. Glover, Jr., Jay D. Hirsch, and Iris H. Robinson.

■ BELOW: (Left to right) Paul E. Anderson, Jr., Alan N. Magenheim, Brian M. Chandler, and Jack McKinley.

■ *(Left to right) John W. Belk, James R. Scott, and Robert H. Bateman.*

tors in oilfield litigation.

Real estate practice within the firm embraces all matters related to acquisitions and sales, permanent financing, and landlord-tenant relationships. Firm attorneys are also experienced in handling construction and development needs (including easement and environmental compliance), real estate syndications, foreclosures, and lien enforcement.

Corporate and securities work within Hirsch, Glover, Robinson & Sheiness ranges from routine business representation to more complex corporate and securities transactions. The firm is involved in structuring and forming corporations and partnerships, venture capital transactions, and in drafting contracts ranging from employment to sales to shareholder agreements.

Banking is a field in which the firm regularly represents bank and non-bank clients in the negotiation and preparation of documents such as commercial and bank stock loans, and for the disposition of assets.

Advice for the firm's clients comes, when desired, through seminars and risk-management meetings that keep clients abreast of changes in the law. The firm is widely known for *Legal Insight*, a legal newsletter sent to regular clients, designed to note and comment upon recent significant judicial decisions and legislation. Hirsch, Glover, Robinson & Sheiness recognizes that enjoying success in the practice of law starts, but does not end, with satisfying clients through responsive and high-quality legal representation.

pellate attorneys provide the post-trial expertise that can be essential to getting or keeping a verdict based upon the law.

The firm's energy practice encompasses

■ *(Left to right) John H. Glover, Douglas K. Eyberg, Dayle C. Pugh, David M. Jones, and Gary M. Alletag.*

all aspects of the oil and gas business, including acquisitions, sales, and exploration and production work. Counsel negotiate and draft mineral leases, joint venture and participation agreements, operating agreements, assignments, and easements. The firm also assists in dealing with applicable state and federal regulatory requirements, and defends operators and service contrac-

CRSS INC.

CRSS Inc. is a prime example of a well-managed company that anticipates future demands and maintains a "performance culture" as well as an "obsessive commitment to client service," according to Tom Peters, author of *Thriving On Chaos*. In just over 40 years the company has grown from a small architectural practice into a major multinational enterprise listed on the New York Stock Exchange (CRX), while avoiding the all too common ills of increasing size.

Two Texas A&M University professors, William W. Caudill and John Rowlett, along with a graduate student, Wallie E. Scott, set up shop in 1946 as architects in offices above a grocery store in College Station, Texas, establishing CRS, an acronym of their last names. The three original partners deserve the credit for laying the foundation that has allowed the firm's business philosophy to evolve even to this day. Originally perceived as mavericks, they later won acclaim for the creativity, innovation, risk taking, and dedication to service that came to epitomize their firm. The final "S" was added after the 1983 acquisition of J.E. Sirrine Co., an engineering organization based in Greenville, South Carolina. J.E. Sirrine, also known as an innovator, founded the company which developed into one of the nation's premier engineering design concerns.

The young Texas company achieved national acclaim initially through Caudill's pioneering research and innovative design of educational institutions. His process included the unique practice of "squatting," or taking a team to a site and working closely with the client to overcome roadblocks and research a final design.

During the early 1960s the company began its phenomenal rise through internal growth and acquisition, moving its head-

quarters to Houston and branching out into health care, housing, and corporate design. In 1971 CRSS became one of the first architecture and design firms to go public.

■ *CRSS corporate headquarters in Houston is a startling demonstration of the company's architectural vision.*

Between 1972 and 1983, under the guidance of former chairman Thomas A. Bullock, and since 1983, under current chairman and chief executive officer, Bruce Wilkinson, and president and chief operat-

ing officer, Richard Daerr, the firm acquired several engineering, construction management, and design firms while expanding into international markets.

Following the downturn in the Middle

■ *The company participated in renovation and designed the award-winning Columbia Suites (INSET) in the Astrodome (ABOVE).*

East "mega-projects" market, CRSS focused on pursuing growth markets in which it has special expertise and expanding into new businesses, which draw on its experience in serving clients in the electric utility and pulp and paper markets.

CRSS today comprises various diversified but synergistic groups. A subsidiary, CRSS Services, offers architecture, interior design, engineering, and construction management services. Another subsidiary, CRSS Capital, Inc., owns and operates independent power/cogeneration plants. Banque Paribas, which has provided more than one billion dollars in project financing for the electrical generation industry, purchased a minority interest in CRSS Capital in 1989.

The company has a major stake in the acid-rain pollution control market through a 45 percent ownership interest in NaTec Resources, Inc., which is a full-service environmental company committed to the cost-effective control of pollutants commonly associated with acid rain (nitrogen oxide and sulfur dioxide). Full-scale tests at coal-fired utility plants have demonstrated that NaTec's proprietary dry sodium injection technology simultaneously reduces emissions of both pollutants.

CRSS, through its subsidiary Global

■ *CRSS designed such diverse structures as the Orange County Performing Arts Center in Costa Mesa, California (TOP RIGHT), and IBM's Federal Systems Division building in Clear Lake, Texas (BELOW).*

■ *MIDDLE: CRSS is responsible, in part, for the look of the famous New York skyline. Buildings in the Merrill Lynch World Financial Center are high-profile examples of the work of CRSS.*

facilities, state-of-the-art transportation, pollution abatement processes, and environmentally safe energy production. Through strategic alliances with other world leaders in engineering and design, the company is reemerging in the mega-project category with such projects as the single largest scientific instrument ever: the superconducting super collider, located in Waxahachie, Texas. CRSS Capital has been cited by the Department of Energy for its pro-environment work in cogeneration and clean coal technology, as NaTec was among the first companies with an efficient and inexpensive method to reduce emissions commonly associated with acid rain.

Given its diversified, innovative approach to business and its consistently high ranking on major trade publications' lists of top design and construction management companies, CRSS Inc. is well positioned for growth through the year 2000 and beyond.

CRSS Inc. is building gateways to the future.

■ *ABOVE: The company has its eye on the future. CRSS has almost half ownership of NaTec Resources, Inc., a full-service environmental company committed to the cost-effective control of pollutants commonly associated with acid rain.*

■ *RIGHT: The Hopewell Cogeneration Facility in Hopewell, Virginia, is another of CRSS' projects.*

Capital Group, Inc., is an insurance-industry specialty program underwriter, an outgrowth of a self-insurance operation.

In 1989 CRSS expanded its international reach by launching a joint venture construction management company in cooperation with Mowlem Management, Ltd., a British construction company. The joint venture is taking advantage of new opportunities in Great Britain. In anticipation of the economic integration of the European Common Market in 1992 and considering opportunities in Eastern Europe, similar alliances will be forged for operations on the European continent.

CRSS has its eye on the future—in Houston, in Texas, and indeed all over the world—and is preparing for it by pioneering in many high-tech sectors of the marketplace, including scientific research

RIVERWAY BANK

Tucked away near the heart of The Galleria, Riverway Bank was established in 1982 as an independently chartered institution. Riverway Bank has carved its niche with the mid- to small-size business that seeks quick executive decisions and a personal touch in services rendered.

In the reshuffling of financial institutions during the 1980s, the larger organizations were acquired by out-of-state owners. They moved, en masse, toward retail banking and created a vacuum for mid-range clients, who were left with little contact with those empowered to make executive

■ *ABOVE AND BELOW: Riverway Bank serves local businesses and professionals seeking sophisticated banking services and a greater level of personal attention.*

addition, many services are customized to address specific customer needs. There is no substitution for the level of service Riverway provides.

Because Riverway offers such high level service, it attracts high level accounts. At most financial institutions of comparable size, accounts average $10,000, while at Riverway the average

decisions in money and account matters. Riverway is filling that gap for local business and professionals seeking sophisticated banking services and a greater level of personal attention.

The net result is a service-intensive bank with parking at the door and an institution where tellers are thoroughly trained to handle all types of transactions. Riverway Bank still proofs each individual check signature and processes all data in house. This enables clients to immediately

inspect their account activity should the need arise.

Riverway serves a diverse group of customers, ranging from individuals and corporations to public entities such as school districts and municipal utility districts. In order to meet the varied requirements of its clientele, Riverway offers a wide selection of traditional products, including many types of depository accounts, as well as financial products such as government securities and repurchase agreements. In

account is in the neighborhood of $60,000. The bank's assets are in excess of $125 million, which includes a high ratio of performing loans with a loan to deposit ratio of roughly 40 percent, compared to industry averages of 80 percent.

Riverway attributes its sucess to having an abundance of capital when it was established. As a young bank, Riverway has been quick to react to changing market conditions. Today Riverway Bank is poised for a stable and prosperous future.

STUMPF & FALGOUT

Stumpf & Falgout is a commercial law firm known for its competence, energy, and integrity. Founded in 1978, the firm has grown consistently and conservatively to a staff numbering more than a dozen attorneys with a strong support team. In 1984 the firm moved to its current location in The Galleria area and has since more than doubled its office space.

■ *From left: Daniel K. Craddock and Fred Stumpf.*

Given the highest rating by the Martindale-Hubbell Law Directory, Stumpf & Falgout's practice consists primarily of litigation, corporate, banking, and real estate work. Additional concentrations include estate planning, bankruptcy, securities regulation, oil and gas work, antitrust, and general civil litigation.

Stumpf & Falgout has a broad-based practice for a small firm and is known for its youthful, aggressive lawyers. While that may give some clients pause, it should be noted that a key factor to the firm's success is its recruitment of the very best and brightest for its staff. Clients are won and maintained by the professional competence and energy of their attorneys.

The firm's size belies the strength of its support materials and staff. The library at Stumpf & Falgout is extensive. Furthermore, the firm has invested in state-of-the-art computer systems and maintains the best in network services. Ultimately this combination of expertise and management benefits the client. The firm keeps its focus on each client and its specific needs.

The firm's clients consist of financial institutions, large and small businesses, and individuals. This diversified clientele has engaged the firm to handle cases and transactions involving complex issues in all areas of law and business. Environmental law is a burgeoning area of the firm's practice in which it has consid-

■ *Michael B. Massey (left) and T.J. Falgout III.*

erable expertise, having successfully handled major environmental litigation. In general the law traditionally lags behind the business world in producing decisions affecting current transactions. Thus, a transaction completely advisable today may not be so in the future. Stumpf & Falgout gives vital, up-to-date advice to clients to reduce their potential future liability and to enhance their business opportunities.

Ultimately clients look at three things when they hire a law firm—experience, competence, and service. The firm is confident in its abilities on all fronts. Based upon its age, experience, staff, and expertise, Stumpf & Falgout is in an excellent position to provide quality legal guidance and professional advice to its current and future clients. The challenge is to take these assets and make the most of them, a task that Stumpf & Falgout approaches with confidence and enthusiasm.   *Photos by Ken Childress*

DE LA GARZA
PUBLIC RELATIONS INC.

The information age, coupled with an increasingly complex and global marketplace, has fueled the public relations industry. The de La Garza agency has built a solid reputation working with a variety of clients to provide them with the services that arena demands.

Established in 1982 by Henry A. de La Garza, the firm is now among the top 10 in the city. After an analysis of a client's needs, specific programs are developed to produce tangible results, including the selling of specific products and

professionally and present their message effectively.

A growing market sector for de La Garza lies within the Hispanic community. The firm was never developed as an "Hispanic" business, but it has nonetheless benefited from the increased recognition of the growing Hispanic market. Hispanic-oriented accounts are responsible for 10 to 20 percent of the firm's business. In the past decade de La Garza has grown to become the largest Hispanic-owned public relations firm in the city.

business writer, in corporate public relations for a *Fortune* 500 firm, and as press secretary for the mayor of Houston and also director of communications for the city. His partner, Randy W. de La Garza, practiced law for 10 years as a senior attorney with a natural-gas pipeline and energy conglomerate. Her areas of responsibility included corporate finance and securities, including investor and shareholder relations and employee communications.

Henry de La Garza offers the best summation of the firm's philosophy:

■ (Left to right) Rosalie Ramsden, designer; Randy W. de La Garza, vice president; Henry A. de La Garza, president; and Bill Heinsohn, photographer.

services, telling the client's story, molding public opinion, and shaping government action.

Among the specialized services offered is a comprehensive media training program, designed for corporate executives and others who must deal with the media. The firm offers its clients the opportunity to deal with the media forcefully and positively. Conducted by instructors with a broad range of experience in the field, clients are trained to handle themselves

The secret of the organization's success is easily pinpointed with a look at the experience of the founding partners. Henry de La Garza has an extensive media background established through his work as an award-winning broadcast journalist and

"Good public relations is doing the right things and communicating those actions to the public. Only then can the public understand and support what you're doing. Public relations, therefore, reflects truth and reality. It begins with needed products, services, programs, and policies that serve the public's best interests. Good public relations can never begin too early and, once begun, never cease. It is the reward for a continuing commitment to responsible communications."

HOUSTON HISPANIC CHAMBER OF COMMERCE

As the end of the century approaches, Houston has grown into one of the nation's largest and most dynamic cities. Playing no small role in this growth has been the city's vibrant and diverse Hispanic community. In recent years the strength and importance of the contributions made by this segment of the community have been reflected by the Houston Hispanic Chamber of Commerce.

The inception of the Houston Hispanic Chamber of Commerce can be traced to a

and the significant roles played by Hispanics in Houston business. The name itself was chosen with careful consideration, reflecting the organization's mandate of promoting both business and the city, within the Hispanic world, both locally and internationally.

Since that fortuitous luncheon the Houston Hispanic Chamber of Commerce has grown to more than 500 active members, encompassing a broad range of enterprises, skills, and interests. The chamber serves an unparalleled net-

keeps members up to date on those activities and profiles prominent Hispanics in the community.

An important development has been the chamber's attention to Hispanic youth and what can be done to improve their skills and chances for the future. One offshoot has been participation in an annual careers day for Hispanic students. This symposium provides them not only with important information about the workplace and what they need to succeed in it, but gives the students role models for that

conversation during a lunch meeting in 1976. At that meeting three men accidentally stumbled on the fact that all had been searching, to no avail, for an organization within the city devoted to fostering Hispanic business. George Hernandez, Jr., Leonel J. Castillo, and Manuel D. Leal resolved to fill that void.

A state charter was obtained and the nonprofit corporation was formed with a 15-member board. Those initial board members, and all board members since, were chosen to reflect the variety of commercial enterprise taking place in the city

■ *Standing (from left) Robert M. Tobias, Jr., first vice president, board of directors; Joseph G. Soliz, director, board of directors; and Bill Healy, Windsor Publications. Seated (from left) Barbara Kazdan, executive director, Houston Read Commission; and Dolores Guerrero, chairman, board of directors.*

working role within the city's Hispanic community. Furthermore, the chamber has expanded its role throughout the years to include providing business information, sponsoring seminars, and hosting innovative programs. A bimonthly newsletter

success.

On the other side of the employment issue, the chamber has approached employers to determine what their needs are and how future employees could be better trained.

The decade of the 1990s has been touted as the decade of Hispanics. The Houston Hispanic Chamber of Commerce stands ready to meet the challenges of this decade in fostering not only economic development for its membership, but providing the leadership required to meet the challenges of the future.

PEPPAR & POST

■ *Karen Post visits with a client in Peppar & Post's lobby. Photo by Barry Rudick*

There are two things about Peppar & Post that any prospective client should know. One, the client should expect to be delighted by the unexpected. And two, clients looking for tired, traditional ideas have come to the wrong shop.

Peppar & Post is a full-service advertising and design agency that gets top results with breakthrough creativity, spiced with vitality. Its style is as distinctive as the flavor of Tabasco. Even though each project reflects the client, people familiar with the agency can recognize a Peppar & Post concept or design a mile away. After all, who else breaks all the rules so audaciously, creating new rules that allow the client to win?

"When a new client comes to us, we challenge the conventional approach to its marketing and advertising needs," says

Karen Post, president and creative director of Peppar & Post. "It's not just a creative whimsy, but good business sense; only fresh ideas cut through the clutter to capture attention and distinguish our client from its competitors. For instance, who says that a financial institution can project stability only with the cliché gray flannel look? We can create visual excitement yet still project a trustworthy image."

Peppar & Post's creativity extends to all areas of the agency's services, which cover practically every area of marketing. Post is

personally involved in design and provides direction for a hot-shot team of designers, copywriters, media planners, public relations specialists, strategy wizards, and other professionals. The team enthusiastically tackles everything from product packaging to corporate identity, that may include annual reports and newsletters, to name a few. Their repertoire also ranges from multimedia presentations and speaker support to corporate events, whether sales meetings or employee incentives, to full-scale integrated advertising and promotional campaigns.

There is another thing prospective clients should know about Peppar & Post: they will never hear the word "no." The agency understands that clients sometimes expect the impossible, so it has made a new rule: anything is possible. If it means working all

night to get the job done (and using suppliers who will do the same) or scouring the streets of New York for the perfect antique gramophone for a photo prop, Peppar & Post will do whatever it takes to make sure the client is absolutely thrilled.

That responsive attitude, along with extraordinary talent, is why the agency is where it is today. By now, the story of Post's entry into the industry is a legend in advertising circles. In 1982 she was basically stuffing envelopes for a public relations company when she convinced a new acquaintance that she could handle PR for his business. Post, whose experience was in visual merchandising, gave herself a crash course at the library, persuaded a tabasco sauce company to donate cases of their product, and mailed out bottles of the hot sauce as invitations to an open house. To her own amazement, more than 700 people attended. Suddenly, at the age of 22, she was in business for herself.

By 1985 business had grown so much

that she formed a partnership, Farb & Post, to handle the activity. With Susan Farb Morris providing public relations, Post was free to expand into other fields such as advertising and design. As the company acquired more *Fortune* 500 clients, it added a third partner and became Farb, Post & Martin. In 1990 Post bought out the partnership and renamed the agency Peppar & Post. (Peppar is a Swedish word for a hot pepper, referring to the dynamic staff.)

While some agencies specialize in only one area, such as advertising, public relations, market planning, or corporate events, Peppar & Post is able to channel its expertise into any area of marketing communications. "We're all specialists in certain areas," Post says. "But at the same time each mem-

ber of the staff is a strong generalist, able to apply creative thinking and winning marketing principles to any endeavor to find effective solutions."

With this dynamic synergy and marketing insight, Peppar & Post is poised as one of the most "fast-forward" firms in the region. The agency has doubled in size each year since it was founded in 1985. Before moving into a different category by expanding into a full-service advertising and design firm, the agency earned a place among Houston's top 10 largest public relations firms; today it commands a position in the vanguard of its industry. It has been praised as a "hot shop" by one of the industry's most important journals and won numerous accolades and awards. Post attributes these successes to the firm's corporate culture, where the primary objective is a stimulating environment. Only those with a passion for creative excellence can stand the heat. Peppar & Post has made a new rule: The sky is no longer the limit.

CULLEN CENTER

Houston's first master-planned complex, Cullen Center provides a strategically located base of operations for more than 100 companies downtown. With immediate connections to freeways, mass transit, and downtown tunnel systems, Cullen Center offers an accessibility unequaled in the central business district.

The 3.5 million-square-foot center covers eight city blocks, including four office buildings, parking for 5,400 cars, a hotel, and three sites for future development. Cullen Center houses a daily population of 6,000 people involved in a diversity of businesses, such as energy, finance, law, accounting, insurance, government, and high technology.

Inside Cullen Center are the conveniences essential to business at its best: hotel accommodations, catering and meeting rooms, restaurants, retail stores, barber shops, dry cleaners, and a car wash. The center also has financial and commer-

■ *Cullen Center anchors the southwestern corridor of Houston's central business district. The center is a 3.5-million-square-foot development situated on eight city blocks.*

cial printers, post offices, access to YMCA fitness center, banks, gift shops, a florist, a travel agency, secretarial services, and microfilming. For tenants, Cullen Center's concierges provide a variety of services from travel arrangements to discounted event tickets.

Cullen Center began in 1948 when oilman/philanthropist Hugh Roy Cullen acquired four acres in downtown Houston just west of the YMCA. Through the years the center, owned by Cullen Center Inc., has expanded to 14 acres.

Hugh Roy Cullen dropped out of school at age 12 and went to work to help support his family. He established himself as a cotton broker, traveling throughout Texas and Oklahoma. After several years of successful cotton trading in Oklahoma, Cullen decided it was time for a change. With his characteristic self-reliance he moved his wife, Lillie Cranz Cullen, and family to Houston, which he believed would become one of the

world's major cities.

His first encounter with the oil business was as a lease man in West Texas. It was his job to acquire leases from farmers and ranchers for future drilling rights. For three years, he drilled wildcat wells in West Texas, eventually acquiring a reputation for bringing in wells where others had tried and failed. His long struggle for success began to be realized.

The Hugh Roy and Lillie Cranz Cullen success story would not be complete without recognition of their philanthropic achievements. Following the development of their Quintana Petroleum Corporation as an established oil company, the Cullens became increasingly involved in community activities. Their support of Houston's charitable and educational institutions became legendary. During their lifetimes the Cullens contributed 93 percent of their fortune to charitable causes. Cullen wanted to see his money spent during his lifetime so that he could enjoy observing the good that it did.

The Cullen family has developed the remaining assets of the estate with the same vision and energy that brought success originally. When Cullen Center was launched in 1959, the $100-million project was dedicated to the late Hugh Roy and Lillie Cranz Cullen. At that time the Cullen

■ *The 20-story 500 Jefferson building was the first to be constructed in Cullen Center. The impressive 372,563-square-foot structure is located on Jefferson at Smith in downtown Houston.*

■ *1600 Smith is the landmark building of Cullen Center. The 55-story tower is a prominent feature of the downtown skyline.*

■ *M.W. Kellogg Tower is a 40-story, 999,141-square-foot office building at Jefferson and Louisiana in Cullen Center.*

land was the largest singly owned, undeveloped tract in the central business district. The original plan called for three office buildings and a hotel. The first phase began with the ground breaking for the 500 Jefferson Building, a 20-story building with an attached 300-car garage.

The Whitehall Hotel, a 276-room hotel, was completed next. The third structure built in the complex was the 600 Jefferson Building, a 20-floor office building with 525-car garage.

In 1971 Cullen Center joined forces with Dresser Industries Inc. to announce the center's tallest building to date, the 40-story M.W. Kellogg Tower. At its completion M.W. Kellogg Tower was the third-tallest building in the city; its 1,600-car parking garage was the largest privately owned parking facility in Houston.

A decade later Cullen Center added another tower to the skyline: 1600 Smith. A joint project with The Prudential Property Company, 1600 Smith has 1.1 million square feet in 55 stories and an attached 3,000-car garage. Since its completion in 1984 the building's lighted dome has become a landmark in the Houston skyline.

During the past two decades Cullen Center has attracted the backing of three major investment partners. Dresser Industries Inc., a diversified manufacturer of energy and industrial products, ventured the development of Dresser Tower with Cullen Center. The Prudential Insurance Company of America, through its subsidiary, The Prudential Property Company, invested in the 1600 Smith project in 1981. In addition, Cullen Center is affiliated with another financial partner, Trizec Properties Inc., a subsidiary of Trizec Corporation Ltd. of Canada. With more than $9 billion in assets, Trizec Corporation is one of the largest real estate investment firms in the world.

Cullen Center has evolved as a vital part of the community, drawing downtowners and visitors alike to its art exhibits and concert performances. The art shows alone have attracted 20,000 visitors to Cullen Center since 1985. By maintaining Cullen Center Park and extensive landscaped plazas, the center provides a welcome respite downtown. Following the footsteps of its founder, Cullen Center continues to give something back to the city that Hugh Roy Cullen so strongly believed in.

■ *600 Jefferson is a 20-story, 419,699-square-foot building in Cullen Center downtown. The project includes an attached 525-car garage and skywalk access to other Cullen Center buildings.*

SHEINFELD, MALEY & KAY

Sheinfeld, Maley & Kay, a Professional Corporation, was founded as a general partnership in 1968. Incorporated in 1989, the law firm has witnessed the city's explosive growth and has been a partner in the challenges and changes faced by Houston's business community.

Sheinfeld, Maley & Kay has developed as a commercial firm with a wide range of client representation in the areas of commercial litigation, real estate, corporate, securities, tax, and banking. These sections, developed initially as a complement to the firm's recognized expertise in business reorganization, have since built their own reputation for excellence.

Litigation is an area of the law that has burgeoned in recent years. The firm's practice includes a wide variety of cases, primarily commercial disputes that involve lender liability, business torts, insurance defense, insurance coverage, real estate, and contract work, along with oil and gas work, deceptive trade practices, bankruptcy, banking, environmental law, fraud, and white-collar criminal claims. Litigators appear in all level and range of courts.

The real estate and banking sectors of Houston's economy experienced some of the greatest growth as well as the greatest decline in the city's recent economic history. Sheinfeld, Maley & Kay responded to those changes and has developed strong commercial lending and real estate sections. Lawyers handle the range of realty matters involved in the purchase, sale, and development of industrial, commercial, and residential property. Their counsel is also provided in matters of joint ventures, partnerships, and syndications. On the lending front the firm's practice includes representation in financing an array of transactions, including commercial lending, as well as lending for mortgage and construction. Other work involves equipment leasing, equity participations, and general bank credit transactions.

Sheinfeld, Maley & Kay's practice of securities, corporate, and partnership areas starts with entity formation, which encompasses capitalization and related shareholder agreements. Subsequent work includes the generation of capital, via private placements to registered offerings, along with maintenance and governance

services, as well as handling mergers and acquisitions, and asset transfers.

Tax is an area of the law in constant change and one that requires diligent attention. The firm's work covers all areas of federal income taxation as it affects individuals, partnerships, and corporations. This can mean tax planning for the preservation and utilization of attributes, particularly in reorganizations. The firm also

represents its clients in adversarial proceedings, whether with administrative branches of the treasury department or in court.

Sheinfeld, Maley & Kay has a well-deserved reputation for excellence in the sophisticated practice of business restructure and reorganization. Handling the legal ramifications of business insolvency formed the foundation of the firm's

practice.

Long recognized as the largest Houston firm in the practice of business reorganization, Sheinfeld, Maley & Kay has developed one of the largest such practices in the nation. Moreover, the firm is unusual in handling both creditors and borrowers. Ultimately the client is the beneficiary as attorneys, skilled in both aspects of reorganization, have the expertise to protect their client's interests.

The firm represents both public and privately held companies, individuals, and partnerships, and a range of financial institutions, including banks and savings and loans. The practice covers the wide array of legal and financial matters pertaining to business restructuring.

As the firm has grown and expanded its practice, the experience of insolvency work has contributed to the acumen of all sec-

tions within the firm. The expertise helps attorneys in business practice and in helping clients plan for the potential of down-

turns. In the past business deals were not as structured as they have since become. Recent experience has sharpened the focus and attention of clients and their attorneys in planning business ventures.

Today attorneys attempt to anticipate problems for their clients and structure business deals accordingly. The expanded practice of Sheinfeld, Maley & Kay gives the client expertise in a wide range of areas required for successful realization of commercial ventures.

The past decade has seen Sheinfeld, Maley & Kay grow into a firm approaching 80 attorneys in size. In 1984 the firm opened an office in Dallas, and it opened another in Austin in 1987. The firm looks forward to a decade of controlled and consistent growth as it continues to strengthen its reputation as a leader in the practice of commercial law.

FERGUSON, CAMP & HENRY, P.C.

Ferguson, Camp & Henry, P.C., was established in 1977 to provide quality personal service to entrepreneurial companies and individuals. Today, as big accounting firms get bigger, it continues to focus on serving privately owned businesses and their owners.

The firm knows that every company, regardless of size, emerging or established, has its own unique problems and special needs. Its professionals work closely with its clients to know and understand their operations, their industry, and their needs. The firm stresses being business advisers first and accountants second.

Ferguson, Camp & Henry, P.C., provides a full range of accounting and audit services, tax planning and compliance services, and personal and business consulting services.

Good financial decisions start with good financial accounting. Every business owner needs accurate financial information in a timely, cost-efficient manner. The firm

■ *Pictured here are (from left) Fran Williams, Paul Kurt, Sharon Henry, John Camp, and Patrice Ferguson.*

enjoys an excellent reputation for the quality and competency of our accounting and auditing practice.

Taxes are a significant cost to businesses and individuals. With the ever-changing federal tax code, the firm constantly monitors the effects that new legislation, regulations, and tax cases will have on its clients and their businesses. Ferguson, Camp & Henry goes beyond compliance; it offers a full range of tax planning services for both businesses and individuals. The firm's strength lies in personalized service by professionals with broad-based knowledge and expertise. By working closely with its clients, the firm can formulate a strategy that will improve their tax position not only today, but years down the road.

In today's dynamic business world, owners and managers are faced with many challenges. As entrepreneurs themselves, the firm knows what it means to need financing, to have accurate management information timely, to know not only where a client's business is profitable, but also to know where it is not. Today, the firm and its clients must deal with competition, diminishing resources, increasing globalization, and fluctuating oil prices, and interest rates.

The firm's goal is to be the client's closest adviser. The key to the firm's ability to meet this goal is the quality of its staff and their genuine desire to assist its clients in accomplishing their business and personal goals and objectives. The professional staff at Ferguson, Camp & Henry, P.C., have a complete technical understanding of accounting, audit, and tax issues. They are technicians through education and by training; they are business advisors through experience and by choice.

14

QUALITY OF LIFE

Medical and educational institutions along with nonsecular organizations contribute to the quality of life of Houston-area residents.

■ *Photo by Mark E. Gibson*

HOUSTON NORTHWEST MEDICAL CENTER

■ *Houston Northwest Medical Center.*

Houston Northwest Medical Center (HNMC) is a full-service, tertiary care medical center located one mile west of Interstate 45.

A major medical complex, Houston Northwest Medical Center has more than 1,450 employees, a medical staff of more than 400 independent physicians, and 494 beds, including 70 beds in its women's hospital, The Women's Atrium.

The Women's Atrium, a 70-bed women's hospital, diagnostic center, and health care facility that opened in July 1989, is just one of a long line of advancements and developments throughout the 17-year history of HNMC.

First opened in 1973, HNMC has grown to become one of the largest health care facilities outside of the Texas Medical Center. Advanced services include open heart surgery, balloon angioplasty, intermediate care (telemetry), medical and surgical intensive care units, a cancer treatment center with bone marrow transplants and linear accelerator, dialysis, an outpatient surgery center, and a pediatric intermediate care

unit. Advanced services in The Women's Atrium include a neonatal special care unit with 24-hour neonatologist.

Other specialized services in HNMC include a medical psychiatric unit, a skilled nursing facility, pediatrics, an endoscopy department with endoscopy suites, a 24-

hour emergency department, and The Women's Atrium.

Advanced diagnostic services include MRI, nuclear medicine, CT scan, and The Women's Diagnostic Center in The Women's Atrium.

Houston Northwest Medical Center attracts thousands of patients each year from more than five counties, including Harris, Montgomery, Walker, Waller, and Liberty counties. It continues to be the busiest, most comprehensive, and fastest-growing medical facility in north Houston.

The Women's Atrium is connected to the medical center via the atrium lobbies of the two facilities. Services in this women's hospital include inpatient medical care, surgical care for selected procedures, cosmetic surgery, obstetrics, gynecology, and diagnostics.

The second floor is devoted to obstetrics with labor/delivery/recovery suites, high-risk observation rooms, private and semi-private postpartum rooms, VIP suites,

■ *The Women's Atrium, which opened in July 1989, is a 70-bed women's hospital, diagnostic center, and health care facility.*

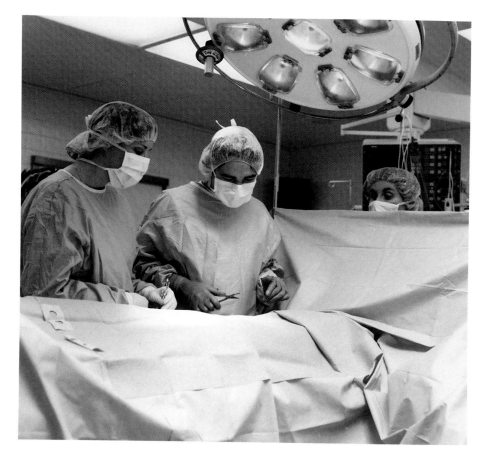

"Concerning Women[SM]." Ongoing classes, health forums, and activities highlight the "Concerning Women[SM]" calendar. The conference center has meeting rooms for groups from 10 to 100.

Amenities of The Women's Atrium include the Personal Touch Beauty Shop, spas with a Jacuzzi on each floor, a deli with extended hours, and a long list of services that includes massage therapy.

Opened in 1984, the Heart Center in Houston Northwest Medical Center provides progressive cardiac care. This includes cardiac catherization, balloon angioplasty (PTCA), digital angiography, special vascular procedures, open heart surgery, nuclear cardiology, laser vascular surgery, intensive postoperative cardiac care, coronary care, and inpatient and outpatient rehabilitation programs.

Important to these services is the 24-hour emergency department, which provides advanced services, including advanced cardiac life support systems and the use of tissue plasminogen activator (+-PA) for patients who benefit from this advancement in emergency cardiac care.

Houston Northwest Medical Center recently opened Texas Tower Satellite, an outpatient center in a nearby physician office building. This satellite provides convenient testing service for patients who see physicians in adjacent office buildings. Services at the center include X ray and a drawing station for laboratory work-ups. Additional services to be offered at the satellite are being planned.

Outreach services of HNMC continue to grow and include an active physician referral service, the Heart Center Speakers Bureau, cancer and other support groups, and an active hospital auxiliary.

well-baby nurseries, an admitting nursery, a neonatal special care unit with 24-hour neonatologist services, operating rooms with recovery for cesarean births, and private family waiting.

The first floor of the facility includes private and semi-private medical/surgical patient rooms, VIP suites, a diagnostic center, a fitness center, a deli, administrative offices, admitting offices, and an education/conference center.

The Women's Atrium Diagnostic Center, located on the first floor, provides mammography, bone densitometry (used for diagnosing osteoporosis), and ultrasound. The center provides education as well as diagnostic testing.

The Women's Atrium is also home to The Women's Fitness Center, a fitness facility just for women. Staffed by degreed professionals, the fitness center provides exercise classes and equipment for a wide

range of fitness levels and abilities. There are also certified prenatal and postnatal exercise specialists on site.

The Education Conference Center is the focal point of an active educational program created by The Women's Atrium called

■ *The Women's Fitness Center provides exercise classes and equipment for a wide range of fitness levels and abilities.*

MEMORIAL HEALTHCARE SYSTEM

Houston is known worldwide for its oil companies, its architecture, aerospace industry, and expansive, entrepreneurial attitude. But for many people who are ill and in need of treatment, Houston means quality health care. From open-heart surgery to transplants to cancer detection and treatment, Houston's health care institutions have led the way in modern medical advances, setting international standards for patient care, education, and research. In this atmosphere of medical excellence, the Memorial Healthcare System has grown to become one of the city's preeminent providers of quality care.

The Memorial Healthcare System began in 1907 as a modest 17-bed facility. Its founder was the Reverend D.R. Pevoto, an assistant pastor at Houston's First Baptist Church, who recognized an urgent need for a quality hospital and committed himself to making that idea a reality. His instincts proved correct. Demand for the hospital's services quickly grew, and within three years the Baptist Sanitarium, as it was then called, had increased its capacity by 50 beds. Though separated from the Baptist Church in 1972, the Memorial Healthcare System remains a nonprofit organization. The purpose and values with which it was founded have not changed, nor has its tradition of focusing on the individual patient's needs.

The Memorial Healthcare System's commitment to the community has shaped and defined its growth. In the early 1960s, when the city's population began moving to the suburbs, Memorial Hospital started one of the nation's first hospital satellite systems, bringing quality, cost-efficient care and innovative medical services to neighborhoods where people live and work. Proof of the success of that decision is in the numbers. Outside the medical center Memorial has 92 percent of Houston's not-for-profit hospital beds, treating more than 150,000 patients annually.

Through its three full-service hospitals, all strategically located near major population centers, the Memorial Healthcare System offers patients comprehensive primary and specialty care that includes treatment of cardiovascular disease, orthopedics, cancer, diabetes, emergency medicine, family practice, ophthalmology, physical medicine and rehabilitation, women's health, otorhino-

■ *Dan S. Wilford, chief executive officer.*

laryngology, plastic surgery, geriatrics, neurology, internal medicine, and psychiatric care.

Memorial Hospital Northwest at Loop 610 North and Ella Boulevard has 175 beds. Memorial Hospital Southeast, with 275 beds, is located in the South Belt-Ellington community, and Memorial Hospital Southwest, a 600-bed facility, is located in southwest Houston at the inter-

section of U.S. Highway 59 and Beechnut. A comprehensive ambulatory care facility located in Sugar Land, just outside the city limits, extends Memorial's services into the outlying communities of southwest Houston.

Memorial channels all its excess revenues toward new and better facilities and equipment and expanded programs. This, together with Memorial's assertive management posture, has allowed the organization to maintain its position as one of the country's leading providers of community medicine, providing quality care at the lowest possible cost to the patient.

In response to recent developments in the health care industry, such as rising costs and resulting changes in insurance programs and payment, Memorial continues to seek ways to improve the quality and scope of its services while helping patients, physicians, and employers control their health care expenditures. More than 60 percent of Memorial's surgery business, for example, is now done on an outpatient

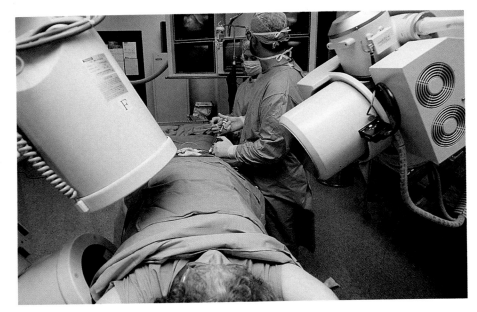

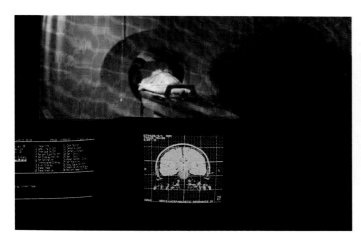

basis, providing a convenient cost-effective alternative for thousands of patients.

Memorial Health Ventures, Inc., is an umbrella for several for-profit subsidiaries that support Memorial's nonprofit mission and provide innovative alternatives in health care. HealthNet, Memorial's own preferred provider organization, allows employers to control costs by designing their own health benefit packages. Partners National Health Plan allows Memorial to expand its benefits to employers and employees through an integrated multiple option that combines a health maintenance organization, preferred provider organization, and indemnity insurance. Memorial Home Health offers skilled nursing, physical therapy, speech therapy, occupational therapy, and medical social services to patients at home, helping them bridge the gap between hospitalization and recovery.

In addition, Memorial has made a major commitment to providing high-quality, cost-efficient health care in rural areas throughout south Texas. Memorial's rural affiliates have access to consulting services, total management contracts for complete hospital operation, and group purchasing agreements, as well as clinical and technical services.

The Memorial Healthcare System's planning department closely monitors trends in the industry to find new opportunities to serve Houstonians. Memorial Women's Health Services schedules educational seminars to help women make sound health care choices. A number of educational classes are also offered, including diabetic classes, CPR, smoking cessation, weight control, and Lamaze classes. A physician referral service helps patients select skilled medical care for all their family's needs. Another remarkable service is Health-Line, a consumer tape library with

messages on a multitude of health problems.

Memorial Senior Services is a direct result of Memorial's attention to the aging of America. In 1984 Memorial became the first health care organization in the city to provide an array of health programs to older Houstonians. Memorial 55+ is a free program providing Medicare and insurance assistance, wellness classes, physician referrals, streamlined hospital discharge, and an extended payment plan. An outgrowth of Memorial 55+, Memorial's annual Senior Concerns Seminar gives older adults an opportunity to hear physicians' advice. University Place, the city's first hospital-affiliated retirement community, offers residents an active life-style and a full social calendar. The Memorial Geriatric Evaluation and Resource Center has also been established to help older adults identify and resolve problems and adapt to the challenges of aging.

As Memorial enters a new decade of community service, providing quality medical care and developing the management systems and procedures to support that care remains paramount. A five-year-old program called Partners in Caring allows Memorial to work closely with members of the board, medical staff, and employees to improve already high standards and deliver excellent service with understanding, compassion, and concern. At the Memorial Healthcare System there is a renewed dedication to the purpose and values of the organization. By being a patient-focused, market-oriented, diversified health care organization, the Memorial Healthcare System will continue to expand its programs and services and provide the finest in community health care through the 1990s and beyond.

■ *Memorial Senior Services is the result of looking at future trends, specifically the aging of America.*

HOUSTON COMMUNITY COLLEGE SYSTEM

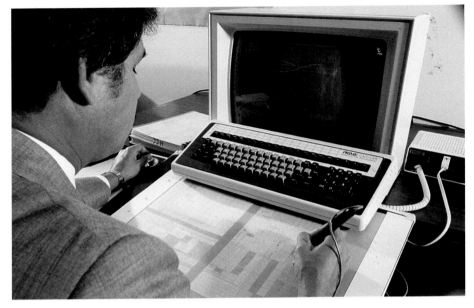

■ *Designers and drafters are gaining a competitive edge in the marketplace by mastering the latest technology in the college's computer-aided drafting program.*

As the city diversifies its economy to meet the challenges of the twenty-first century, the Houston Community College System will continue to play an essential role in providing the professional resources that will be required to do so.

HCC was established in 1971 by the voters of the Houston Independent School District when it became apparent the city was facing a growing need to provide postsecondary education. Prior to the inception of HCC, the city was the only of one its size lacking a public provider of occupational and technical education. In 1989 HCC separated from the school district to begin a new phase in its continuing expansion.

Proof of that expansion is in the numbers. Since 1971 the system has had a total enrollment of more than a half-million students, making it the third-largest community college in Texas today. More than 24,000 people are enrolled in HCC's adult-literacy program. In addition, the college has received a $17-million grant from the Texas Education Agency to provide educational services to the 35,000 adults who received eligibility status under the federal amnesty program.

The reasons for the success story are plentiful. First and formost is an extensive curriculum with more than 100 programs to select from. They run the gamut from accounting to welding, fashion design to paramedic training. Those courses are taught by a dedicated faculty of several hundred, all of whom have extensive experience in their fields.

The college plays a vital role with its user friendly approach. It lures the students who have realized advancement requires education. It nurtures the mother returning to the work force. It aids the displaced worker in finding a new career. And it polishes the skills of professionals required to upgrade their training in a changing marketplace.

More than 65 percent of enrollment is comprised of those students returning for continuing education in their professions, due to the strong ties that HCC has always maintained with the business community. Good illustrations of these ties can be found in the maintenance training for the Metropolitan Transit Authority, all of which is conducted by HCC. In addition, the college also provides microcomputer training to employees of Texaco Marine Services, now essential with the computerization of shipping. In a sense HCC caters to the marketplace by developing the specific curriculum required by the business community. HCC has the facilities and faculty to handle the job.

When companies relocate they transfer key people and look to its new community for most of its employee recruitment. Houston must have a well-trained employment base in order to lure that new growth, and HCC is providing that talented pool of employees. Beyond that, Houston Community College plays a critical role as the institution that ensures education for the community, thus serving the city as a whole.

■ *The Houston Community College Fire Academy trains firefighters to meet the needs of fire departments that serve the greater Houston area.*

TEXAS CHIROPRACTIC COLLEGE

Texas Chiropractic College is one of 15 acredited chiropractic colleges nationwide and only two statewide. People are usually surprised to learn that it is the second-oldest such institution in the United States. Established in San Antonio in 1908, the college has been in continual operation since then. In 1965 the college moved from its original site to a location 25 miles from downtown Houston in Pasadena, Texas—home to the 18-acre campus ever since.

The college has continued to expand, adding classrooms, a library, auditorium, cafeteria, and an outpatient clinic that provides last-year students with the opportu-

ited institution, with the majority of course work in the sciences. Once accepted, their curriculum is a rigorous preparation for the practice of chiropractic as a primary health care profession. Away from class, students can take their pick from a wide range of social and professional organizations or simply enjoy the campus pool and volleyball courts.

Innovative programs have been developed. One program enables students to participate in mock trials as expert witnesses. Qualifying interns may participate in six-week observational rotations with the Hermann Hospital Department of Orthopedics. The college is the only one

■ ABOVE: Students at Texas Chiropractic College attend lecture sessions in modern, well-equipped classrooms.

■ LEFT: The Learning Resource Center houses classrooms, laboratories, faculty offices, the Mae Hilty Memorial Library, and the bookstore.

that offers a preceptorship program to all students.

"Today Texas Chiropractic College stands strong as a nonprofit institution dedicated to the mission of providing high-quality education," says Dr. S.M. Elliott, president. "A talented and dedicated faculty, modern facilities, and a commitment to excellence supports the strong professional curriculum."

Texas Chiropractic College is accredited by the Council on Chiropractic Education and Southern Association of Colleges and Schools and is recognized by the Federation of Chiropractic Licensing Boards.

■ RIGHT: Interns treat the general public during the three trimesters they function in the outpatient clinic. Taking and reading X rays are only part of the skills fine tuned during this time.

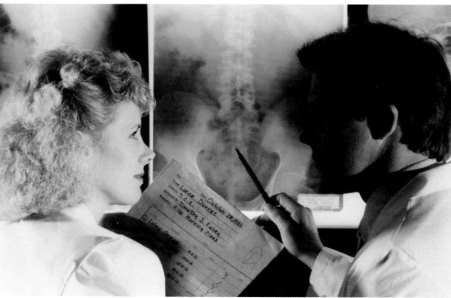

nity for internship. The latest addition to the clinic is a computerized tomography (CAT scan) unit. Keeping abreast of the latest technology is essential in the training of students, as well as Doctors of Chiropractic, who need to maintain their state licenses.

Students may pursue degrees in Doctor of Chiropractic, or the bachelor of science in human biology. Operating on a trimester system, the college enables most students to complete their training in three and one-third years. All students applying must have completed 60 semester hours at an accred-

ST. LUKE'S EPISCOPAL HOSPITAL

At St. Luke's Episcopal Hospital quality is no accident. Providing patient care that is not only clinically excellent but compassionate has been the hallmark of St. Luke's since it opened in August 1954.

St. Luke's has become one of the nation's preeminent hospitals by knowing its purpose: to provide quality, cost-effective care while advancing clinical expertise through education and research. St. Luke's has earned a reputation for quality that is reflected in the synthesis of the human touch and state-of-the-art technology. This quality has become the inimitable signature of St. Luke's Episcopal Hospital.

The 949-bed St. Luke's Episcopal Hospital provides the community with an important health care resource, offering its patients unparalleled services and technology. Patients hospitalized there span the spectrum from the low-risk obstetrics patient who spends only 48 hours in the hospital to the patient with multiple problems requiring the depth of expertise available only at such a tertiary care facility.

With two dozen clinical services covering more than 40 specialties, St. Luke's has earned a position of leadership in the world-renowned Texas Medical Center and an international reputation among referring physicians and patients alike. Patients from throughout Texas, the United States, and from more than 60 countries have come to St. Luke's to be treated by experts in a number of fields, including cardiovascular surgery, high-risk obstetrics, orthopedics, hand surgery, and urology.

St. Luke's serves physicians-in-training as well. Affiliations with Baylor College of Medicine, The University of Texas Medical School at Houston, and the Texas Heart Institute (THI) enable St. Luke's to provide residents with guidance from clinical experts and experience in technologies that enhance every aspect of their medical training.

The majority of St. Luke's active staff holds faculty appointments at Baylor and/or The University of Texas, and most are board certified in a medical specialty. Since physicians on staff fully integrate their teaching and clinical practice, St. Luke's affirms its dedication to medical education while maintaining its independence as an institution whose primary focus is patient care.

The St. Luke's medical staff is made up of nearly 1,400 community-based and academic specialists, many of whom are known internationally. These physicians are at the core of our outstanding patient care. And St. Luke's employees are also among the finest in health care—proud of what they do and of the care they provide.

■ *For both patients and physicians, the new 29-story, twin-spire tower is one of the most convenient and user friendly medical facilities ever designed.*

The trend-setting Division of Nursing, for example, has earned St. Luke's Episcopal Hospital national recognition as a

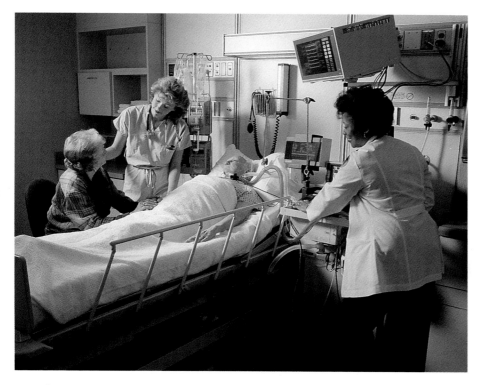

■ *In the high-tech environment of St. Luke's intensive care units, family interaction and support are important parts of a patient's recovery process.*

center for nursing innovation. Through its shared governance, collaborative practice model, clinical ladder, nursing support services department, and continuing education opportunities, nursing at St. Luke's has attained a professional status that is seldom achieved. Few, if any, nursing departments in the country can claim as many innovations in leadership—as well as clinical and technological advances—as this dynamic and dedicated group of people.

St. Luke's medical and nursing services are strengthened by outstanding support services that include pharmacy, pathology, respiratory services, radiology, nuclear medicine, physical medicine, nutrition services, social services, pastoral care, patient services, and information services. A staff of more than 3,000 technical and support personnel, more than 1,100 nurses, and 250 volunteers provide direct patient care or support services for the approximately 31,000 adult inpatients, 8,000 outpatients, 19,000 emergency room patients, and 3,000 newborns seen annually at St. Luke's.

St. Luke's has long been the site of dramatic advances in medical care, and its association with THI has provided the opportunity for many of these innovations.

Founded by Denton A. Cooley, M.D.,

in 1962, the Texas Heart Institute is one of the world's leading centers for the study and treatment of cardiovascular disease. Its successes have brought national and international patients to St. Luke's.

The Texas Heart Institute's heart transplantation program is one of the largest and most successful in the nation. THI and St. Luke's have participated in such historic milestones as the first successful cardiac

transplantation in the United States, the first human implantation of a total artificial heart, the perfection of treadmill tests, the refinements of pacemakers, the use of disposable oxygenators and nonblood priming for open-heart operations, the use of non-invasive nuclear techniques, improved medication for high blood pressure, and treatment of heart disease with calcium blockers and antiarrhythmic drugs.

These two institutions have also been on the forefront of technology in using percutaneous transluminal coronary angioplasty (PTCA), a technique using a balloon catheter for dilating the coronary artery to increase blood flow, and in using lasers to widen peripheral and coronary arteries blocked by atherosclerotic plaque. With a range of experience no other facility can match, more open-heart procedures, heart transplants, and cardiac diagnostic procedures have been performed here than at any other institution in the world.

The Texas Heart Institute and St. Luke's Episcopal Hospital rank as world leaders in nonsurgical therapies. With the

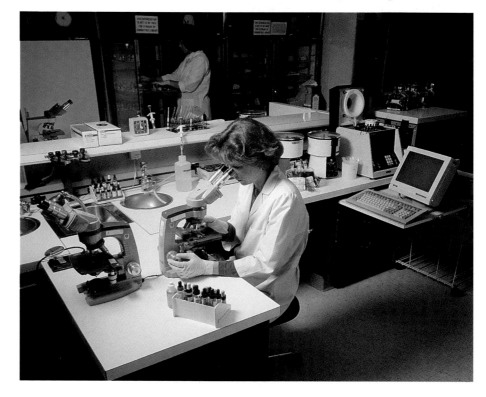

■ *The blood bank is one of the many professional support services that strengthen St. Luke's medical care.*

opening of its expanded Cardiac Catheterization Laboratory in the fall of 1988, St. Luke's Episcopal Hospital became the home of the premier cardiac catheterization facility in the world. With a capacity for more than 10,000 procedures a year, this lab has no equal in size or level of sophistication. A pioneer in laser-assisted angioplasty for coronary and peripheral vessels, the St. Luke's cath lab sets the pace for the future of cardiac intervention.

The 36,000-square-foot laboratory is designed for optimum efficiency of operations and patient flow and includes two research labs, five interventional labs, and three double-tabled swing labs. The swing labs, a classic example of St. Luke's leadership in engineering and design, promote cost savings and efficiency by permitting one imaging unit to swivel overhead be-

■ *In the Noninvasive Adult Cardiology Laboratory, patients undergo routine treadmill testing in conjuction with nuclear medicine imaging, a procedure that evaluates the distribution of blood flow to the heart and helps determine the nature of cardiac disease.*

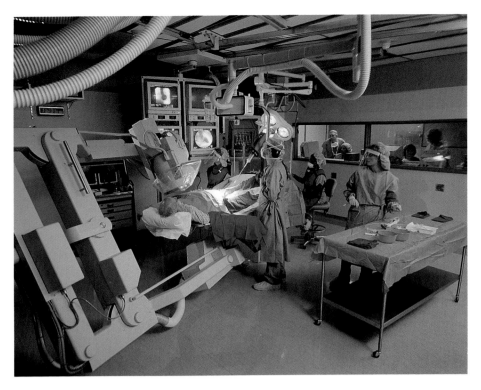

tween two identical treatment tables, allowing staff to examine one patient while preparing for another, thus increasing patient capacity per unit by more than 50 percent. With full integration of the helistop, operating rooms, cath labs, emergency center, intensive care units, and coronary care units, surgical and medical backup for cardiac patients is only a heartbeat away.

St. Luke's Cardiac Catheterization Laboratory is an essential part of the full-service

■ *The cath lab, which is equipped to treat more than 10,000 patients each year, sets the pace for the future of cardiac intervention.*

cardiac care that St. Luke's Episcopal Hospital and the Texas Heart Institute provide. It is also one more example of the comprehensive, quality care that patients receiving treatment at St. Luke's have come to expect.

Though St. Luke's has been both a partner and a pioneer in cardiac care, it has also attracted public attention for many other innovations in the areas of internal medicine, nuclear medicine, general surgery, obstetrics and gynecology, urology, orthopedics, and hand surgery. Because St. Luke's employs the most advanced imaging tools—ultrasound, magnetic resonance imaging, computed tomography, and nuclear imaging—patients have come to expect the very best in both diagnosis and therapy. Everything—from an integrated computer system that supports laboratory, pharmacy, and dietary ordering and tracking systems, to manned satellite pharmacies on each nursing floor—is geared toward comprehensive patient care.

As the trend from inpatient to outpatient care continues, the facilities in which these treatments and procedures are carried out must be clinically effective and efficient. A new 29-story medical office tower supports this health care trend by allowing physicians both the latest in communication linkages and easy access to their patients and hospital services.

Designed by world-renowned architect. Cesar Pelli, the medical tower with its twin

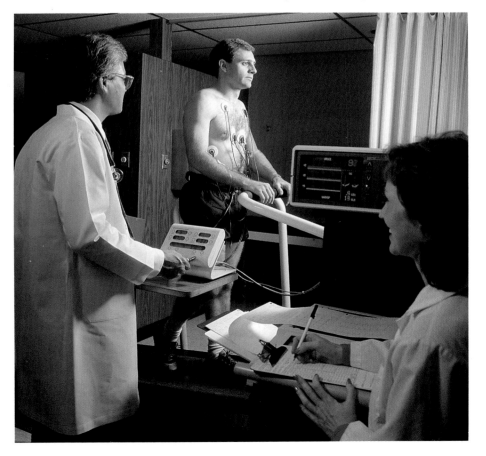

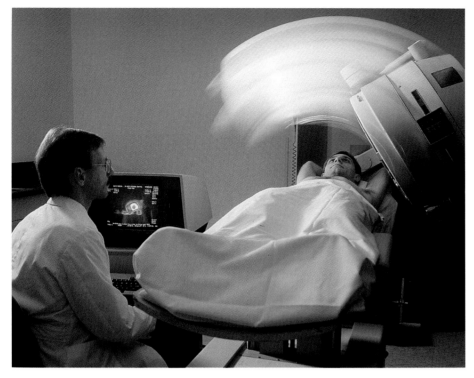

spires is destined to be a Houston landmark. It contains more than one million square feet of office, hospital, retail, and parking space, making it one of the largest medical professional buildings in the world. Not only is it one of the most architecturally striking medical buildings in the country, but also—through its ambulatory center and electronic communications with the hospital—one of the most convenient and "user friendly" medical facilities ever designed for patients and their physicians.

The tower also houses the outpatient services of ambulatory surgery, radiology, laboratory, endoscopy, physical therapy, occupational therapy, cardiology, urodynamics, and community health education. A skybridge connecting the tower to the hospital allows convenient access for physicians and patients alike.

In addition to providing a full spectrum of outpatient services and diagnostic laboratories, St. Luke's offers the following clinical services: anesthesiology, cardiovascular anesthesiology, cardiovascular surgery, emergency center, family practice, general surgery, hand surgery, internal medicine, neurology, neurophysiology, neurosurgery, newborn and premature, nuclear medicine, obstetrics and gynecology, ophthalmology, oral and maxillofacial surgery, orthopedic surgery, otolaryncology, pathology, physical medicine and rehabilitation, plastic surgery, radiology, transplantation, and urology.

And when inpatient or outpatient hospital services are not the answer, St. Luke's

home care department supports the trend toward providing as much care as possible outside the hospital walls. The department is fully staffed by registered nurses who make visits to area patients in their homes and to out-of-town patients in their hotel rooms. They coordinate a wide range of patient care, including nutritional counseling, social services, medications, physical therapy, speech pathology, and other services.

Consistent with St. Luke's emphasis on wellness of the total individual, the hospital offers a wide variety of services and programs designed to help the community take positive steps toward better health. From community-wide health screenings and health fairs to an active speakers bureau and physicians referral service, these programs are an integral part of St. Luke's commitment to quality health care.

The mission of St. Luke's Episcopal Hospital has changed very little during the life of the hospital. There has been no need. The emphasis on providing quality health care has always been the cornerstone of its purpose. Patients needing medical care have come to expect the very best of what the medical world has to offer. At St. Luke's Episcopal Hospital their expectations are met.

HOUSTON'S FIRST BAPTIST CHURCH

Few institutions have witnessed and been party to as much Houston history as First Baptist Church. The church was first chartered on April 10, 1841, in the new Republic of Texas. Since the organization of those first 20 members, First Baptist has seen its membership grow a thousand-fold and today is generally recognized as the largest church in the city.

In 1972 church members voted to move from downtown to the current site, located on more than 12 acres at Loop 610 and the Katy Freeway. A spacious and state-of-the art facility, the church hosts more than 5,000 members each Sunday. Scores of classrooms provide plenty of places for Sunday school and the myriad other activities offered to members and guests. Furthermore, First Baptist Church has remarkable broadcasting facilities that extend the church's abilities and ministry.

■ *First Baptist Church Houston at 7401 Katy Freeway.*

■ *John R. Bisagno, pastor of Houston's First Baptist Church.*

An integral part of First Baptist's growth has been the leadership of its pastor, Dr. John Bisagno. Unanimously elected by the church leadership in 1970, Bisagno has given the church a vision and role in responding to the challenges and needs unmet in today's society. A leader with a willingness to try new ideas, Bisagno imbues his staff and congregation with confidence and a measure of his loving and positive attitude.

Among his visions is the outreach of the church to the unmet needs encountered in society. The church has developed an expansive outreach ministry, having established 28 mission churches throughout the greater metropolitan area. These missions, often located in apartment complexes, care for the spiritual needs of communities from a variety of ethnic and socioeconomic back-

grounds, with services in a host of languages.

First Baptist Church has extended its spiritual outreach by developing its broadcast ministries. A phenomenal outgrowth has been the church's annual Christmas pageant. Featuring what has become a cast and crew in the hundreds, this pageant began in 1970. It has grown to become a part of many Houstonians' annual Christmas traditions and 45,000 people now view one of its many performances. Countless thousands more watch the annual broadcast on a local network affiliate. Today "Pageant: A Christmas Spectacular" is syndicated to more than 55 markets, three countries, and three cable networks.

While some might be intimidated by the size of Houston's First Baptist Church, members form lasting associations through the church's Sunday school programs. The church has continued to expand its ministry to meet a variety of needs, including diet, health, addictions, youth ministry, and groups for single, married, elderly, divorced, or widowed people.

Photo by Charlene Faris

15
MARKETPLACE

Houston's service industries and facilities offer both residents and visitors the finest in accomodations.

■ *Photo by Bob Rowan/ Progressive Image*

MARRIOTT WEST LOOP– BY THE GALLERIA

Nestled among business skyscrapers less than a mile from the heart of Houston's "second downtown," the Marriott West Loop–By The Galleria is a full-service hotel, with an emphasis on service. One of the hotel's biggest selling points is its location, three blocks from the city's premier shopping district and just off the Loop, which gives it tremendous accessibility.

The hotel is midway between both airports, five miles from downtown and the Astrodome, seven miles from the Texas Medical Center, and less than two miles from the city's lovely Memorial Park.

By definition, full-service implies everything travelers needs to make their trip a

successful one. The hotel industry is a competitive one where innovations are quickly copied and trends develop rapidly. Since most hotels offer roughly the same amenities, the business edge belongs to those who can deliver the best service. As general

manager Siamak Djalali says, "Service sells a hotel. It's the bread and butter of the industry."

This Marriott must be thriving: 50 percent of its guests have stayed here before, and based on the results of their voluntary

■ *ABOVE: With more than 300 rooms and many special features created with the business traveler in mind, Marriott West Loop-By The Galleria is conveniently located between both airports and five miles from both downtown and the Astrodome.*

■ *RIGHT: The Marriott West Loop features a fully equipped health club with an indoor pool and full exercise room, in addition to a hydrotherapy pool, sauna, and outdoor sundeck.*

■ *Dining options at the Marriott West Loop include a complete restaurant, a lounge, room service, and even outside catering.*

survey, 94 percent of the guests rate the service as excellent. But service is not the only seller here; the hotel itself is a big part of the picture.

Guests have more than 300 rooms to choose from. In addition to the standard choices, Marriott also offers quarters for the traveler's special needs.

A perfect example of tailoring one's product to the changing market is the First Lady Queen rooms. Developed in response

■ *Recently opened and among the first of its kind in a hotel, as well as in the immediate area, the Punch Line Comedy Club lets guests unwind and enjoy live entertainment without leaving the hotel.*

to the growing number of traveling female executives, these rooms are located immediately next to the elevator, thus eliminating a long walk down the corridor. The rooms' standard features include hair dryers, full-length mirrors, an iron and ironing board, and bathsheets in lieu of regular towels.

The Glass Palace, a five-story glass atrium, is a big plus for this hotel. The soaring space lends itself to any function, including the many weddings held there. The adjacent health club offers a wide range of activities: everything from indoor pool to a full exercise room, with the five-station Pro Master gym, stationary bicycle, rower and treadmill, in addition to a hydrotherapy pool, sauna, and outdoor sundeck.

Along with the Glass Palace the hotel has a newly renovated Grand Ballroom: 5,000 square feet that either can be divided into five separate meeting areas or seat up to 400 people for dinner. Almost another 4,000 square feet of meeting space is also available.

Dining options include a complete restaurant, a lounge, room service, and even outside catering. Recently opened and among the first of its kind in a hotel, as well as the imme-

diate area, the Punch Line Comedy Club gives guests a chance to unwind or entertain without going out. It also brings in nonguests and gives them an opportunity to get to know the hotel and staff.

The hotel business is a good way to monitor the pulse of an economy. In 1988 hotels in the area experienced a 7 percent increase in occupancy, a good reflection of the steady improvement in what had been a downturn.

With almost 400 hotels nationally the Marriott name needs little introduction to the traveling public. There are seven full-service Marriotts and two Residence Inns in the greater metropolitan area, representing a strong commitment in Houston.

For those unfamiliar with the history of the Marriott corporation, it is the quintessential American success story. Beginning in 1927 with an A&W root beer shop in Washington, D.C., the corporation has grown to become a giant in the hotel and food service industries.

Within its hotel business, Marriott has five distinct operations. In addition to the full-service hotels familiar to most, the corporation also has a level of compact hotels, which differ only in their slightly smaller, more compact size. These are traditionally located in secondary cities.

There are also The Courtyard Hotels by Marriott, with extended amenities designed for the economy-minded business traveler. The All Suites group is just that: a facility composed of independent suites. There's also the Residence Inns chain, which is a combination of the All-Suite product and the Courtyard format. Finally, there is the Fairfield Inn chain, dedicated to the budget-minded traveler.

Going beyond business, Marriott has a commitment to the community. In 1989 more than 300 Houston employees participated in the March of Dimes Walkathon. The corporation has also designated the Children's Miracle Network for sponsorship. Beyond this, Marriott by the Galleria is a member of Houston Proud, the Houston Chamber of Commerce, and a multitude of community associations.

J.W. MARRIOTT HOTEL

saunas, steam room, and a whirlpool. Taken with the indoor/outdoor swimming pool, and the racquetball and tennis courts on site, the hotel provides its guests with plenty of options for un-winding.

Beyond the amenities for its guests, the J.W. Marriott has more than 35,000 square feet of meeting space. Adjacent to the hotel is the 20,000-square-foot exhibition center. Within the hotel, the ballroom itself is 9,000 square feet, and is one of the largest and finest in the Galleria area. The remaining 10,000 square feet is spread throughout various meeting rooms.

Backing up these meeting areas is a staff with the expertise to deliver exactly what the function requires, from society events to business conferences. The food-service staff excels at making each event a special occasion.

The J.W. Marriott is a leader in the city in general and in The Galleria area in particular. The hotel industry was not immune when the city's revenues declined, but occupancy rates are now on the rise and stabilizing. The city has worked hard to meet the challenge and promote itself and the qualities of its facilities.

That the Marriott corporation believes in the strength of the city is evidenced in the number of operations it maintains here. Including the J.W. Marriott, the firm has five Marriott-managed hotels and two franchise operations. It is one of the largest providers in the food-service industry as well. Coupled with its other chains, such as Residence Inns, Marriott provides the traveling public with a tremendous cross section of resources.

Those resources extend to its operations as well. In the case of the J.W. Marriott, the moment it became a Marriott operation,

Across the street from one of the finest shopping centers in the Southwest in metropolitan Houston is the J.W. Marriott Hotel. Built in 1983, the hotel came under Marriott management in December 1988. Both the Marriott organization and the investor saw a beautiful facility in a good and growing market.

Built as a luxury hotel, this is one of only four Marriotts given the J.W. designation: one is in Century City, Los Angeles; one is in Atlanta, Georgia; and the flagship hotel is in Washington, D.C. Guests can look forward to a cut above the already high standard of excellence the Marriott group prides itself on.

The hotel has 482 beautifully appointed rooms, including several on the concierge level. These rooms provide guests with a concierge who can assist them in whatever is necessary to ensure they have a successful

■ *The J.W. Marriott Houston is a luxury hotel with 482 beautifully appointed rooms and 35,000 square feet of meeting space.*

stay—from opera tickets to floral deliveries. Guests also have access to a lounge on that floor where complimentary continental breakfast is served in the morning, and hors d'oeuvres are served in the evening. This gives the traveler a quiet place to unwind and often the opportunity to exchange ideas with others in business.

In conjunction with the concierge level is the set of suites with extra amenities such as bathrobes, hair dryers, ironing boards, and a special consideration for comfort. The J.W. Marriott also has an executive health club in house with exercise equipment, men's and women's locker rooms,

the organization's network kicked into place. The hotel was immediately linked with the Marriott reservations system, and managers from the reservations group visited the hotel personally in order to better understand the facility. The newsletter that goes to members of Marriott's frequent traveler program featured an insert detailing the new hotel and its amenities.

The Marriott philosophy of doing business has always included its employees. Their motto is: take care of your employees

■ *Across the street from one of the finest shopping centers in the Southwest, the J.W. Marriott Hotel has the finest amenities including an executive health club, an indoor/outdoor pool, racquetball and tennis courts, and a professional staff.*

and they'll take care of your guests. The organization's resources extend to all its employees, and Marriott provides them with the opportunities to excel and rise within

the corporation. Many of the firm's top managers today have worked their way through the ranks, with some having started their careers as food-service attendants.

That membership in a larger organization gives the J.W. Marriott Houston the reputation and the responsibility that has made the Marriott organization what it is—a commitment to service with attention to detail and a striving to exceed their guests' expectations and establish consumer loyalty.

THE WYNDHAM WARWICK &
THE WYNDHAM GREENSPOINT

Loving care was taken in the restoration of the lobby's Portuguese marble floors and the crystal chandeliers. A priceless Aubusson tapestry, woven in France almost 300 years ago, depicts the story of Diana, goddess of the moon, hunting, and action. These are just some of the wonderful pieces that adorn the Wyndham Warwick and preserve its heritage.

All of the hotel's 300-plus rooms were freshly painted, redecorated, and the bathrooms were modernized. Among standard features are remote-control television and clock radios, and hair dryers and coffee makers are available. Supplementing these are the services standard in a first-class hotel: a concierge, safety deposit boxes, business services, a hair salon, and gift shop.

One area that has long been a favorite of guests is the pool and its environs. This has been expanded to include an exercise group, along with saunas for men and women. Tennis, raquetball, and varied health equipment is readily available at a nearby health club.

The Wyndham Warwick offers its guests a variety of options in dining. The Hunt Room, a richly paneled, intimate room, is

■ *The Wyndham Warwick*

■ *The Wyndham Warwick main lobby.*

The Wyndham Warwick is a luxury hotel located in what is one of the nicest spots in Houston—adjacent to the Museum of Fine Arts, overlooking Hermann Park, with a grand view down Main Street, where oaks form a canopy as they line the boulevard.

Originally built in 1926, the Wyndham Warwick was purchased in 1988 by the Begemann Group. Wyndham Hotels and Resorts joined the venture in 1989 and assumed the management of the hotel. The commitment was made to restore the hotel to its glorious tradition, as well as adding the modern amenities essential to a world-class hotel and filling the expectations of today's traveler. This landmark reopened on November 15, 1989, and reclaimed its stature as one of the city's grandest hotels.

Among the major changes was a complete renovation of the lobby area. The registration area was moved, a concierge desk was added, and bar was built off the lobby.

■ *The Wyndham Warwick offers functional meeting space with spectacular views.*

the place for fine dining at lunch and dinner. The Café Vienna is the spot for informal breakfast, lunch, and dinner. The lobby lounge offers a splendid view of the Museum of Fine Arts and the fountains, making it a perfect meeting place. To complement these choices is a fine room-service menu offered 24 hours per day.

The Wyndham Warwick has increased its options to serve guests by creating better meeting space. The renovations converted some vendor and commercial space to expanded group facilities. The Warwick also added a beautiful ballroom to the 12th floor by converting what had been the Warwick Club. The end result is a ballroom that was booked solid during the month immediately following the hotel's reopening in November 1989. The hotel is now better designed to handle larger groups and meetings.

Beyond its physical beauty there are few words to describe the convenience of the Wyndham Warwick's location. It is, simply, ideal. The Texas Medical Center lies within a half-mile, the downtown business district is within five minutes, and the hotel is at the heart of the museum district.

The Warwick is the latest commitment by the Wyndham group to the hotel business in Houston. The city's northwest sector has experienced tremendous growth, and the Wyndham Greenspoint is centrally located within this thriving area—just 10 minutes from the Intercontinental Airport and across the street from Greenspoint Mall and its 175 stores.

In contrast to its cousin downtown, the Wyndham Greenspoint is a contemporary 15-floor building with a 45-foot atrium serving as the focal point with its dramatic glass skylights and lush landscaping. With almost 500 hotel rooms, each of which is equipped with the best in guest amenities, the Wyndham Greenspoint can handle a variety of business needs. For the discerning traveler the hotel offers its concierge-level floor. For all its guests the Greenspoint provides the level of service expected in a Wyndham hotel.

A state-of-the-art athletic facility offers a pool and sauna, and the adjacent Greenspoint Club has a running track, racquetball and squash courts, and Nautilus weight-lifting equipment for the complete workout.

Dining and entertainment options range from the Atrium Café, which as its name implies provides informal dining nestled among the foliage, to the ambience of the sidewalk café found at Alfresco Dining Pavilion. The Bay Tree Ristorante offers lunch and dinner menus specializing in the cuisine of northern Italy. An intimate lounge, Crucible, is the perfect place for entertaining with cocktails, and dancing.

Both the Wyndham Warwick and the Wyndham Greenspoint are owned by the Trammel Crow Company, long known as one of the nation's largest commercial and residential realtors. The Wyndham Hotels and Resorts subsidiary has become one of the fastest-growing hotel management companies within the industry, operating more than 20 luxury hotels in 14 U.S. cities and three Caribbean islands.

■ *The Wyndham Warwick junior suite.*

ADAM'S MARK
HOTEL

Located in the Westchase Business Center, the Adam's Mark is among Houston's best hotels. It is a secret it wants to share with those who have not yet experienced the hotel's service.

The Adam's Mark, which is Houston's second largest hotel, hosts 604 well-appointed rooms that open up to a dramatic 10-story atrium. But more than a large quantity of rooms make the Adam's Mark a delight. Most visible are the number of places to meet and dine. Guests may choose the Fountain Court, located on the atrium level among the fountains, trees, and *Checkmate*—the bronze sculpture by Herb Miguery. They might prefer Quincy's, Houston's hottest high energy night club, or Pierre's, a quiet lounge with live entertainment complementing a romantic ambience.

For fine dining featuring American western cuisine, there is the Marker, whose reviews, and those of its chef, have been glowing. On the lighter side is the Pantry on the Plaza, a cozy sidewalk café.

The Adam's Mark has 31,000 square feet of meeting space. The Exhibition Center, with almost 15,000 square feet, has the capacity for 100 booths and their infrastructure. The Grand Ballroom can accommodate almost 1,000 people for banquets and 1,100 for receptions. In addition, there are a variety of break-up rooms, adjacent to larger meeting spaces, and 49 suites. Combined, these cover most of the requirements the business client demands.

The Adam's Mark has the largest hotel climate-controlled year-round indoor/outdoor pool, a Jacuzzi, sauna, and health club. The hotel is minutes from a tennis and racquetball club, along with three public golf courses. Services available include same-day laundry and cleaning, notary public, and Fax machine. Next door is the Carillon Center, filled with restaurants, Spellbinder's Comedy Club, and much more.

Locale might not have been an impetus to its success, but the continued growth in the Southwest, coupled with the completion of the city's outer beltway, have put the Adam's Mark in an enviable position. It is seven minutes from The Galleria for easy visits, and four minutes from Fame City. The 1,000 free parking spaces are

■ *ABOVE AND BELOW: The Adam's Mark, located in Houston's Westchase Business Center, hosts 604 well-appointed rooms that open up to a dramatic 10-story atrium.*

another plus.

Since its opening in 1980 the Adam's Mark has successfully targeted the national convention market. Today's meeting planners are very sophisticated and are looking for the best in service at a reasonable price. The Adam's Mark Hotel has been on the mark in providing what they need. Future plans call for aggressive marketing on the state and local level, along with the social market.

BIBLIOGRAPHY

Brown, Thomas E. and Scott Miller. *Layman's Guide to Oil & Gas Investments and Royalty Income.* Houston: Gulf Publishing Company, 1985.

Buenger, Walter L. and Joseph A. Pratt. *But Also Good Business—Texas Commerce Banks and the Financing of Houston and Texas, 1886-1986.* Texas A&M University Press, 1986.

Feagin, Joe R. *Free Enterprise City.* Rutgers University Press, 1988.

Fehrenbach, T.R. *Lone Star.* American Legacy Press, 1983.

Harris, Phyllis. *Houston's Gallery of Architecture.* Houston Chapter of the American Institute of Architects, 1989.

Houston: A Profile of its Business, Industry and Port. Pioneer Publications, Inc., 1982.

Jankowski, Patrick. "Houston's 150 Years: A Persistence of Visions." *Houston Magazine,* January, 1986.

McAshan, Marie Phelps. *A Houston Legacy.* Hutchins House of Houston, 1985.

McComb, David G. *Houston: A History.* University of Texas Press, 1981.

Meinig, D.W. *Imperial Texas.* University of Texas Press, 1969.

Nevin, David. *The Texans.* Time Life Books, 1975.

Orban, John III. *Money in the Ground—Oil and Gas Investments Explained.* Oklahoma City: Meridian Press, 1985.

Pratt, Joseph A. *The Growth of a Refining Region.* Greenwich, Conn: JAI Press, 1980.

Presley, James. *Saga of Wealth—The Rise of the Texas Oilmen.* Texas Monthly Press, 1983.

Sibley, Marilyn McAdams. *The Port of Houston, A History.* University of Texas Press, 1968.

Texas Comptroller's Office. "Economic Outlook for Houston and the Gulf Coast Region." June 28, 1989.

The 1986-87 Texas Almanac. Dallas: A.H. Belo Corp.

The 1988-89 Texas Almanac. Dallas: A.H. Belo Corp.

von der Mehden, Fred R., ed. *Ethnic Groups of Houston.* Rice University, 1984.

NEWSPAPERS
The Houston Chronicle
The Houston Post

PERIODICALS
The Houston Business Journal
Texas Monthly

PATRONS

The following individuals, companies, and organizations have made a valuable commitment to the quality of this publication. Windsor Publications gratefully acknowledges their participation in *Houston: Gateway to the Future.*

Adam's Mark Hotel★
AIM Management Group Inc.★
S.C. Arthur Andersen & Co.★
Barwil Agencies (Texas) Inc.★
Bechtel Corporation★
Brae Burn Construction Company★
Brooks/Collier★
Butler & Binion★
Chevron Companies★
Computel Business Communications★
CRSS Inc.★
Cullen Center★
de La Garza Public Relations Inc.★
The Dow Chemical Company★
Emily Investments Inc.★
Entex★
Ferguson, Camp & Henry, P.C.★
Fluor Daniel Inc.★
Global Marine Inc.★
Hirsch, Glover, Robinson & Sheiness, P.C.★
Houston Chronicle★
Houston Community College System★
Houston's First Baptist Church★
Houston Hispanic Chamber of Commerce★
Houston Lighting & Power Company★
Houston Northwest Medical Center★
Houston Shell and Concrete Company★
Houston Ship Repair Inc.★
Kerr Steamship Company, Inc.★
KHOU Channel 11★
K-NUZ AM/K-QUE FM★
KZFX Z-107 FM★
McDonnell Douglas★
McFall & Sartwelle★
J.W. Marriott Houston★
Marriott West Loop-By The Galleria★
Memorial Healthcare System★
William M. Mercer, Incorporated★
Peppar & Post★
Pioneer Concrete Of Texas★
Port of Houston Authority★
Riverway Bank★
St. Luke's Episcopal Hospital★
Sheinfeld, Maley & Kay★
Sterling Chemicals, Inc.★
Stewart & Stevenson Services, Inc.★
Stumpf & Falgout★
Sunbelt Hotels, Inc.★
Texas Chiropractic College★
Universal Weather and Aviation, Inc.★
Wholesale Electric Supply Co.★
The Wyndham Warwick & The Wyndham Greenspoint★

★Participants in *Houston: Gateway to the Future.* The stories of these companies and organizations appear in chapters 9 through 15, beginning on page 148.

DIRECTORY OF CORPORATE SPONSORS

Adam's Mark Hotel, 258
2900 Briarpark Drive at Westheimer
Houston, TX 77042
713/978-7400
Steven J. Musatto

AIM Management Group Inc., 203
11 Greenway Plaza, Suite 1919
Houston, TX 77046
713/626-1919
C.T. Bauer

Arthur Andersen & Co., S.C., 212-213
711 Louisiana, Suite 1300
Houston, TX 77002
713/237-2323
H. Devon Graham, Jr.

Barwil Agencies (Texas) Inc., 182
1235 North Loop West #1000
Houston, TX 77008
713/862-5575
Gilbert Nilsson

Bechtel Corporation, 214-215
3000 Post Oak Boulevard
Houston, TX 77252
713/235-3547
Cindy Delulio

Brae Burn Construction Company, 172
6655 Rookin Street
Houston, TX 77074
713/777-0063
Timothy A. Pixley

Brooks/Collier, 209
3131 Eastside, Suite 100
Houston, TX 77098
713/520-9990
Robert A. Brooks

Butler & Binion, 210-211
1600 First Interstate Bank Plaza
Houston, TX 77002
713/237-3111
Louis Paine

Chevron Companies, 198-199
1301 McKinney
Houston, TX 77010
713/754-2285
Mickey Driver

Computel Business Communications, 202
2500 Central Parkway R-2
Houston, TX 77092
713/686-3456
Julie H. Williams

CRSS Inc., 220-223
1177 West Loop South, #900
Houston, TX 77227-2427
713/552-2093
Phyllis K. Winn

Cullen Center, 230-231
1600 Smith, Suite 4800
Houston, TX 77002
713/951-6100
Robert Skinner

de La Garza Public Relations Inc., 226
24 Greenway Plaza, Suite 1405
Houston, TX 77046
713/622-8818
Henry A. de La Garza

The Dow Chemical Company, 196-197
400 West Sam Houston Parkway South
Houston, TX 77042-1299
713/978-3647
Mary Jane Mudd

Emily Investments Inc., 176
6666 Harwin Drive, Suite 190
Houston, TX 77036
713/789-5753
Emily Guillen

Entex, 166
Post Office Box 2628
Houston, TX 77002-7345
713/654-5100
Benny M. Hill

Ferguson, Camp & Henry, P.C., 234
1800 Bering Drive, Suite 950
Houston, TX 77057
713/783-5200
John Camp

Fluor Daniel Inc., 170-171
One Fluor Drive
Sugarland, TX 77478
713/263-2039
Jan Kelly

Global Marine Inc., 192-193
777 Eldridge
Houston, TX 77079
713/596-5832
J.C. Martin

Hirsch, Glover, Robinson & Sheiness, P.C., 218-219
917 Franklin at Main
Houston, TX 77002-1779
713/224-8941
Stephanie Glover Burke

Houston Chronicle, 162-165
801 Texas Avenue
Houston, TX 77002
713/220-7525
Robert F. Thomas

Houston Community College System, 242
22 Waugh Drive
Houston, TX 77007
713/869-5021
Charles A. Green

Houston's First Baptist Church, 248
7401 Katy Freeway
Houston, TX 77024
713/957-6740
Thomas J. Williams

Houston Hispanic Chamber of Commerce, 227
601 Jefferson, #2320
Houston, TX 77002
713/759-1101
Juanita B. Shihadeh

Houston Lighting & Power Company, 154-155
611 Walker
Houston, TX 77001
713/229-7124
Stephen Gonzales

Houston Northwest Medical Center, 238-239
710 FM 1960 West
Houston, TX 77090
713/440-2480
Linda Smith

Houston Shell and Concrete Company, 178
5111 Woodway
Houston, TX 77001
713/621-8510
J. Dan Nixon

Houston Ship Repair Inc., 188
Box 489
Channelview, TX 77530
713/452-5841
Edward T. Motter

Kerr Steamship Company, Inc., 183
2 Northpoint Drive, Suite 9000
Houston, TX 77060
713/931-2500
Charles Weihe

KHOU Channel 11, 158-159
1945 Allen Parkway
Houston, TX 77001-0011
713/521-4317
Garen Van de Beek

K-NUZ AM/K-QUE FM, 160-161
4701 Caroline
Houston, TX 77004
713/523-2581
Davis Morris

KZFX Z-107 FM, 156-157
3050 Post Oak Boulevard, Suite 1100
Houston, TX 77056
713/968-1000
John R. Dew

McDonnell Douglas, 150-151
5301 Bolsa Avenue
Huntington Beach, CA 92647-2048
714/896-1300
Tom Williams

McFall & Sartwelle, 216-217
909 Fannin, Suite 2500
Houston, TX 77010
713/951-1000
Al Machemehl

J.W. Marriott Houston, 254-255
5150 Westheimer
Houston, TX 77056
713/961-1500
Bradley A. McCreedy

Marriott West Loop-By The Galleria, 252-253
1750 West Loop South
Houston, TX 77027
713/960-0111
Marie Hayes

Memorial Healthcare System, 240-241
7737 Southwest Freeway, Suite 200
Houston, TX 77074
713/776-5484
Dan S. Wilford

William M. Mercer, Incorporated, 208
1221 Lamar Street, Suite 1200
Houston, TX 77010
713/951-0060
Scott C. Sustmam

Peppar & Post, 228-229
520 Post Oak Boulevard, Suite 350
Houston, TX 77027
713/623-6161
Judi Martin

Pioneer Concrete Of Texas, 173
800 Gessner, Suite 1100
Houston, TX 77024
713/468-6868

Port of Houston Authority, 184-187
1519 Capitol Avenue
Houston, TX 77252
713/226-2153
James D. Pugh

Riverway Bank, 224
Five Riverway
Houston, TX 77056
713/552-9000
Deborah J. Parker

St. Luke's Episcopal Hospital, 244-247
Texas Medical Center
6900 Fannin, Suite 540
Houston, TX 77030
713/791-4375
Dan Wise

Sheinfeld, Maley & Kay, 232-233
1001 Fannin Street
Houston, TX 77002
713/658-8881
Robbin R. Dawson

Sterling Chemicals, Inc., 194-195
333 Clay, Suite 3700
Houston, TX 77002
713/650-3700
David Heaney

Stewart & Stevenson Services, Inc., 204-207
2707 North Loop West
Houston, TX 77251
713/868-7700
C.J. Stewart

Stumpf & Falgout, 225
1400 Post Oak Boulevard, Suite 400
Houston, TX 77056
713/871-0919
Herb Holloway

Sunbelt Hotels, Inc., 177
2600 Citadel Plaza Drive, Suite 507
Houston, TX 77008
713/868-2815
Ron E. Jackson

Texas Chiropractic College, 243
5912 Spencer Highway
Pasadena, TX 77505
713/487-1170
Gabrielle Greenwade

Universal Weather and Aviation, Inc., 152-153
8787 Tallyho
Houston, TX 77061
713/944-1622
Marjorie Evans

Wholesale Electric Supply Co., 174-175
Post Office Box 230197
Houston, TX 77223-0197
713/748-6100
Clyde G. Rutland

The Wyndham Warwick & The Wyndham Greenspoint, 256-257
5701 Main Street
Houston, TX 77005
713/526-1991
Mark Vann

INDEX